The World's Twenty
Largest Churches

Kurt & Layse
Johanson

Lincoln Christian College

The World's Twenty Largest Churches

JOHN N. VAUGHAN

BAKER BOOK HOUSE
Grand Rapids, Michigan 49506

Copyright 1984 by
Baker Book House Company

Library of Congress
Card Catalog Number: 84-071187

ISBN: 0-8010-9297-3

Printed in the United States of America

To

My Mentors

Dr. Elmer L. Towns
American Church Growth

Dr. C. Peter Wagner
World Church Growth

and

My Supportive Flock

Briarcrest Baptist Church
Memphis, Tennessee

Contents

Churches of Africa:

Churches of North America:

Churches of Latin and South America:

Foreword

One reason why many pastors fail to lead their churches into vigorous growth is that they themselves have never experienced church growth. They grew up in static churches, they were assigned to work in static churches during seminary days, and their pastoral experience has been in static churches. When they read a book on church growth, their understanding is limited by their experience. Some have very little faith that it could happen to them. Others even develop theological reasons why it shouldn't.

John Vaughan's book is a godsend, not only for those pastors who lack growth experience, but for all church leaders and faithful Christians who want to put their finger on the pulse of what God is doing in the world. It will go a long way in closing the credibility gap. It will help Christians believe that God is still doing great works which surpass even those recorded in the Book of Acts. Just by reading this book one can vicariously experience what it feels like to be part of dynamic, growing churches.

This book is the first one ever to identify and describe large, growing churches on an international scale. I salute John Vaughan for the dogged and determined research which was necessary for the book. I hope that this pioneering effort will be the beginning of a whole series of books which will encourage God's people everywhere. It will provide a substantial stimulus to complete the Great Commission in our generation.

Not only does John Vaughan describe these large churches with fascinating detail, but he also analyzes them with church-growth eyes. His concluding chapter "The Future and Large Churches" is upbeat and optimistic. One of his conclusions is that such churches are growing because they "refuse to set limits on God." Vaughan makes no apology for size. Nor does he fail to point out that the quality of ministry in these churches usually matches the quantity of members.

As you read this you will be impressed by the majesty of God. Each church is unique. Some of their philosophies of ministry are similar, but they differ significantly from one another. Yet God blesses many approaches to reach new people for Christ and nurture believers in their spiritual growth. God is much bigger than denominational emphases or national boundaries.

I feel tremendously indebted to John Vaughan for giving us this magnificent book. As you read I'm sure you will feel indebted, too.

C. Peter Wagner
Fuller Seminary, School of World Mission
Pasadena, California

Acknowledgments

This book is possible only because many pastors, staff members, researchers, librarians, denominational executives, mission boards, family, and friends have been willing to share information, time, influence, and concern for God's story of His superchurches. Special appreciation is expressed to Alice Webb for her help in typing and proofreading the manuscript.

To the best of my knowledge the information shared in these pages is true and correct and reflects an accurate picture of each church.

It is hoped that this project will prove valuable in the further discussion of church growth and that some of the ideas provided here will prod churches to grow not only numerically but also spiritually.

John N. Vaughan
Briarcrest Baptist Church
6000 Briarcrest Avenue
Memphis, Tennessee 38119

Introduction

W hen *The Complete Book of Church Growth*[1] was released
in 1981, it contained a list of the largest American churches ranked by
size of church membership. Highland Park Baptist Church of Chattanooga, Tennessee, with 54,989 members, appeared as the largest Christian congregation in the nation. Second on the list was First Baptist
Church of Hammond, Indiana, with 52,255 members.

Both are Independent Baptist churches with common goals, priorities,
and a focus on the absolute authority of the Bible as God's Word. Both
are unapologetically committed to the urgency and command of Jesus
Christ to evangelize every lost soul with the gospel.

Repeatedly, however, questions were raised concerning the ranking of
Highland Park as the largest church in America. Comments were made
about Highland Park being "the church with all the mission chapels."
The implication was that since all of the church's members did not meet
under one roof, at the same location, a valid comparison could not be
made between these two large churches.

Also, until this new ranking appeared, First Baptist had appeared in
previous lists as being the largest church. However, previous lists, compiled by Dr. Elmer Towns of Lynchburg, Virginia, ranked churches by

1. Elmer L. Towns, John N. Vaughan, and David J. Seifert, *The Complete Book of Church
Growth* (Wheaton, Il: Tyndale, 1981).

average weekly Sunday school attendance. The third list in *The Complete Book of Church Growth* does indicate that the First Baptist Church still maintains the nations's largest Sunday school.*

These questions led me to examine methods of ranking churches. After months of research, interviews, and travel for my chapter on "The Fuller Factor" in *The Complete Book of Church Growth,* I realized the need for a single volume on the large churches listed in those pages.

I needed information on the superlarge churches in countries outside the United States and the data could be gathered only from an assortment of sources. As readers of world church-growth literature know, Dr. Donald McGavran and Dr. Peter Wagner of Fuller Theological Seminary in Pasadena, California, are without equal in Third World church-growth research.

Also without question is the value of key research data gathered by Dr. Elmer Towns, dean of Liberty Baptist Seminary, in the arena of both the largest and fastest-growing churches inside the U.S. Each has had a marked influence on the other in their sharing of information. Fuller's church-growth faculty has increasingly examined American churches in light of principles observed from the mission field while Dr. Towns has become increasingly involved in world church growth. I owe much to all three men.

At the encouragement of Dr. McGavran I began to gather data for a book on these strategic churches of the world. After developing a sixteen-page questionnaire for the project, the Lord brought Dr. Joseph Underwood of the Southern Baptist Foreign Mission Board to aid me in selecting a research oriented team of missionaries in the cities involved in the study. Team members are identified in the following chapters.

Many other churches came into view as months passed. I cannot begin to catalog the multitudes of books, articles, miles of travel, interviews, and telephone calls around the world involved to make these chapters possible.

The suggestion for ranking the churches and including North American congregations came from Dr. Elmer Towns. As the data began to pour in, however, I made an interesting discovery. Some of the churches reported small Sunday schools and large worship attendance, while others reported the opposite.

Once a church's total membership, Sunday school average attendance,

---

* In 1981, First Baptist regained its position as the nation's largest church.

and average worship service attendance is identified, how can variances be compared?

The solution I used is a helpful church-growth procedure developed by Dr. Charles Mylander and named by Dr. Peter Wagner. Described by Mylander in his book, *Secrets of Growing Churches,* the end product of the calculation is called a "composite membership." The composite is determined by adding the average weekly morning worship attendance, the average weekly Sunday school attendance, and the total adult church membership. When these figures are added and divided by three, the result is a composite membership total. Because of the variety of recording procedures used by churches around the world, the "adult church membership" was modified for this study to include all members.

All information was gathered by personnel on-location or by telephone interview with each church's pastor or the person designated to speak for him. To my best knowledge, this practice has been followed in every case. Many times information was shared openly and without reservation. At other times repeated contact was necessary. In some instances information was very difficult to obtain.

Where information essential for an accurate calculation of composite membership was unobtainable, such churches are omitted from the composite membership list of the churches. The omitted churches, however, are listed in the categories of information received from the churches. Usually only one item was unobtainable, but this alone can make a substantial difference.

There is a descriptive chapter in this book about many, even most, of the world's largest congregations. Researchers of American church growth have known for decades that the largest churches in the U.S. tend to be Baptist congregations. Outside the U.S. it is becoming increasingly obvious that Pentecostals predominate among the large churches.

Many more than twenty churches are included in the four lists of the appendix section of this book. In the primary list of churches by composite membership, four different nations, eight states in the U.S., and eight denominational or church groups are represented.

Newly discovered congregations, such as the Soong-Eui Methodist Church of Inchon, Korea, are still being researched. Also, a recent chapter has been written on the Grace Community Church of Panorama City, California, in *The Complete Book of Church Growth.*[2]

---

2. Ibid. Readers also may be interested in the chapter on Mt. Olivet Lutheran Church of Minneapolis, Minnesota, in *Great Churches of Today* (Minneapolis: World Wide Publications).

The Soong-Eui Methodist Church, Incheon, Korea. The Rev. Ho Moon Lee serves as pastor of this rapidly growing congregation.

Each chapter profiles the strategies, ministries, leadership, and, if available, measurable growth information. The churches included in this study were mailed copies of the chapter which dealt with their church and were invited to submit revisions and corrections prior to publication.

Each suggestion for possible churches that had any probability of being included in the listings of the world's twenty largest churches has been examined. Neither time nor expense has been spared in this venture.

Without doubt, the publication of this book will generate attention on this topic. Experience in gathering information with Dr. Elmer Towns on churches in the United States suggests that there are unknown churches which rightfully belong in this list of the world's largest churches. Such churches are invited to contact me at the Briarcrest Baptist Church, 6000 Briarcrest Avenue, Memphis, Tennessee 38119 U.S.A.

Concerning Brazilian Churches

The Brazilian models used in this book are representative of the super-churches in that country. The structure and strategies used by many of these churches tend to be significantly different from other models. They are treated as a unique kind of church.

While other churches, even those with satellite chapels, usually focus their ministries in their own metropolitan area, Brazilian superchurches frequently extend their chapels to other cities and even to other states.

For example, the Sao Paulo based *Congregacao Crista* is listed in Dr. David Barrett's *World Christian Encyclopedia* as having 3,500 congregations with 600,000 adults among its affiliated membership. Thirty percent of their total membership resides in the neighboring state of Parana. *Brasil Para Crista* (Brazil for Christ), also of Sao Paulo, reports that 5,000 of its satellite congregations are located outside the city of Sao Paulo. Recently, the mother church is reported to have released all of the chapels as autonomous churches.

After consultation with internationally respected Pentecostal leaders, a listing of these major superchurch centers of Brazil is provided for the interested reader and researcher. Without question, these churches should be the major focus of another book. I have encouraged several Pentecostal leaders to write this much-needed story. These churches appear to operate more like denominations or denominational church-planting agencies than the congregations listed in the present study. The strong, continued identity of satellite chapels with the mother church and their continued membership in the mother church makes comparison with other types of churches difficult.

Concerning Churches Using Cell Groups

Especially among Korean congregations, the use of small classlike groups called cells has become an accepted way of reaching the masses evangelistically and of following-up on both new and present members of the churches. In contrast with Sunday school classes, these groups usually have fewer than sixteen members and meet in homes, offices, and factories away from the church buildings. Cells usually meet on a day other than Sunday. That day is usually Friday.

Readers unfamiliar with this organizational pattern among churches influenced by the Full Gospel Central Church in Seoul, Korea, need to be aware of this strategy for growth.

Eight of the twenty churches listed in the composite membership appendix in the back of this book have cell groups. In the cases of Central Church, Sung Nak Baptist Church, and Chung Hyeon Presbyterian Church, all in Seoul, Korea, the cell group attendance far exceeds Sunday school attendance. Appendix E provides detailed information for making this comparison.

Originally, consideration was given to including the cell group attendance in the composite totals. For three reasons it was decided not to take this approach: (1) for continuity, not all twenty churches have cell groups; (2) these groups meet on days other than Sunday; and (3) if included in this study, weekday ministries in all churches would need to be considered. Some churches have extensive weekday ministries, for example, Mt. Olivet Lutheran Church in Minneapolis. Finally, some churches keep detailed records and statistics on these ministries; others do not, and consider them of little value.

Very similar to the Brazilian model is the one being adopted by the Miracle Center of Benin City, Nigeria. New churches are organized from new converts in the city-wide evangelistic crusades conducted by Benson Idahosa, who was recently designated bishop.

Concerning Roman Catholic and State Churches

Early in the study, the research office of the Vatican was contacted for information on the largest Roman Catholic congregations. Their response, through the U.S. office, indicated that they did not have information on their churches identified in this manner. They suggested that the Kennedy Directory Offices in Washington, D. C., be contacted. Contact with this office revealed that the only means of determining these churches was by the size of their ministry staff since parish, but not congregational information, is retrievable.

State churches pose a difficulty similar to that of the Brazilian super-churches when making comparisons. National cathedrals are not included in this study for this reason. State churches and their cathedrals, as more than architectural structures, are an area that merits the attention of other researchers.

Concerning House Church Movements in Asia and Communist Countries

The church of Jesus Christ is very much alive and well in countries dominated by communist governments. While very restricted in many places because of Communist opposition to unregistered group gatherings, Christians in these countries are among our strongest believers. It would be unwise to reveal too much information about these ministries at this time. Readers should be aware, however, that extensive research is being conducted by others in this area.

Churches of Asia

1

The Limits of Growth

At thirty years of age, the trusted employee of an African shoe factory is converted. Within one year, and with twelve dollars from his own pocket, he rents a storefront building. From this obscure beginning a church is raised which has given birth to more than a thousand churches in West Africa.

In North Korea more than one-third of the nation's population escaped across the border into South Korea. Driven by the rapidly advancing Communist army, twenty-seven young refugees found refuge in an abandoned Shinto shrine. Since 1949 this seed group has blossomed into the largest Presbyterian congregation in the world with sixty thousand members.

A retired government transportation specialist in Santiago, Chile, leads the eighty-thousand-member Jotabeche Methodist Pentecostal Church. Today, with a sanctuary seating fifteen thousand, only one-fourth of the church members can be accommodated at one time. Sections of the city rotate the use of the church auditorium.

In Seoul, Korea, a recent Bible college graduate and his future mother-in-law erected hand-sown fragments of army tents as a shelter for newly arriving refugees. Within two years five pioneers became three hundred. Now, almost twenty-five years later, an average of ten thousand new converts each month join the largest church congregation in recorded history with more than 400,000 members.

Each member is part of a system of cell groups which never exceed sixteen members. In each group every member is known by name and by face. Worshipers stagger their attendance during the seven worship services in the 10,000-seat sanctuary each Sunday.

Almost every large church began with only a few committed members. Each endured and conquered the battles of small vision, the prophets of doubt, and the social, political, and financial barriers. Growth has, at times, been at the partial loss of smaller neighboring congregations.

Almost all of the large superchurches have reproduced themselves many times by creating smaller satellite chapels. Some chapels grow to be giants themselves while others remain small. Some even elect to remain as satellite chapels or missions of the parent church.

First Baptist Church of Dallas began with only eleven members and today has 22,732 members, seventeen satellite chapels, and ten other preaching points.

Bible Baptist Church of Cebu City, Philippines, began as a meager, fourteen-member group from the streets of the city. Less than thirty years later over three thousand people attend worship services and ten thousand come to Sunday school through the mother church, its seven chapels, and the thirty-five extension classes that meet away from the main church.

A mere twenty-seven organizing members meeting in a county south of Los Angeles in 1960 claimed their area for God. At the time the growing group bought its present worship center. Local law prohibited churches from building in Anaheim. Today ten thousand people attend the center each Sunday morning.

The sixty chapels and parent Highland Park Baptist Church of Chattanooga, Tennessee, did not begin with their current membership of 57,322. Only twelve people met on Ivy Street in the Orchard Knob community in 1890 to form the Orchard Knob Baptist Church. During the first thirty years of chapel ministry, approximately fifteen chapels became self-supporting, autonomous congregations.

These stories can be duplicated in South Africa, Korea, Nigeria, El Salvador, Brazil, and many other places. This book records the faith experiences of the world's largest churches.

While it is recognized that not every church can, will, or perhaps even ought to surpass the 1,000-membership mark, many churches are living far below their growth potential.

For many congregations, if petty excuses for nongrowth were laid aside, if outgrowth fellowship were given priority over ingrowth fellowship, if an aggressive evangelism strategy were to complement follow-up and nurture strategies, and if obedience to the Bible mandates for growth replaced blinding barriers, multitudes of nongrowing churches would begin to grow.

Preoccupation with Bigness?

Just how many superchurches are there in the United States? While large is defined by some as an attendance or even a total membership ranging from 250–500, the superchurch ceiling has continued to rise during the 1970s.

According to the most recent research, there are at least 107 superchurches with memberships of more than 4,400 members. I am confident that there are still other churches that belong in this listing of U.S. congregations.

In 1971, Jerry Falwell and Elmer Towns wrote:

Historians will probably look back on the decade of the 70's as the beginning of the large church movement. They believe that over 300 churches will be raised up in this country that will be averaging over 2,000 in attendance in this decade. This amounts to one large church for each of the 300 major metropolitan areas of America.[1]

A decade later Towns gave an update on the projection of 300 churches averaging over two thousand members in attendance by 1980. Although there were twelve Sunday schools averaging more than two thousand in 1968, he reported forty-nine that large in 1980.[2] A new listing, however, indicates that at least one hundred churches now average two thousand attendants in weekly Sunday worship services.[3]

Does it not seem reasonable to pray as a Christian community that there be at least one superchurch in each of the nation's major urban centers? Elmer Towns writes, "I have often preached that the greatest church since Pentecost is yet to be built. Why not? We have tools at hand to build a greater church than any previous generation ever had."[4] He

1. Elmer Towns and Jerry Falwell, *Church Aflame* (Nashville: Impact Books, 1971), pp. 37, 40.

2. Elmer L. Towns, John N. Vaughan, and David J. Seifert, *The Complete Book of Church Growth* (Wheaton, IL: Tyndale, 1981), p. 15.

3. Ibid., pp. 349–53.

4. Jerry Falwell and Elmer Towns, *Capturing a Town for Christ* (Old Tappan, NJ: Revell, 1973), p. 5.

Table 1   Profile of U.S. Superchurches, 1980–83

Size of Membership	Approximate Number of Churches
4,400– 4,999	25
5,000– 5,999	30
6,000– 6,999	20
7,000– 7,999	5
8,000– 8,999	2
9,000– 9,999	5
10,000–10,999	4
11,000–11,999	4
12,000–12,999	3
13,000–13,999	2
14,000–19,999	4
20,000–49,999	1
50,000 +	2

Adapted and revised from lists in *The Complete Book of Church Growth* by Elmer L. Towns, John N. Vaughan, and David J. Seifert (Wheaton, IL: Tyndale, 1981), pp. 342–345.

goes on to stress that the saturation of our cities with these tools is only as effective as our willingness to yield them to the anointing power of God's Holy Spirit.

Much change has occurred since the early 1970s when Falwell could say,

> . . . there has never been a church that approximates the size of the church of Jerusalem. . . . This is supernatural growth. With these 5,000 men, there were 5,000 women nearby, and very likely . . . at least 10,000 or 15,000 children. So at this point the church in Jerusalem numbered above 25,000. Now the population of Jerusalem in that day was about 200,000, as best we can determine.[5]

Carl S. Dudley, professor of church and community at McCormick Theological Seminary in Chicago, stresses that "History is on the side of the small church. Bigness is the new kid on the block . . . By the turn of the century (i.e., nineteenth) the average congregation still had less than one hundred fifty members."[6] He also mentions that while "15 percent of the largest churches reach 50 percent of the membership; 50 percent of the smallest churches serve 15 percent of the members."[7]

In a world where the population was reported to be 4.6 billion in 1980,

5. Towns and Falwell, *Church Aflame*, pp. 34–35.
6. Carl S. Dudley, *Making the Small Church Effective* (Nashville: Abingdon, 1978), p. 23.
7. Ibid., p. 22.

and doubling every thirty-three years, the church had best insure it is effective, whether it is small, medium, or large.

Realizing that the small church will continue as a viable force in the Christian church movement, it is also helpful for the large church to be encouraged in the tasks it is uniquely equipped to accomplish.

The emergence of the New Testament church of Acts 6:1-7 from a single-cell organizational structure to a multicell structure is outlined by Dr. George W. Peters.[8] Much research has established the simple, and even resistant, nature of the single-cell organization. The strength of the single-cell group is its ability to survive; its weakness is its resistance to growth and the large influx of outsiders.

Peters traces the transition in the early church with its tensions resulting from unmet needs in the single-cell pattern. The solution adopted was to divide the enlarged group to natural substructures. Notice that the church remained intact as one unit but was reorganized to insure a shared ministry among the members and leaders. Almost every large church has become large because it took courageous steps to reorganize along the path to growth.

The emergence of the New Testament church is carefully described:

> . . . the Christian church begins to emerge in Acts 6:1-7 when the necessity for organization surfaces. A division of labor is necessary in the quality community. There are several stages in the movement toward structure in the Christian church—from being (1) strictly person-centered (the apostles), to being (2) structure-centered (James is the leader), to becoming (3) a pyramid system (James, the elders, the deacons, the congregation). The multi-level structure replaces the person-centered operation. . . . The organization is forming its own organization; the church is becoming an institution. The structure provides for a division and apportioning of labor and assigning of responsibilities.

> . . . Fellowship, as it is often advocated and practiced, is no substitute for organization; and sooner or later the organism will suffer seriously, cease to function dynamically, or progressively disintegrate.

> . . . such tension is wholesome and is indicative that the organism is alive. . . . The two belong together. Structure without function is like a corpse. However, an organism of function without structure is like a paraplegic—unable to be coordinated and to move in an orderly manner.

8. George W. Peters, *A Theology of Church Growth* (Grand Rapids: Zondervan, 1981). Used by permission.

In either case, growth or progress is impossible. Thus structure is necessary for the church to function effectively.[9]

An illustration of one church using both group structures is Central Church in Seoul, Korea. At the beginning of 1983, the church reported a total of 17,772 cell groups. Each group has an average of fifteen members. Even with 267,000 members, every involved member is known both by name and face.

One of the major focuses of this book is to allow the reader to merely observe what is done correctly by the large church which allows it to grow in a godly and New Testament manner.

Over a decade ago. Elmer Towns noted a research project conducted at Trinity Evangelical Divinity School:

> The average church member was on a speaking basis (called people by their first names) with sixty individuals, whether the church had sixty, 600 or a thousand members. Therefore, it is wrong to accuse the large church of being impersonal. The average person will speak to approximately sixty people no matter what the size of the church.[10]

Recent History and the Large Church

The accounts of historic revivals and evangelistic crusades glow with reports of multitudes gathering to hear the Bible preached. George White-field is reported to have spoken to an audience of 20,000 in his farewell message delivered at Glasgow, Scotland, in 1753. Dwight L. Moody, during a tour of Great Britain, preached 285 times to a total audience of 2,530,000 people.

But what about individual congregations? Were there any large congregations functioning prior to the 1970s and the advent of its super-churches? A brief summary given below may best answer these questions:

1832—*Chatham Street Chapel* (Second Free Presbyterian Church) of New York City was led by Charles Finney to meet in a renovated theater seating 2,500–3,000. By 1889 the Sunday school enrollment had reached 6,027 with 1,867 children in the church nursery.

1860—*Plymouth Church*—Brooklyn, New York. Henry Ward Beecher regularly preached to 2,000 each Sunday.

9. Ibid.
10. Towns and Falwell, *Church Aflame*, p. 42.

1861—*Metropolitan Tabernacle*—London. Built while Charles H. Spurgeon was pastor. Capacity of the Tabernacle was 5,000. When the building burned in 1898, it was rebuilt to seat 3,000.

1883—*First African Baptist Church*—Richmond, Virginia. Registered 2,675 members.

Sixth Mt. Zion Baptist—Richmond, Virginia. Black pastor John Jasper founded the church with nine members and led the church to reach 1,068 members. The building included 1,000 seats on the main floor with additional seats in the side galleries.

1890—*Bethany Presbyterian Church*—Philadelphia. Wilber Chapman as pastor was fortunate to have department store magnate John Wanamaker as a member. On Easter Sunday, 1891, the "world's largest Protestant church" was dedicated. Regular attendance averaged 3,000 to 5,000.

1890—*First Baptist Church*—Dallas, Texas. Built in 1890, prior to coming of George W. Truett as pastor. He served as pastor almost one-half century in this auditorium built to seat 2,800.

1894—*Chicago Avenue Church*—Chicago. Built while Dwight L. Moody was pastor, the capacity is 2,200. There are 1,200 seats on the main floor and 1,000 in the giant horseshoe balcony. Attendance averaged 2,700. At the funeral of evangelist Billy Sunday, a crowd of 4,400 was reported.

1922—*Angeles Temple*—Los Angeles. This center for Four Square Gospel leader Aimee Semple McPherson was built for 5,400 attendants. In 1922, there were 31 weekly healing services held in this auditorium.

1924—*First Baptist Church*—Minneapolis. Under William Bell Riley's term as pastor the 2,634-seat sanctuary was constructed. Membership reached 3,550 by 1942.

1928—*First Baptist Church*—Fort Worth, Texas. J. Frank Norris built the "World's Largest Sunday School" at this location with a peak attendance on Sunday morning of 12,000 in 1928 and an average attendance of 5,200. While pastor of the the Fort Worth church, he also built the Temple Baptist Church in Detroit in 1934 with 800 members. It grew to 8,597 members by 1943. Between the two churches, he held the world record of one man serving a combined membership of 25,000 members.

1949—*Akron Baptist Temple*—Akron, Ohio. Built in 1949 to seat 2,500 by Dr. Dallas Billington. Prior to 1946 this church reported

21,000 members. The Sunday school attendance averaged 6,300 and the largest adult class had 2,500 in attendance. The record attendance for the church was 10,221 on Easter Sunday, 1943. During a 33-year period this church started over 200 new churches.

1968—*Temple Baptist Church*—Detroit. Led by G. Beauchamp Vick, this congregation built a 4,500 theater-seat auditorium for regular crowds of 5,200.

In 1949, Louis Entzminger compiled and published a list of the nation's largest Sunday schools. The first ten churches in that listing as they appeared were:[11]

1. First Baptist Church—Fort Worth, Texas
2. Temple Baptist Church—Detroit, Michigan
3. First Baptist Church—Birmingham, Alabama
4. Dauphin Way Baptist Church—Mobile, Alabama
5. First Baptist Church—New Orleans, Louisiana
6. First Baptist Church—Shreveport, Louisiana
7. First Baptist Church—Minneapolis, Minnesota
8. Jarvis Street Baptist Church—Toronto, Canada
9. First Baptist Church—Houston, Texas
10. Broadway Baptist Church—Knoxville, Tennessee

Exactly two decades later the September, 1968, issue of *Christian Life* magazine contained an article, "10 Largest Sunday Schools in the U.S. Today." The listing compiled by Elmer Towns, Sunday school editor, drew immediate response. His book, *The Ten Largest Sunday Schools*, was released within months of the article.[12]

The previously untold success story of the superchurches in America encouraged the churches of the nation. Each year for almost a decade, an annual listing of the churches with the one hundred largest Sunday schools appeared in the September issue of *Christian Life*. Looking back at the 1970s, Towns wrote:

At the beginning of the seventies there was only one Sunday school aver-

11. Louis Entzminger, *How to Organize and Administer a Great Sunday School* (Fort Worth: Manning, 1949), pp. 111–14.

12. Elmer L. Towns, *The Ten Largest Sunday Schools* (Grand Rapids: Baker, 1969).

aging over 5,000 in attendance. Today there are five Sunday schools that size. Research has shown that only twelve Sunday schools averaged more than 2,000 in attendance in 1968. Today there are forty-nine that large.[13]

Across the nation at Fuller Theological Seminary in Pasadena, California, other voices were announcing churches in other countries experiencing even greater growth. Dr. Donald McGavran had written several books and Dr. Peter Wagner had written two books of special interest to America's growing churches. These books told the story of superchurches in Chile, Bolivia, Mexico, Argentina, and Brazil. The American public became aware of a church in Santiago, Chile, with an auditorium seating 15,000 worshipers and of another in Sao Paulo reported to seat 25,000.

About that time news releases in the U.S. began to give photos and reports of Seoul's 20,000-member Full Gospel Central Church and its pastor Dr. Paul Yonggi Cho. By the end of the decade, growth reports announced 80,000 members with goals of 100,000 and even 200,000 in sight. Even the future goal of 500,000 now seems attainable.

The 1970s was a significant decade. A glimpse of the giants of the Christian world is provided with the hope that churches will be encouraged and challenged to be all that God intends them to be in the decade of the 1980s.

13. Towns, Vaughan, and Seifert, *The Complete Book of Church Growth*, p. 13.

2

Imagine . . . 500,000 Church Members— Full Gospel Central Church
Seoul, Korea

Paul Yonggi Cho was seventeen when the Korean War came to a formal end in July, 1953. During the three-year military action, an estimated eight million South Koreans were driven from their homes and 600,000 homes were destroyed.

In the midst of this rubble and awesome poverty Cho vowed, "I reject a life of disease and poverty. I rise above the condition of myself! Poverty might be somebody's root, but it is sure not going to be mine. . . . Someday I'm not going to be ragged and poor! I'm going to be a medical doctor. I've been a nobody long enough. . . ."[1]

Don C. Jones, missionary to Korea for the Southern Baptist Convention and adminstrator of Korean Baptist Mission in Seoul, gathered primary research data.

1. Nell L. Kennedy, *Dream Your Way to Success* (Plainfield, NJ: Logos International, 1980), pp. 69–70.

Two years later the young Buddhist contracted what appeared to be a hopeless case of tuberculosis. Cho, almost thirty years later, vividly re-members:

> One afternoon I was working as a tutor. Suddenly I felt something oozing up from deep inside my chest. My mouth felt full. I thought I would choke.
>
> As I opened my mouth, blood began to gush out. I tried to stop the bleeding, but blood continued to flow from my nostrils and mouth. My stomach and chest soon filled with blood. Severely weakened, I fainted . . . I was nineteen years old. And I was dying.[2]

His doctor gave him no hope. Cho was told that he had, at most, three or four months to live. Out of such despair he invited Jesus Christ to do what his unanswered prayers to Buddha could not do.

Today Dr. Paul Yonggi Cho is pastor of the most researched church on earth. The Full Gospel Central Church of Seoul, Korea, was projected to reach a membership of 200,000 by the end of 1981, According to early 1981 reports from the church, an average of 264 new members were added daily, in the first quarter of the year. Imagine growing at a rate of more than 8,000 new members during a one-month period. By 1984 the rate of growth increased to 10,000 new members monthly.

Church reports from January, 1984, reveal a total membership of 350,000 with 316 pastoral staff members; 20,805 deacons and deacon-esses; 19,839 cell groups, with attendance at the cell groups averaging 297,585; and a weekly all-night prayer service attendance of more than 12,000. Also, the total number of baptisms reported for 1980 was 12,000. When you consider that Seoul is a city of over eight million people, church attendance of even 350,000 seems small. While some critics minimize the impact of superchurches like Central Church, many feel the response should be praise and prayer for continued growth in cities with large populations of unreached peoples.

Assisted by his mother-in-law, Jashil Choi, and missionary John Hur-ston, Pastor Cho ministered faith, hope, and healing to an expanding congregation surrounded by great need.

Many observers are quick to credit the cell group meetings as the major key to the growth of Yoido Full Gospel Central Church. Leaders within the congregation, however, stress that the cells are channels of growth rather than causes for growth. Reasons for the church's expansion include the pastor, his pastoral and volunteer staffs of men and women

---

2. Paul Yongii Cho, *The Fourth Dimension* (Plainfield, NJ: Logos International, 1979), pp. 1–3.

Table 2   Two Decades of Growth

	1982*	1980	1975	1970	1960
Church Membership	230,000	133,000	22,992	8,252	800
Weekly Cell Groups	15,358	9,000	755	167	76
New Members per Day, Average/Time Period	133	60	8	2	2

*Based on the above data, the church experienced an explosive growth rate of 1,512 percent during the past decade (1970–1980).

of faith, organizational strategy, and, foremost, the role of the Holy Spirit and the power of answered prayer.

Allen Swanson serves as a Lutheran missionary in Taiwan and, after attending the All-Chinese Church Growth Seminar in the Central Church, writes:

> Dr. Cho shared with delegates the importance of prayer to evangelism. Church growth does not result from simple application of specific principles. It is born and nurtured through prayer. Calculations based on the time spent in prayer during regular services revealed that members of Central Church spend 260,000 hours in prayer every month.[3]

When God Sets the Limits

In one sense, Dr. Cho has served only one church. However, it can be said that the pastor has served three churches. Each time the church moved, a portion of the congregation remained in the former location to continue the existing ministry, while the majority of the congregation moved with the pastor.

The small tent-church founded on May 18, 1958, by Paul Yonggi Cho has a steady history of growth. The tent-church was established in a postwar climate of poverty. It was originally located at Taejo Dong, a slum area of the city. Following graduation from Full Gospel Bible Institute in Seoul, in March, 1958, Cho's plan was to further his studies in America. Meanwhile, Mrs. Joshil Choi, an honors graduate of the same school, became the object of his concern.

Dr. Cho sensed an urgent need to help her organize a church in the Taejo Dong area. He was convinced that she needed a building. She had no money to buy bricks and insisted that their goal should be to convert thirty people before he left for the United States.

3. Allen Swanson, "Not in Vain," *World of Faith* 1 (Winter 1980): 2–17.

Some of the 275,000 members of Dr. Paul Yonggi Cho's Full Gospel Central Church gather at the immense facility in Seoul, Korea.

Together they bought a U.S. Army tent that provided the shelter needed for the people. Frequent sewing and patching kept the tent in good repair while straw mats covered the ground beneath.

Shortly after its erection, the tent was leveled beyond repair by typhoon Sarah. Temporarily the preaching continued in Mrs. Choi's newly built house. When the crowds became too large for the house, a second tent was pitched in front of her house.

Miracles began to happen and the community knew that the tent was a place of hope to those in need. Since there was no bell to announce the Sunday service, Dr. Cho would stand on a hill and call the people to come to the church.

Membership of the tent-church soon grew beyond the goal of thirty to fifty members. The power and presence of God in the new all-night prayer and singing service in the tent would not allow Cho to leave for America. Several life-changing lessons were learned about the power of specific prayer. Two members had now increased to three hundred.

Pastor Cho was drafted in 1960 for a term in the army of the Republic of Korea. He selected John Hurston, a new missionary to Korea, to be the church's leader during his absence. The prayers of the church for their pastor were answered when Cho received a medical discharge after serving only seven months.

When he returned Cho discovered that the church had increased by two hundred members during a revival meeting. The unexpected growth required the church to relocate on October 15, 1961, to the Sodaemoon West Gate area downtown. The church was renamed the Full Gospel Revival Center.

A nucleus of eight hundred members moved from the Taejo Dong congregation and left behind the tent-church that had cost five thousand dollars. Almost two hundred members remained with the land and tent at the former site.

Dedication day for the new 1,500-seat building in the West Gate area was February 18, 1962. Dr. Cho's biographer, Nell Kennedy, reported that during the service a crippled man who had crawled in on his knees later left walking. Another man, totally deaf, left with "his hearing completely restored."[4] With only three staff members, a significant decision was made. Only God could set the limit on how large Full Gospel Revival Center would grow.

The center's name was changed to Full Gospel Central Church on May

---

4. Kennedy, *Dream Your Way to Success*, p. 181.

13, 1962. This event marked a change in emphasis from revival center to the building-up of a strong and stable church membership. Two years earlier, Cho's ministerial license had been revoked due to his young age and the manner of worship. Now his license was reinstated. The church was affiliated with the Assemblies of God denomination.

Missionary John Hurston returned the church's full leadership to its Korean founder. The interim pastor shared years later, "Cho had been serving as their pastor all along; I was merely holding the position for him until he got the paper back that made it legal for him to be there."[5]

The membership of eight hundred soon increased to two thousand by 1964. Value of the prefabricated worship center grew to $100,000 by 1964. In 1967 a 500-seat balcony and five-story front educational building were added.

The year 1964 was critical for both pastor and congregation. Increased growth now required four worship services. Church membership was growing at a rate of about fifteen new members daily and would reach an attendance of 7,500 by 1965.

During an afternoon service when Dr. Cho had baptized hundreds of new believers for almost two hours, he collapsed onto the floor from total exhaustion. He had been interpreting for a guest speaker when the crisis occurred.

While confined at the hospital for a week of rest and recovery, his doctor advised him to change professions. Dr. Cho refused to follow this recommendation. Determined to preach again, he returned to his pulpit the next Sunday and was able to stand for eight minutes. Again he was taken to the hospital.

During the days that followed, the young Korean leader began reading through the Bible, starting at Genesis 1:1. He had been reading for less than a week when he was captivated by Exodus 18:18, "You will surely wear out, both yourself and these people who are with you, for the task is too heavy for you; you cannot do it alone." (NAS) The plan described in Exodus 18 became the blueprint for the future growth of Full Gospel Central Church.

The next Sunday the pastor called the deacons, deaconesses, and elders to share his vision from God. That gathering gave birth to the "cell group" system that has aided the expansion of the gospel throughout Seoul. His leaders expressed their initial fright and lack of training to assume such

5. Ibid., pp. 182–83.

a shared ministry. Pastor Cho assured them that he would teach them what they needed to know.

> It took almost five years to gain back what he had lost. His concentration span was shortened, his memory often failed him, he grew tired easily, and he had sleepless nights without reason. . . .
>
> At twenty-eight, he had tried to do everything himself, to monopolize the church. . . . Like Moses, he had tried to solve every situation. . . . In his own eyes he had become the mighty Cho. Now Jethro was telling him to select able men out of all the people.[6]

Many men hesitated to grasp the invitation. He enlisted those who were agreeable and then began enrolling women. The enlistment of women to lead mixed groups of men and women was against all accepted Korean custom. Pastor Cho and his congregation attribute its success to the leadership and protection of the Holy Spirit. By May, 1981, there were almost 3,000 deacons and over 9,000 deaconesses.

On March 1, 1965, Paul Yonggi Cho married Sung Hae Kim, the daughter of his friend and associate, Mrs. Jashil Choi. He was twenty-nine and his bride was twenty-three.

Sung Hae and her husband would have three sons. Their oldest son, Hee Jae, almost died. This experience gave an intensified awareness of the power and presence of the Holy Spirit in their home.

The Move to Yoido Island

In 1966, the famous pastor of Seoul's Central Church became general superintendent of the Assembly of God churches in Seoul, and chairman of the board of the Full Gospel Bible College. One year later, at age thirty-one, he served on the advisory committee of the Pentecostal World Conference. That same year a five-story educational and office addition to the West Gate Church was built and the church published a monthly magazine, *World of Faith*. *World of Faith* became *Church Growth Magazine* in 1983 and has a circulation of 10,000 distributed to 75 countries.

Cho is careful to explain that the Holy Spirit is always his senior partner on every platform. He believes that the Holy Spirit has the unique ability to keep his focus on the solutions, not the problems. An amazing example is the miracle that emerged for both Central Church and the city of Seoul.

6. Ibid., see pp. 206–9 for details of the event.

In 1966 the Han River overflowed its banks causing much destruction in Seoul. During the inspection of damages caused by the flood, Il Suk Cha, the vice-mayor of Seoul, realized that Yoido Island sat in the middle of the Han River, much like Manhattan. As the flood waters dropped, Yoido Island became the location for the new Congress Hall and urban center for Seoul. Only one church was scheduled by the urban planners to be located on the island and this site was won by Central Church after Cho's interview with a congressman. The eyes of Pastor Cho must have gleamed when he learned that the congressman's mother attended his church on Sunday nights. Eventually, the vice-mayor and his wife were converted and baptized.

Credit was arranged for purchase of the church site and ground-breaking services were held on April 6, 1969. When the church relocated to Yoido Island about 1,000 members remained behind with another pastor and 8,000 followed Pastor Cho. The 10,000-seat auditorium was completed in five years at a cost of $2.5 million.

The church buildings are located on the northwest corner of Yoido Island, south of the main business district of Seoul, but still in the heart of the city. Directly across the street from the church is the headquarters building of the Korean Baptist Mission.

Due to the oil crisis and the refusal of banks to make large loans, many members of the church lost their jobs and debts began to accumulate. The pastor's salary was volunteered to pay the interest on the church loans. Church staff salaries also went unpaid until the economy improved. These troubles became a severe test of courage and faith for the pastor, his family, staff, and congregation.

Hundreds of members began to gather regularly for prayer and praise in the church's unfinished basement. Members began to bring their treasures. Some sold their houses and moved into apartments. Others pledged one year's salary and lived by faith alone. Finally, the loans were paid off and the buildings completed.

By 1972, the church averaged an annual increase of nearly 1,000 members. Billy Graham was the first man invited to preach in the new sanctuary that year. The Tenth World Pentecostal Conference was hosted by the church in 1973.

Official dedication of the worship center was set for September 24, 1973. Across the front of the new auditorium a large blue banner proclaimed Mark 9:23 in white and gold lettering, "If Thou Canst Believe, All Things are Possible to Him That Believeth."

Associate Pastor Jashil Choi established Prayer Mountain as a fasting and prayer retreat in the summer of 1974. An estimated 200,000 people visit the center annually. Pastor Cho expanded the prayer center to seat 5,000. On September 4, 1982, a new 10,000-seat sanctuary was dedicated for the Osanri Haven of Prayer (Prayer Mountain), with 150 grottoes for private prayer. The church, by 1979, was giving regular monthly support to more than sixty other churches. Over fifty churches have organized in outlying areas. They serve members who cannot travel to Yoido Island each week.

Construction continued with the erection of the $1 million, ten-floor World Mission Center dedicated in January, 1977. This multi-purpose building also houses the Church Growth International training center, begun in November, 1976. By 1983, over 242,000 pastors and lay leaders from forty different countries had been involved in over 150 seminars. Church Growth International is supported by an international board of directors from twenty countries. A genuine ecumenical spirit is demonstrated in the ministry of the World Mission Center building, which is next to the main auditorium of the church.

Central Church meets in eighteen assembly areas. Eight are located at the Yoido Island complex of buildings. Ten rented halls are used for children's church services. The buildings on the church's property have three major assembly areas capable of accommodating less than 1,000 people, three areas for 1,000–2,000 people, and two areas for more than 2,000 attendants.

The congregation that meets on Yoido Island provides regular Sunday school classes. For example, in July, 1981, when most American churches competed with the "summer slump," there were over 9,000 children and young people attending Sunday school at Central Church. By January, 1984, attendance more than doubled to a total of 20,875. If this total can be maintained throughout the year, Central Church will have the largest Sunday school in the world.

Sunday school curriculum is published by the congregation. Except for the international classes, all literature is written in Korean. Boys and girls meet together in the same classes and are not separated by sex. Worship services are designated for adults. By 1976, the increase in attendance led to the need for four worship services. By the winter of 1980 six services were needed. Seven services were required by 1981. Attendance in each of the services will average 15,000 with over 50,000 adults attending weekly. The congregation has seven choirs with 2,000 members and two orchestras with a total of 120 members.

Table 3   Sunday School Profile of Central Church, 1980

	Enrollment	Age Grouping	Teacher/Pupil Ratio	Total Classes
Preschool	2,850	Birth-Age 6	1:15	175
Children	4,270	Ages 7–12	1:20–40	265
Junior High	2,600	Ages	1:30–40	160
Senior High	2,400	13–18	1:20–40	130
*Adults**				
Total	12,120		1:20–35	730

A class is provided for approximately 2,000 deaf members in Canaan Chapel, which seats 2,200 people.
*Most adults meet in cell groups during the week.

The Cell Group Concept

The cell groups have probably become the universal trademark of Full Gospel Central Church. Two questions about the church center around current membership and the present number of cell groups.

A cell group is a cluster of church members who meet weekly in a home, factory, office, or other place for the purpose of evangelism and Christian fellowship through singing, prayer, Bible study, offering giving, announcements, sharing of needs, and praises and ministry to one another.

Adult cells are organized into groups that meet weekday mornings while the children are in school, and into men's and children's groups that usually meet at night during the week. Some groups are mixed with both men and women. Previously, the cells were called home groups and there were more mixed groups.

This is a most workable plan for Central Church because of the difficulty of seating over 100,000 church members in buildings designed to seat 18,000. One major reason for its success is that it is, above all, the structure for lay involvement.

Many problems emerged as the home groups evolved into the current cell groups. The first problem was to convince the leaders that they could accomplish the challenge of directing a congregation. A second barrier was the role of women in leadership positions within the congregation. A third decision had to be made about the role of the house of each believer in worship, instruction, evangelism, and ministry. Was it a valid center of authority? How does it relate to the main place of worship where the body of believers traditionally assemble on Sundays?

Karen Hurston, daughter of Dr. John W. Hurston, indicates that the method had great difficulties during the formative years.

Allowed to teach what they felt best, some groups fell into heresy. Others faltered with inadequate direction, and a few became instruments of personal ambition. The cell units needed a firm hand of guidance. Sporadic training sessions were initiated. For a short time, cassette tapes of Dr. Cho's sermons were played during weekly Bible studies.[7]

Seven levels of leadership in the cell group strategy have developed since 1964, with an eighth under consideration. By 1967 the church had begun 125 cell groups with a membership of 7,750 and 2,267 families.

In 1974 when the church began printing a weekly outline of cell group Bible studies, the city was divided into twenty-one ministry areas, and each of the ministry areas was supervised by a member of the pastoral staff. These three actions made it possible for additional decisions.

In 1974 there were four significant developments relating to organizational changes, leadership philosophy, and training needs.

First, the city was mapped off into five large districts and then subdivided into thirty-five smaller sections. Each of the thirty-five sections was assigned an average of twenty-two cell groups already located in the same geographical neighborhood.

Second, to provide standard training for the leaders serving the various levels of responsibility and accountability, weekly and annual training programs were developed.

Third, an interesting crisis occurred during this period. The cell groups began to multiply so rapidly that there were no longer enough deacons and deaconesses to lead the groups. This need required new ways to enlist, qualify, and train a broader base of leaders.

Fourth, "the home cell unit system became the pastoral care department of the church."[8]

Once these decisions were made, dramatic and highly visible growth occurred. From the time of the ground-breaking service in April, 1969, until the dedication of the new 10,000-seat church building on September 24, 1973, the Lord added an average of three new members each day.

Once the new building was opened, the ratio of members to the number of cell groups was reduced from one group for every 53 church

7. Karen Hurston, "Freedom to Mature: Home Cell Units in Central Church," *World of Faith* 3 (Summer–Fall 1980):2–11.
    8. Ibid.

members in 1969, to one group for every 32 members by 1973. This means the number of cell groups almost doubled from 152 cells in 1969 to 394 cells in 1973.

Even though the church has experienced explosive growth from 8,000 members in 1969 to more than 350,000 today, it has continued to hold the size of the cells to about fifteen members to ensure maximum care for the personal and spiritual needs of each member.

This amazing accomplishment is made possible by the Holy Spirit's leadership in (1) the willingness of cell members to divide and create new cells when membership reaches between 8 and 16 members, (2) the training of an assistant cell leader in each group who is ready to assume the leadership of one-half his group once it divides, (3) the high accountability exercised by the church through the various levels of leadership, (4) the intense commitment to evangelism, Bible study, and concern for the daily needs of fellow group members, and (5) the intense loyalty to the greater ministry of services at Central Church, Dr. Paul Yongii Cho, and the team of more than 200 pastoral staff.

Five kinds of cell groups are operative at Full Gospel Central Church at this time. There are efforts to institute groups among businessmen. As of May 31, 1981, the groups totaled 12,757 in the categories shown in table 4.

All cell leaders are expected to attend one of the three training meetings at the main facility every Wednesday. The lesson to be taught in the cell group is presented by Dr. Cho on video tape. The attendance at the Wednesday training meeting averages 1,200 teachers. Most of these are new cell leaders.

More experienced cell leaders meet with their section heads in their neighborhood districts. "Baptism with the Holy Spirit" is a requisite for all levels of leadership above the assistant cell leader rank. Baptism is desirable for assistant cell leaders but is not required.

Membership in Full Gospel Central Church is by written application

Table 4 Cell Group Categories

Type of Cell Group	Men	Women	Youth	Children	Teachers
Total Cell Groups	1,296	7,882	336	3,034	209
Total Cell Members*	18,000	110,500	5,000	45,000	3,000

*Averaged to the nearest 500.

with a three-month waiting period. During that time, the applicant's faithfulness to his local cell group is a major factor in his or her acceptance or rejection. Once approved and officially received, water baptism is usually postponed until the summer months.

Several weeks, usually four or five, are planned during July and August for baptizing new believers. Each of the twelve geographical districts of the city schedules the baptism of their candidates. A total of 12,000 new members were baptized during the 1980 year.

Inactive attendance in the life of the church for a period of two years is considered just cause to remove a person's name from the membership roll. While a name can be removed at any time, upon request and approval by the appropriate leader, every January the rolls are reviewed and adjusted.[9]

Organizing to Evangelize

Dr. Donald McGavran, senior professor of Missions and founding dean of Fuller Seminary's School of World Mission and Institute of Church Growth (1965–1971) believes that Central Church may be the most organized church in the world.

As of 1982, over 115 missionaries had been sent out by the church. They planted more than eighty Korean churches in sixteen countries. In the United States, seventy-four missionaries lead sixty-six churches, with a membership of 8,132.

Media is taken seriously by the congregation in its strategy to communicate the gospel to the world. Yongsan Publishing Company is the printing and distribution ministry of the church. More than forty titles are distributed through that office.

Church Growth International television began in the United States in January, 1981. In June, 1983, a weekly half-hour program entitled, "Dr. Paul Yonggi Cho's World Discovery," was broadcast in all fifty states, reaching an estimated ten million homes. The first telecasts for the Republic of Korea began in April, 1980, and in Japan in June, 1980. Television programs produced in the Yoido church are viewed in both

9. A guidebook to the concept, principles, and organization of cell groups is *Caught in the Web* by Dr. John W. Hurston and Karen Hurston. The book is published in English by Church Growth International in Seoul. Included are the six biblical principles behind the cell system; detailed job descriptions and organizational charts; twelve elements that lend themselves to growth; twelve guidelines for an understanding of the pastor's role in the development of lay leadership; how a person becomes a member of a cell group; and sample copies of report forms used by the cell group leaders. An update report on the cell groups and how they function can be found in a special edition of *World of Faith* (Summer–Fall 1980) also published by Church Growth International.

New York City and Los Angeles. These cities have the largest Korean populations in the United States. In a recent article, Dr. Cho writes, "As I prayed, God impressed me with the bold goal of winning ten million Japanese to God in the decade of the 1980s."[10]

Various ministries also provide outreach and fellowship to special interest groups such as career youth, university students, men and women, military, and businessmen.

Every Sunday 150 members of the church's Evangelism Department spend eight hours in personal witness activities. All members are expected to witness regularly. In addition to the men's Evangelism Department there are about one thousand young people who witness in small groups. Also, an estimated 1,200 highly-trained soul-winners teach and encourage members to be active witnesses. Special seminars are taught several times each year to equip members with more effective witness skills. Dr. Cho challenges each family to reach another family each year. Amazing results have come from that challenge.

Dr. Cho confides, "If God were to answer your vague prayers, then you would never recognize that prayer as being answered by God. You must ask definitely and specifically. The Lord never welcomes vague prayers."[11]

The Lord continues to send new believers to the Full Gospel Central Church at a rate of almost 120,000 a year, 10,000 a month, 2,308 weekly, 330 daily, 13 hourly, or one every five minutes. Leaders of the church consider goals to be statements of faith to be claimed by God's people. Upon entering the new facility, the congregation set a five-year, total membership goal of 50,000 by the year 1978. That goal was achieved in only four years. A new goal of 100,000 members by 1981 was surpassed two years ahead of schedule in 1979. Early in 1981 membership exceeded the 150,000 mark. By early fall that same year, total membership reached the 200,000 mark. Central Church is the largest single church in Christian history and continues to grow.

Dr. Cho shares:

I have explained that the growth of our church is based upon goal-setting and the establishment of home cell groups. I have more than realized the goals I have set so far. At the beginning of 1980 we had 100,000 members in Full Gospel Central Church. Now I have set 500,000 as my goal to be

10. Paul Yonggi Cho, "Outreach: Life of the Church," *World of Faith* 1 (Winter 1981):3–4.
11. Cho, *The Fourth Dimension*, p. 17.

reached by 1984, the year in which we celebrate the 100th anniversary of Christianity in Korea.[12]

How does the congregation plan to achieve the 500,000 goal? By crusades or city-wide evangelistic meetings? Each cell group will accomplish the goal as they each ask the Holy Spirit's direction in selecting one family each year to win to salvation in Jesus Christ—one family each year. As each cell, composed of ten to fifteen families, prays, invites, and shares with those around them, the goal will be reached. Imagine . . . 500,000 church members!

12. Paul Yonggi Cho, *Successful Home Cell Groups* (Plainfield, NJ: Logos International, 1981), p. 81. This is the most recent publication on home cell groups.

3

The Church of the Changed Life— Kwang Lim Methodist Church

Seoul, Korea

Kim Sun Do was born in North Korea on December 2, 1930, and graduated from medical school before the onset of the Korean War. He escaped from the North in 1950 and joined the South Korean army. During the horrors of the war, Kim Sun Do promised the Lord that if He would protect him, he would serve Him with his life. After the signing of the cease-fire, Kim Sun Do kept his vow and entered Methodist Seminary in Seoul.

After graduating from the seminary he served a church in Seoul for five years before he began a ten-year term as an Air Force chaplain. As a chaplain, he had the opportunity to study counseling and pastoral care at the Wesley Theological Seminary at the American University in Washington, D.C.

Written by H. Cloyes Starnes, Southern Baptist Convention missionary to Seoul, Korea. Adapted by the author.

In 1971 Kim Sun Do was appointed pastor of the Kwang Lim Methodist Church. The first Sunday he preached there were only 170 in attendance at the morning worship service. Pastor Kim's first goal was to have 500 in attendance. Although the attendance increased each year, the crowded conditions in the center of Seoul hindered further growth.

In 1976 Pastor Kim attended Robert Schuler's Institute for Successful Church Leadership in California. At this time God gave him a vision of direction for the Kwang Lim Methodist Church in Seoul.

Although New Year's Day in 1979 was cold, with ice and snow, Pastor Kim went out in search of a new location for the church. The most rapidly developing section of Seoul is the area south of the Han River, in the southeastern part of the city. God led Pastor Kim to a pear orchard in this section where he knelt beneath the trees and prayed, "Oh, God, make this holy ground and I will build your church here."

This was such a deep spiritual experience for Pastor Kim that he began a fast which continued for twenty days. On two other occasions during the building of the new church he fasted for twenty days. Pastor Kim says that he can continue the normal work of his ministry, although he may go to the mountains for brief periods of prayer, during a fast. He testifies that he feels much stronger physically and spiritually and his preaching seems to be anointed with special power.

Before contacting the owners of the pear orchard, Pastor Kim led his church in a vote to sell their present church property. He had faith that God would help them. The negotiation for the new land was not easy. There were six owners and the price was twice the revenues received from the old church property, but God helped the members raise the money to pay for this new land. At first, the city government refused to give permission for the construction of a church building on that location. But Pastor Kim and his people triumphed. After meeting in a tent for eight months they moved into a beautiful new church with an auditorium which seats 4,300.

The church had no building fund when they started. A deacon of the church was the president of a large construction company which offered to build the new church building. The church has paid almost one million dollars for the new building since 1979 and planned to complete payments during 1982.

When the church members moved into the new building they had an attendance of approximately 1700 and did not fill the lower floor of their new auditorium. However, by January of 1982 the total attendance of the three morning services exceeded 5,000. The church budget for 1982 was almost $2.3 million.

Pastor Kim emphasizes positive thinking and faith in his sermons. He believes that there is a serious credibility gap in the life and ministry of many churches. For this reason he places much emphasis on ministering to the real needs of his people. He seeks to involve many of the church members in some kind of ministry.

Every Thursday morning he leads a lay leaders' workshop, "The Academy of Lay Ministers." This meeting includes all of the Bible teachers and mission society leaders. There are seventeen men's and seventeen women's missionary societies in the church. For instance, there are about 50 medical doctors in the Luke's Mission Society, about 60 college and university professors in the Philip's Mission Society, and about 50 business executives in the Philemon's Mission society. During the church's 28th anniversary celebrations in 1980, the members of the Luke's Mission Society gave free medical counsel to all who came to the church and the members of the Philip's Mission Society gave free educational and vocational counsel. On Good Friday each year Holy Communion is served throughout the day, and, at the same time, members are encouraged to donate blood at the church.

The church partially supports about fifty rural churches. They also support a prison chaplain's and hospital chaplain's ministry. A member of the church's pastoral staff ministers to college students. The church also partially supports a number of seminary students.

Though Pastor Kim emphasizes the importance of ministering to the social needs of people, he does not preach a social gospel. He believes that the problems of society cannot be solved until the hearts of people are changed. The 1982 motto for the Kwang Lim Church was "The Church of the Changed Life."

Pastor Kim's ministry is positively evangelistic. He regularly gives opportunity for people to come forward and make public profession of their faith in Jesus Christ during the Sunday morning services. The church averages about thirty public professions each Sunday.

In 1981 Pastor Kim had a tremendous evangelistic ministry to the men in the military reserve forces in Seoul. The church offered the use of their auditorium to the reserve trainees if the pastor could speak to each group. In this way Pastor Kim has been able to present the principles of Christ to 30,000 reservists. As a result, some 800 men have professed Christ as

Providing an evangelistic ministry to the people of Seoul, Pastor Kim Sun Do preaches in the 4,300-capacity auditorium of the recently completed Kwang Lim Methodist Church.

Table 5 Growth of Kwang Lim Methodist Church, Seoul, Korea

	1982	1981	1980	1975	1970	1965	1960	1955	1950
Church Membership	11,486	12,200	5,590	1,820	680	502	220	168	82
Worship Attendance	5,646	4,970	2,970	1,003	305	200	180	100	40
Sunday School Enrollment		1,500	1,300	380	155	130	95	85	35
Sunday School Attendance Elementary through High School	4,095	1,020	980	270	135	105	70	50	25
Baptisms	2,740	2,100	1,240	480	175	110	42	35	20
Total Home Bible Study Groups	692	380	243	32	6	5			
Total Offering (in millions)	2.3	1.2	.15	.04					

Savior and joined the church. Pastor Kim also gives training in evangelism and witnessing to his leaders in the Thursday morning workshop.

As a result of Pastor Kim's effort to bridge the credibility gap in his ministry he has not received a salary from his church since the beginning of construction on the new building.

In July of 1980 the first Church Growth Seminar was held in the Kwang Lim Church. Pastor Kim Sun Do was the featured lecturer. There were 278 pastors from several denominations enrolled.

The congregation has made gigantic strides since its original thirty-five members crossed into South Korea at the end of the Korean War. Those early days spent in an abandoned Japanese-built Buddhist temple as a branch of the Kwang Hi Moon Methodist Church proved to be essential for the development of the church. Within three decades Kwang Lim became the second largest Methodist congregation outside the United States and the third largest Methodist church in the world. In the first months of 1984, the congregation had 13,500 members, a pastoral staff of 25 ministers, a total of 1,234 deacons and deaconesses (494 deacons and elders and 740 deaconesses), a Sunday school attendance of 2,518, and a total of 750 cell groups with 3,250 in attendance. The church operates one mission church and partially supports 102 other satellites.

As indicated by the 1984 data, Kwang Lim has continued to grow as it reaches the multitudes for Jesus Christ.

4

The World's Largest Presbyterian Church— Young Nak Presbyterian Church
Seoul, Korea

Every four hours a new Christian congregation is organized in the Republic of Korea. Church bells echo daily at five o'clock in the morning to call believers to prayer in Korea's 18,000 Protestant and Evangelical churches. Over 2,000 churches are in the capital city of Seoul.

According to Samuel H. Moffett, professor of Ecumenics and Missions at Princeton Theological Seminary, "Korea's Christians grow four times as fast as the population. One estimate says Koreans build six new churches every day. Protestants outnumber Catholics about six to one, and well over half of the Protestants are Presbyterians."[1]

The world's largest Presbyterian church is the Young Nak Presbyterian

H. Cloyes Starnes, missionary to Korea for the Southern Baptist Convention, gathered major research data for this chapter.

1. Samuel H. Moffett, "The Church in Asia: Getting on the Charts," *Christianity Today* 17 (October 2, 1981):25–39.

Church of Seoul. L. Nelson Bell wrote several years ago, " . . . on any given Sabbath it has been estimated that more people worship in Seoul's largest Presbyterian church than in all churches of that denomination in all of Japan."[2]

Young Nak began as a tent-church. It ministered to refugees escaping the invading Communist army as it marched through North Korea at the end of World War II. Army tents provided shelter since building materials were scarce.

The 60,000-member Young Nak Presbyterian Church provided the motivation for Dr. Paul Yonggi Cho in 1961 to build Central Church, the largest church in the world. At that time the Presbyterian congregation was ten times larger than the smaller, but rapidly growing, Assembly of God church. Dr. Cho recalls:

> In those earlier days the Young Nak Presbyterian Church was the largest church in Seoul. It had about 6,000 members, and that proved to be a challenge to me. In fact, one day, without anyone else knowing about it, I took a measuring stick and went over to the Presbyterian church in order to take its exact measurements. . . . It seated more than 2,000 persons.
>
> In my ambition, I then said, "I will build a church larger than this, and the Lord will fill it."[3]

In 1984 Young Nak Church reported a total membership of 60,000 with more than 10,000 households; twenty pastoral staff members; fourteen pastoral assistants (unordained seminary students serving a two-year internship before ordination); 4,000 deacons and deaconesses (1,500 men and 2,500 women); 1,562 cell groups with 56,200 attendants; a worship attendance of 25,785; and a Sunday school attendance of 12,400. Church membership, Sunday school attendance, and worship attendance almost doubled during the five-year period from 1975–1980. Contributions grew from $600,000 to $3,000,000 during the same period.

The growth of this superchurch reflects the growth of Korean churches. From 1940 to 1961 the Korean Protestant community more than tripled its membership. It almost doubled again during the 1960s, from 1.3 to 2.3 million members, and more than tripled during the 1970s to 7 million members.

2. L. Nelson Bell, "Korean Missions: Triumph and Shadow," *Christianity Today* 10 (February 18, 1957):1–16.

3. Paul Yonggi Cho, *Successful Home Cell Groups* (Plainfield, NJ: Logos International, 1981), p. 2.

As these congregations begin the 1980s, 20 percent of the Korean population professes to be Christian, among Evangelicals and Protestants alone. Assembly of God Korean missionary Nell L. Kennedy notes, "Only the Philippines with its large Roman Catholic majority, outstrips Korea in the ratio of Christians to the general population."[4] Currently, Evangelicals and Protestants are growing at a rate seven times faster than the general population.

Samuel H. Moffatt, commenting on the frequent splits and splinter groups generated by rapid growth, observes:

> Korean Christianity seems to split as fast as it grows. All the larger denominations suffered schisms in the 1950's and most of those divisions remain. Yet rightly or wrongly, the divisions seem to stimulate growth, not hinder it.[5]

Communist Influence on Church Growth

The Young Nak Presbyterian Church had only two pastors throughout its forty-year history. As founding pastor, Dr. Han Kyung Chik served the congregation twenty-eight years, 1945–1973. His successor, the capable and energetic Dr. Cho Choon Park, celebrates his eleventh anniversary as pastor in 1984. Both men are graduates of Princeton Theological Seminary.

Dr. Han was born in North Korea on December 29, 1902, to a Confucian father. He was allowed to enroll in a Christian school founded by Presbyterian missionary Samuel A. Moffett. At the age of fourteen he became a Christian and developed friendships with missionaries.·

In 1915, Han transferred to the O-San Academy in Chung Joo. While enrolled in this school he developed an appreciation for his Korean heritage from his Christian teachers.

Only five years earlier Korea had been annexed as a province of the growing Japanese Empire. The standard of living was altered noticeably as agriculture, industry, banking, and transportation were modernized by the imperial war lords from the South.

Japan ruled Korea, often with brutal force, until 1945. During the forty-year occupation many Japanese were sent from Tokyo to occupy and assume control of Korean farms.

Laws were passed forbidding the use of the Korean language. The

4. Nell L. Kennedy, "Troubled South Korea Manages a Very Big Bash for Missions," *Christianity Today* 16 (September 19, 1980):24–44.

5. Moffett, "The Church in Asia," p. 39.

name of the country and even its citizens were renamed with Japanese substitutes. Korean families were separated and some were sent to Japan for resettlement.

Missionaries who remained in Korea often were not allowed to preach or teach, and Koreans were limited to one worship service each week. These were the conditions when Han Kyung Chik entered the O-San Academy at age thirteen. The climate would become even more tense.

In 1921, at age nineteen, he entered Soong Sil (Union Christian) College in Pyeng Yang. He was a frequent guest and a secretary to Dr. William N. Blair. His love and loyalty for Korea grew. During those years he received direction from God concerning his future. Larry Ward, executive vice-president of World Vision, recalls the event:

> . . . as he walked along the beach one day, he suddenly felt that God was speaking to him. The young student stopped, fell to his knees, prayed for what must have been hours. When he finally arose, he knew what he had to do. God had called him to the ministry. . . .[6]

Despite the complications created by the Japanese occupation and the limited opportunity for travel, Dr. Blair was able to arrange for his young friend to enter Emporia College in Emporia, Kansas. Han received his Bachelor of Arts degree in 1926. He enrolled in Princeton Seminary and graduated in 1929.

The intensity of his studies exhausted him. For two years he was hospitalized for tuberculosis in Albuquerque, New Mexico. This detour in his plans would serve to increase his sensitivity for the sick and poor throughout his future ministry.

He returned to Korea in 1931, at age twenty-nine, and taught one year in a Christian high school before moving to Sinuiju. This northwest frontier of Korea, located across the Yalu River from Manchuria, is where Dr. Han pastored a Presbyterian church. Three years later his congregation had grown to approximately 1,500 members.

> By 1935 . . . relying on their own financial resources, they began construction of a large church building. Within three years they had paid for it. Han served this same church until 1941, when—with the outbreak of war

6. Larry Ward, "Dr. Han Kyung Chik, Korea's Quiet Dynamo," *World Vision* 3 (March 1968):12–18. This article is a most valuable piece of literature on the early history of Young Nak Presbyterian Church. The author is indebted to Larry Ward and *World Vision* for this rare article.

The Young Nak Presbyterian Church—that denomination's largest—has been pastored by only two men during its forty-year history. Dr. Han Kynung Chik (top) was the founding pastor; he was succeeded in 1973 by Dr. Cho Choon (bottom).

in the Pacific—he was imprisoned by the Japanese who regarded him as pro-American. Within a few weeks he was released, but was forbidden to preach.[7]

During the war he ministered in an orphanage and in a home for the elderly. This second detour in his life would equip him for the future social welfare ministry at Young Nak Church.

The year 1945 held many surprises. Liberation had come at last. After Japan's defeat, U.S. troops occupied the southern half of Korea and Russian forces occupied the northern half. A separate Korean government was formed in each half. For two years the two Korean governments, the United States, Russia, and Britain were unable to devise a satisfactory plan to reunite Korea. In 1947 the problem was put into the hands of the United Nations.

In July, 1948, representatives of the newly-elected national assembly elected Syngman Rhee, a Christian, President of the Republic of Korea. Three of the first presidents of the Republic of Korea have been Christians and have been an encouragement to growth of the churches.

Rapid church growth was about to occur throughout South Korea, especially in Seoul. Seoul is the Cinderella story for missionary response in Asia. Historically, Seoul has been more resistant to the gospel than other sectors of the peninsula. A series of four successive military invasions would awaken the city to the gospel of Jesus Christ.

The first invasion was a Communist-inspired rebellion on the southern island of Cheju-do in April, 1948. The following October 19, a contingent of government troops joined the rebel cause. Widespread Communist guerrilla activities occurred throughout South Korea.

The second, and most important, invasion occurred at dawn on June 25, 1950. North Korean troops led by Soviet officers launched a full-scale attack across the 38th parallel. Two days later the U.N. Security Council sent a fifteen-nation army to aid South Korea. The Korean War had officially begun.

The North Korean army made rapid advances. By September they controlled most of South Korea until the U.N. troops drove them north across the 38th parallel as far as the Yalu River and the Manchurian border. The third wave of troops opened the way for Christians from Seoul to return home to rebuild. The fighting continued until a truce was signed in July, 1953.

7. Ibid.

Table 6   Church Growth—Young Nak Presbyterian Church

	1980	1975	1970	1965	1961	1955	1950
Church Membership	34,864	19,576	13,337	11,386	5,797	3,000	27
Home Study Groups	673	293	210	144	93	80	1
New Members per Day, Average per 5 Years	8.4	3.4	1	3	1.5	1.6	1.6
Ratio of Home Study Groups to Membership	1:52	1:67	1:63	1:79	1:62	1:37	1:27

The Communists had dismantled the organized church in North Korea. Samuel H. Moffett reports:

They wiped out the organized church in the north, where almost two-thirds of Korea's Christians were living. . . . More than one-third of the entire population of North Korea escaped across the border between 1945 and 1950.[8]

Accompanied by twenty-seven refugees, Dr. Han slipped across the border. Claiming an abandoned Shinto temple as their new center, the small group began to multiply. Refugees continued to stream across the border located just twenty-five miles north of Seoul. This group of twenty-seven refugees organized Young Nak Presbyterian Church. Table 6 summarizes the growth of the church from 1950 to 1980.

The smell of freshly-dug earth has been an identifying mark of Young Nak since 1949. At great sacrifice the congregation launched seven major construction projects in the last thirty years.

Due to the Communist invasions and subsequent military occupations of Seoul, the original sanctuary, with its seating capacity of 1,850, was finally completed after six years. Immediately after the building was dedicated, Communists invaded the city.

An elder of the church, Kin Eunak, returned to examine and pray for the safety of the church and its sanctuary each day. Miraculously, the structure had not been destroyed. Soldiers were about to ignite a bonfire to burn the church when the elder was discovered, arrested, and told that he would be executed immediately. His request for five minutes to pray was granted before he was martyred on the front steps. An unexpected counterattack on the city scattered the Communists and the building was

8. Samuel H. Moffett, "The Gospel in Korea: Struggle and Triumph," *World Vision* 8 (September 1973):17–9.

spared. A monument in front of the sanctuary honors the devotion of this son of the congregation.

Three years later the first educational building, with a seating capacity of 1,200, was completed at an expense of $470,000. Another eight years elapsed before the missions building, with its smaller 1,000-seat auditorium was dedicated in 1965. In 1973, the present Christian service building was constructed at a cost of $800,000.

By 1973 the congregation surpassed the 13,000-membership mark. The next year a staff apartment building was built to accommodate the fourteen associate pastors and their families. In 1975, the five-story Dr. Han Kyung Chik Memorial Building was built to train an estimated 650 people daily. The final addition, built in 1978, expanded the main auditorium to a 3,750-seat capacity. This expansion cost $1,000,000.

The church buildings are located in the center of the business district in this city of almost nine million people. There are several hospitals in the immediate area. The large Catholic Cathedral is located next to Young Nak. In the same district are large office buildings and elegant shops, department stores, and the largest Western hotels. There are very few private residences in the area. The upper floors of many shops serve as living quarters.

Training God's Army

Young Nak Presbyterian Church is affiliated with the Jesus Presbyterian Church of Korea. Almost 4,000 congregations constitute the total membership of 1,234,270.

The Bible is the basic textbook at Young Nak. Versions currently in use include the Korean Revised Version, the 1977 Good News For Modern Man, and the 1967 Revised Version published by the Korean Bible Society.

Although graded literature is provided by the denominational publishing house, in the Korean language, the church staff adapts and supplements the materials to the needs of their own people. All teachers of adult classes prepare their own teaching materials and reproduce them for the class.

The Korean language is used in most classes. There are three Bible study groups taught in English: one for college students, one for adults under age thirty-five, and one for adults over age thirty-five.

A trademark of the church is the variety of other learning opportunities provided for members and their friends. Koreans are known for their academic interests. The Korean literacy rate of 90 percent is one of the highest in the world. Training provided by the church, in addition to the Sunday school, includes both Sunday and week-day classes.

Among the 167 classes taught at the main facility are two classes for mothers of preschoolers, classes designed for new members, and Hebrew and Greek classes.

Weekday Bible studies are provided by the church. An estimated 150–200 members attend the daily meeting with a different age-group scheduled each day. Approximately 600 individuals attend these classes which survey the entire Bible in one year.

In the evening Bible school is provided for 120 students. This is a two-year program. Also, every Friday afternoon approximately 180 senior citizens gather for Bible study.

In 1980, two classes began meeting daily for two hours at the church. The course is composed of twelve different Bible studies weekly and is primarily attended by women.

Every Monday morning the 3,000 leaders of the 673 community groups, which meet every Friday evening, meet at the church. The pastors prepare them to lead the next meeting.

The Lutheran Bethel Bible Series course is taught to one young people's group. One group studies great Christian hymns. A couples class, age forty-five and older, studies hymnology.

The typical worship service at Young Nak Presbyterian Church is very similar to a conservative Presbyterian congregation in the United States.

Table 7   Sunday School Profile of Young Nak Presbyterian Church, 1979–80

	Attendance	Age Grouping	Teacher/ Pupil Ratio	Total Teachers
Preschool	607	Birth–Age 6	1:14	45
Children	911	Grades 1–6	1:22	42
Youth	1842	Grades 7–12	1:37	50
Young Adults	595	Ages 19–34	1:99	6
College	450	Ages 18–24	1:90	5
Middle Adults	726	Ages 35–44	1:80	9
Older Adults	1615	Age 45 +	1:162	10
Teacher	100			
Mothers	100			
Total	7396			

Each service is approximately one hour long. The first twenty minutes includes the call to worship, recitation of the Apostle's Creed, three hymns, scripture reading, and special choir music. Following the twenty-five minute sermon there are the offerings, announcements, two hymns, and benediction.

The 3,750 available seats are filled each Sunday for the prayer meeting at dawn (5 AM) and the eight worship services: 7 AM, 8:30 (children and students); 10 AM; 11:30 AM; 1:30 PM, 3 PM, 5 PM (children and students), 7 PM. The Sunday morning worship service is broadcast on two radio stations. Traditional Wednesday night prayer services are held at seven o'clock, and this service, too, is broadcast. Members also conduct a Friday noon prayer meeting.

Young Nak congregation has five chapel choirs. The church's orchestra is a regular part of the Sunday evening worship service. There are also five age-graded children's and student choirs.

The church could be described as an evangelistic Evangelical church, conservative in doctrine, but not radically fundamentalistic. It is similar to conservative and evangelistic Southern Presbyterian churches in the United States. Doctrine and church polity would also have much in common with Southern Presbyterians. A Southern Baptist would feel comfortable with the worship climate and spiritual warmth of the church. The congregation has been led in two revival meetings by Baptist evangelist Dr. John Haggai.

Like most Korean churches, Young Nak believes that a personal conversion cannot be verified in children. Candidates younger than age sixteen or seventeen are not baptized.

A one-year waiting period for baptism is required after a person makes a profession of faith in Christ. During this time attendance in the new member class, an examination on the church's doctrinal beliefs, a personal testimony of a personal conversion experience, and a one-month special class immediately before being baptized are required.

The mode of baptism is usually sprinkling. The church will immerse any candidate upon request. No one is allowed to partake of the Lord's Supper until having been baptized. The ordinances of the Lord's Supper and baptism are observed only four times each year.

Priorities at Young Nak

Even the casual observer will soon detect the three priorities of the congregation: evangelism, religious education, and social welfare.

Evangelism. An estimated 18 percent of the baptisms each year at Young Nak are new believers, according to church leaders. A total of 3,000 members participate in or support the church's visitation and evangelistic activities each week.

An army of 1,000 well-trained soul-winners lead the evangelistic activities of the church. Another 2,000 to 3,000 members are improving their skills alongside the main force.

In 1974 the new pastor, Dr. Park, began a new program for training soul-winners. During the subsequent years 958 church members have been trained in twenty-two training classes.

Five members are enrolled from each of the fourteen church parishes. Seventy members are trained every five weeks. They meet for two hours on two evenings each week. The 1980 goal was eight new classes during each training period with 500 new volunteers trained.

Dr. Park and his staff prepared a textbook for the training program. In addition to the time spent in the classroom, evangelistic visitation is included in the training to insure exposure to personal and productive evangelism methods. Frequently, one-day seminars are conducted by the church for various age groups in evangelism.

The men's evangelistic and missionary organization reports 800 members. The Women's Missionary Society contains 2,200 members. These groups established twenty-two new churches in 1980. An Open-Air Evangelistic Society of 150 members also is active in the city.

Dr. Park's personal and church goals are related to evangelism and church growth. He is more concerned about training his people as effective personal evangelists than promoting large evangelistic crusades.

Young Nak Church started new churches in Korea since 1945. The strategy has been to help each satellite become a self-supporting, independent congregation rather than a daughter church continually dependent of Young Nak.

Since 1947 over 150 new churches have been established that are now self-supporting. Fifteen other churches are still supported by Young Nak. In their overseas missionary work, the congregation sent its first missionary to Thailand in 1956.

Chaplains are maintained and provided by the church for hospital, industry, and military ministries in Seoul. The church has built a servicemen's center at the large army training camp and they continue to support a military evangelist-counselor there. Every Sunday open-air evangelistic meetings are held by the Open-Air Evangelistic Society.

Religious Education.   The church's membership is divided into seventeen parishes with one ordained minister and one unordained seminary-graduate staff member responsible for each parish. Each parish is divided into many church communities with four elders or deacons responsible for each. There are 673 well-organized church communities.

On Friday nights there are regular meetings in homes across Seoul, with an average attendance of fifteen in each home. All ages attend and the majority are women. Korean homes are small and the rooms are crowded. Everyone brings Bibles and hymnbooks and uses them as they take notes on the Bible study.

Leaders of these meetings are selected from the mature Christians. These leaders meet at the church every Monday morning and are taught the material to be studied. These teaching and worship materials are prepared at the church and distributed weekly.

Each week reports are made from each of these community group meetings and are sent to the central church office. Reports include updates about sickness among members, graduations, deaths, marriages, births, and other news of importance. Information concerning visitors in the church worship services is passed on to the community where the visitor lives. Visits are made within the first two weeks.

The church has 2,118 unordained deacons who work in the church community organization and on church committees. Each year the parish pastors recommend men and women for election as deacons and deaconesses.

All candidates are carefully screened and then recommended to an annual meeting. The session nominates candidates for ordination as deacons and elders to the congregation. The pastors and elders of the church make decisions on all church policies.

The first Sunday of each month, following the worship service, all new members of the church meet with the Visitation Committee and all pastors of the church. Refreshments are served and there is a slide presentation on the history of the church. Included in the presentation is a summary of all the church programs and activities.

Following the slides, the pastor encourages all the new members to grow in the Christian life. He stresses how church programs are designed to meet the growth needs.

New members are asked to attend the new member class in the Sunday school for six months. Then they are asked to study in a regular class for one additional year before being considered as a candidate for baptism. At that time they are interviewed and questioned by elders and pastors before being baptized. New members are sometimes excluded from official church membership.

Retreats and camps are valuable tools used by the church. Church facilities can accommodate 400 people. During the summer months, tents are used for the four, week-long camps. Each camp has 2,000 in attendance.

The congregation owns a small retreat center in the mountains for use by its pastors and their families. These facilities accommodate about ten people.

A deaf congregation of 500 members is an active part of the church life at Young Nak. The church also operates a Woman's Seminary designed to train visitors from the church. Enrollment for this group averages almost ninety.

Social Welfare Ministries. The church's strategy of reaching the city has taken several shapes in addition to the channels mentioned above. The myriad of social ministries include the school, the kindergarten with its enrollment of 120, clothing and food distribution, free medical clinics, the deaf ministry, an orphanage, a home for the elderly, a widows' home, and a servicemen's center.

The school system maintains an enrollment of 3,000–4,000 students. A special focus is placed on junior and senior high school students.

Free medical assistance is available through a team of 160 physicians and 160 nurses. This clinic service began in 1980.

An orphanage and a widows' home each care for 100–200 residents. A home for the aged cares for less than fifty persons.

Goals For Growth

Pastor Cho Choon Park has proven to be a man mighty in Spirit. Philippians 4:13, "I can do all things through Christ which strengtheneth me" is his favorite Bible verse.

His personal and church goals are related to evangelism and church growth. The future of Young Nak Presbyterian Church is unquestionably linked to the vision of the pastor, his ability to comprehend God's will, and the willingness of the people to follow the pastor's leadership.

Six goals for the church have been identified by Dr. Park. First, Dr. Park visualizes the 1980s as the decade when the church will continue to double and even triple in membership. This means that the membership could grow from 50,000 to 150,000 members.

A second goal is to buy land on the south side of Seoul to build a new

15,000-seat auditorium. An educational space for 10,000 members is planned on land already purchased in the same area. When this phase is completed, a total of one hundred buses would be needed for a bus ministry to the city.

Third, Dr. Park's wishes to convert the Woman's Seminary into a junior college.

Fourth, plans are being made to expand the educational foundation work which operates the church's middle and high schools.

Fifth, the Social Welfare Society of the church plans to build a social welfare building.

Finally, the church has the goal of sending out 100 crosscultural missionaries during the eighties. Eight missionaries have been sent out and two are ready to leave.

Since the age of twenty-two, when Dr. Park first preached to a group of 550 Sunday school students, God has guided and provided for him. Much has been accomplished under God's leadership since the pastor was called to serve as a deacon and as pastor of Young Nak. The future is bright for the world's largest Presbyterian church as it continues to evangelize in the shadow of Communist North Korea.

5

Healing in Jesus' Name— Sungrak Baptist Church
Seoul, Korea

Sungrak Baptist Church is another rapidly growing Korean superchurch. It was founded in 1969 with 85 members. By January, 1984, membership had swelled to 19,730.

Sungrak is located on the outskirts of Seoul in a rather poor neighborhood. The climate of the church is very religious; the atmosphere is subdued, but full of the Holy Spirit.

Forty-two-year-old Ki Dong Kim has served as the senior pastor since the church began. Pastor Kim came from a family with no religious background. He was converted at the age of nineteen and two years later began to preach. He holds degrees from seminary as well as graduate school.

In January 1984, 507 deacons and 973 deaconesses, 7 ordained pastors, and 75 staff members served the church. Twelve branch chapels and eight missions are operated by Sungrak.

Don C. Jones, missionary to Korea for the Southern Baptist Convention and adminstrator of Korean Baptist Mission in Seoul, gathered primary research data for this chapter.

A Church with Strong Preaching

The 3,200-seat sanctuary is filled to capacity at each of Sungrak's four Sunday morning worship services. Each service lasts almost two hours. The main sanctuary is capable of seating five times the number of attendants that the educational facilities can accommodate. This is obviously a church with strong preaching from the pulpit.

Each service is saturated with prayer. Prayer is designated seven times in the order of service. After the opening congregational hymn, silent prayer and the Lord's Prayer follow. Another hymn is sung intensely.

A most unusual event then occurs in this Baptist congregation. For approximately three minutes all hands are lifted toward heaven in prayer.

The offering follows congregational singing and the reading of Scripture. Unlike some churches where the offering is a brief, rushed event, the pastor and members of Sungrak have established this as a time charged with adoration and praise to God.

Next, the congregation sings "Hallelujah" for five minutes, the announcements are read, and a prayer of thanksgiving is offered. Following a forty-minute sermon preached with resounding authority, the congregation again prays and sings a hymn. All four services are filled with music—from the congregation, the orchestra, and the 120-voice choir. The service is concluded with a welcome to newcomers. As members exit the six-story building, they wait on the curb for the white-gloved traffic policeman to stop traffic and allow them to make their way back to their homes.

Table 8   Profile of Growth—Sungrak Baptist Church

	1984*	1982	1981	1980	1969
Church Members	19,730	12,320	6,845	3,874	85
Worship Attendance		9,960	5,200	3,000	85
Sunday School Attendance	9,730	4,750	420	350	60
Baptisms		1,200	750	550	70
Teaching Units		24	16	9	1
Cells (Home Groups)	767	330	200	120	16
Cell Attendance	7,670				
Offering in Dollars		700,000	400,000	150,000	30,000

From interview and questionnaire.
* January, 1984.

An Adult-Centered Sunday School

Many members remain for Sunday school or meet their classmates in one of the four additional locations in Seoul. Approximately 4,000 adults are joined by 500 young people, 200 children between the ages of seven and ten, and 250 preschool children. These 5,000 Sunday school attendees are led by a team of 109 teachers.

The preschool, children's, and young people's classes contain ten to fifteen pupils per teacher. Due to a space shortage, each adult group contains an average of 175 pupils.

Extension Bible schools are conducted at Tae Gu, Pusan, and Kwang joo. Attendance varies from twenty to one thousand people in each place. These adult gatherings are led by teachers trained at Berea Academy for a minimum of two years. Bibles are used by all attendees and hymn singing is followed by Bible study. These extension classes are available day and night for anyone wishing to study the Bible on weekdays.

Sungrak Baptist Church publishes its own Sunday school curriculum. All materials are written in Korean. Age-graded materials are provided for kindergarten, grades 1 to 4, grades 5 to 6, junior high, and senior high. In the adult classes, men and women meet together. The children's and young people's classes have the boys and girls meeting in separate groups.

An estimated 500 members participate in or support the church's weekly visitation and evangelistic activities. There are approximately 16,000 soul-winners in the congregation. Pastor Kim estimates that 40 percent of all persons baptized in 1983 were new believers. Soul-winners are trained weekly through home services and the Berea Bible Study.

New members are assimilated into the life of the church through the

Table 9   Profile of the Sunday School, Sungrak Baptist Church, 1982–83

Age Groups	Approximate Attendance	Age of Groups	Pupils per Teacher	Total Number of Teachers
Preschool	250	4–6	10	25
Children	200	7–10	10	20
Youth	500	11–19	15	42
Adults	3,800	20–80	173	22
Totals	4,750		43*	109

* Average for total Sunday school.

Located on the outskirts of Seoul, the Sungrak Baptist Church is growing rapidly. Under the guidance of senior pastor Ki Dong Kim, membership climbed to more than 19,000 in 1984.

weekly home meetings. There is no waiting list or period before new members are baptized. The only requirement is an assurance of salvation.

The two major factors contributing to the growth of the church are the Bible-centered messages from the pulpit and the demonstrations of the power of God to heal.

The key scripture passage claimed by the pastor as a promise for the congregation is Psalm 23. The motto of the congregation is, "Make Disciples." Sungrak places a strong emphasis on resurrection and eternal life.

6

Raising Up Workers for the Kingdom—Chung-Hyeon Presbyterian Church

Seoul, Korea

In 1973, the Chung-Hyeon Presbyterian Church sent out its first foreign missionary, Rev. Paul M. Suh, to Indonesia. Ten years later, the congregation supported seventeen missionaries serving in ten countries and partially supported ten additional missionaries. Territories touched by the church include Japan, Hong Kong, Taiwan, Egypt, Australia, Argentina, Paraguay, Chile, Belgium, and West Germany.

Chung-Hyeon is the second largest Presbyterian church in the world. In January, 1984, the church had a membership of 11,099 with a Sunday

Data from a questionnaire designed by the author and filled out by members of Chung-Hyeon Presbyterian Church was used in this chapter. Missionary Don Jones, administrator of the Korean Baptist Mission for Southern Baptists, updated the information.

Dr. Hyung Chul Yoon, associate pastor in Christian Education for the Chung-Hyeon Presbyterian Church and a graduate student at Fuller Theological Seminary in Pasedena, California, shared valuable information in an interview in Pasedena.

The booklet, *This Is Chung-Hyeon Church*, published by the church, is quoted frequently.

school attendance of 5,000 excited believers. Approximately 477 deacons and 1,115 deaconesses serve the congregation. A large ministry staff contains 56 pastors and 45 employees.

A Brief History of Chung-Hyeon Church

Chung-Hyeon Presbyterian Church was founded on September 6, 1953. One month later the congregation moved to its present location. A makeshift tent served as a worship center. By November both primary and adult Sunday school departments had been organized. The older children's and young people's departments soon followed.

The church's present building was constructed in 1955, the year that the name Chung-Hyeon Presbyterian Church was adopted. One month later the church's young people organized a mission church on the outer edge of Seoul. On September 8, 1957, Rev. Kim Chang-In was ordained and named senior pastor on the church's fourth anniversary.

"Raising Up Workers for the Kingdom of Heaven" was adopted as the motto of the church in January, 1963. At the same time, "I love Thee, O Lord, my strength" (translation is from Korean to English; Psalm 18:1) was designated as the official promise verse of the church. In September of 1963, the congregation joined the General Assembly of the Presbyterian Church in Korea. Broadcast evangelism began in 1967. In 1968 the church bought a parcel of land for a prayer retreat and burial ground.

Table 10   Profiles of Growth, Chung-Hyeon Presbyterian Church

	1984*	1982	1981	1980	1970	1955
Church Members		14,000				
Worship Attendance		6,000	4,055	3,699	2,018	528
Average Sunday School Attendance	4,998	4,200	3,348	2,870	1,406	333
Baptisms		427	461	400	178	35
Teaching Units		16	15	15	9	2
Cells (Home Bible Study Groups)	747	338			51	9
Cell Attendance	1,891	845				
Total Offering (Dollars) in millions		$1.42	$1.1			
Member Households		4,233	3,729	3,363		

From interview and questionnaire.
* January, 1984.

The 1,800-seat sanctuary has been replaced with the newly-built 11,000-seat auditorium. Prior to the construction of this new building, the Chung-Hyeon Presbyterian Church conducted five worship services each Sunday morning in addition to the dawn prayer meeting customary to Korean Christians. Five choirs aid the various worship services.

Church leaders began to organize groups like the Church Officers Association (1953), the Women's Evangelism Association (1954), the Men's Evangelism Association (1954), the Christian Education Committee (1961), the Police Evangelism Association (1966), and the Evangelical Overseas Mission Association (1968).

Pastor Kim Chang-In, age sixty-six, is the sixth pastor of Chung-Hyeon Presbyterian Church. He has served nine congregations: five in North Korea, two in Pusan, and two in Seoul.

Pastor Kim's father died when Kim was eight years old. He describes his mother as a "most godly" mother. He was converted at age fourteen and began preaching at age seventeen. A graduate of Korean Theological Seminary, he has been offered honorary degrees but has refused them. He has three sons and two daughters.

Pastor Kim views preaching as food for the soul and his goal is to feed the saints "digestible meals" by preaching the Word of God simply and plainly. He has a passion for evangelism, and stresses that in the fight against Satan to save souls, the "evangelist, like a soldier, must be well-trained and fight with a 'do-or-die' spirit." A worship service without a choir is unthinkable to him. All five Sunday worship services and the Wednesday prayer service are served by choirs.

His personal life goal is to live a life of integrity like Joseph and Daniel. His favorite biblical book is Psalms and favorite Bible doctrine is the sovereignty and glory of God.

Imagine . . . 100,000 Tracts a Month

"Evangelism Church" is a nickname given to Chung-Hyeon Presbyterian Church. Members unapologetically share the gospel person-to-person, door-to-door, and in the streets of Seoul. Members of the congregation distribute an estimated 100,000 gospel tracts each month.

By the church's first anniversary, several new congregations had been started. In Sungnak's thirty years of ministry thirty-eight new churches have been planted and support has been given to thirty churches. Fifty mission churches have been established by this congregation.

Evangelization of the industrial and business sector of Seoul is coordinated and conducted by the Chung-Hyeon Industrial Mission. Also, each

Rev. Kim Chang-In, senior pastor at
Chung-Hyeon Presbyterian Church
in Seoul, is one of 56 pastors
serving the congregation of 11,099
members.

Sunday school department has its own mission projects. Since 1972 the congregation has aided its members by providing worship opportunities and Bible study with employees in their place of work weekly or monthly.

Radio evangelism extends the ministry of the church. Each week the gospel is shared five times on three networks.

Concerning the ecumenical movement, Pastor Kim comments, "Though we regard churches of different denominations as churches of God and want to help and cooperate among nations, these ecumenical attitudes can never be confused with liberal, heretical or other unhealthy groups. We have never approved of the World Council of Churches."

Other local mission activities include rural evangelism training teams, financial assistance to army chaplains, and hospital and campus evangelistic events.

Approximately 2,000 members actively participate in the church's visitation and evangelistic activities each week. In addition to the home visitation cell leaders, there are an additional 150 active soul-winners in the church.

Pastor Kim notes that approximately 40 percent of the total baptisms in 1983 were new believers. "Once each year, in May, we train many soul-winners as a part of Total Mobilization of Evangelism. Most of the officers, teachers, and leaders in the church are trained for a week every year during this period."

New members are introduced into the life of the church by a process that begins with the Newcomer's Department of the Sunday school. Adults coming to the church for the first time study in this department for six months.

The Catechumen Department is an extension of the Newcomers Department. It also is a six-month class offering lectures on basic Christian doctrine and the Christian life. New members are baptized when they have completed both classes.

Soul-winners lead newcomers into these Sunday school groups and may attend with their new converts. Usually newcomers attend alone and are encouraged by teachers.

Christian Education: Raising Up Workers

For more than two decades, the church's motto has been, "Raising Up the Workers for the Kingdom of Heaven." Today the church has sixteen Sunday school departments. Each department has a full-time pastor and one or two evangelists. The church stresses that this is unique in Korean churches.

Pastor Kim writes, "Besides the Sunday worship services, all of the Sunday schools have their own chapels. We don't use the 'mother church' model, though Sunday schools have their own pastors and evangelists as leaders."

As of May, 1983, these sixteen departments had thirty-five pastors and evangelists, 645 teachers, and 5,525 members. The teacher training department, organized in 1971, has trained over 1,200 Sunday school teacher candidates.

A curriculum published by the denomination is used throughout the Sunday school. All classes are taught in Korean. One Bible, one language, and one curriculum are used in this church. Classes are not separated by sex.

Sunday schools usually have an additional meeting on weekdays. These meetings emphasize Bible study and fellowship. The exception would be the infant department meeting on Thursday which aims at education for mother's care of babies in a Bible context.

Youth and college departments have many small group meetings which gather on weekdays. The adult and senior departments meet only on Sunday.

The Chung-Hyeon Bible Institute has twenty-three classes throughout the week. Founded in 1973, the institute is responsible for the layman's Bible study and the training of lay leaders. There is also a correspondence Bible study course and cassette-tape Bible study course for those who cannot attend the class.

There are special two-week training programs at the beginning of each year for all church leaders. All members who have some position, including Sunday school teachers and choir members, are trained according to their ministries.

Table 11   Profile of the Sunday School,
           Chung-Hyeon Presbyterian Church, 1983

Age Groups	Approximate Attendance	Age of Groups	Pupils per Teacher	Total Number of Teachers
Preschool	1,244	Birth–6	13	93
Children	1,291	7–12	7	190
Youth	1,498	13–23	10	146
Adults	1,492	23+	9	172
Total	5,525		9 Average	601

Home visitation is a priority at Chung-Hyeon. The city is divided into five districts which are again subdivided into cells. Approximately 747 cell groups are scattered across the city. Many leaders are trained through these neighborhood groups.

A cell group usually contains five families and is lay-led. This shepherding ministry to families of the church centers around the Home Visitation Committee composed of five pastors, five women evangelists, and elders. A special effort is made to visit members who have just moved into a new home, or who have experienced the birth of a child, a wedding, hospitalization, or a funeral. A major effort is made once each year to visit the home of every member. Cell groups are designed to keep a personal touch among the members as the church continues to grow even larger.

Home visitation small-group meetings always have Bible study with the text written by the Home Visitation Committee. Small group leaders teach these groups.

The power of prayer is a vibrant priority at Chung-Hyeon. A prayer retreat was built by the church in 1978. It was financed by special offerings. The center cost $800,000 and includes a prayer chapel which holds 500 people, dormitory which can accommodate 500 men and women, and a dining hall which can accommodate 400. Two church buses shuttle members and visitors to the retreat center.

Recent building projects include three main structures: the chapel, a main auditorium; the education building; and the mission center building. A new parking area occupying two basements accommodates an estimated 600 cars. This parking facility is the largest in any Korean church.

The Twelve Principles of Church Growth

Twelve specific principles have been attributed to the growth of the second largest Presbyterian church in the world.

1. The presence of the Holy Spirit.
2. The faithful pastors in their ministry of shepherding and evangelizing.
3. Bible preaching. The biblical principles of stewardship of time, talent, and money have been a key element of church growth in the congregation.
4. A trained laity. A well-trained laity has been an important key to growth. The intense years of Japanese domination and persecution

motivate the lay leaders and pastors to raise up an army of workers for the kingdom of heaven. Members are trained in evangelism, home visiting, and devotional Bible study.

5. Clear goals and strategy. Since its earliest days the church has repeatedly reached its goals and performed its intended ministry because of effective blueprints and plans.
6. The priority of evangelism. The church has a world vision for the conversion of souls to Jesus Christ. Members are mobilized in Seoul to evangelize their home districts and to send teams of Christian workers to establish new churches in other areas.
7. Christian education. Good leaders make good workers in the process of "Raising Up Workers for the Kingdom of Heaven."
8. Fellowship. The church must have a demonstrated concern to care for its members by visiting homes and places of work during week days and by encouraging fellowship in groups.
9. Missions. Members seek to reach the "hidden people" in North Korea and plant new churches through the sending of missionaries.
10. Modernized facilities. The congregation prepares for the birth of the multitudes that will be born spiritually during coming years.
11. A strong faith. Pastor Kim always stresses the need for a pioneering faith to break through all the barriers in doing God's work. He says, "We believe we can receive anything we need from God the Father, although we have nothing now in our hands. God has always filled our hands."
12. Fervent prayer. Many Christians of the Chung-Hyeon Church are eager to pray. They pray at the dawn prayer meetings and at the all-night prayer meetings. Through their unceasing prayer God gives power for church growth.

Philippine Strategy for Growth— Bible Baptist Church
Cebu City, Philippines

The Republic of the Philippines is a maze of more than seven thousand islands stretching over one thousand miles from north to south in the western Pacific Ocean. Inhabitants of the 700 populated islands speak 160 dialects.

Bob Hughes, an Independent Baptist missionary, began his ministry among the multitudes of Cebu City in 1957. Dr. Hughes and his wife Helen started this hopeful work with a meager fourteen people converted in the streets of Cebu City. By 1964, sixty-nine attended ten Sunday school classes.

The crowded second-floor, storefront building where the small group gathered was filled to capacity when attendance reached forty. The need for more space led to the construction of a new building in 1964.

As a result of the Saturday afternoon Good News Clubs begun in 1964, attendance began to increase.

Total Involvement—The Key to Growth

Major advances occurred in 1964 when the church's founding pastor, Dr. Bob Hughes, adopted the "Total Involvement" concept of evangelism.

Table 12 Growth Profile

	1982	1972	1970	1964	1957
Auditorium Capacity	3,000	3,000	600	400	40
Sunday School Attendance*	9,220		600	69	14

* Sunday school attendance includes extension classes.

This two-week training involved, initially, eighteen members in soul-winning, teaching the Bible in Sunday school, and visitation.

The method included memorizing what became known as the four verses: Romans 3:23, Romans 6:23, John 1:12, and Revelation 3:20. Within six months, every Sunday school teacher knew these four verses, knew how to teach better, and knew how to witness. This information became a requirement for all Sunday school teachers.

People reaching people is the secret to growth at Bible Baptist Church. The Sunday school grew from sixty-nine to six hundred by 1970. The sanctuary exceeded its 400-seat capacity with 600 in attendance. Two years later, in 1972, the present 3,000-seat sanctuary was completed.

Dr. Elmer Towns observes:

> Missionary Bob Hughes, Cebu City, Philippines, might be more responsible for these trends to mission Sunday Schools than any other. His Sunday School jumped from 1,000 to over 20,000 weekly by mobilizing workers to go to the multitudes by jeeps and buses then bring them to hundreds of satellite schools in washeterias, store porches, garages and any other building with a roof.[1]

The twenty-two, full-time staff workers (including three ordained pastors) who lead the ministry team of 9,000 members, believe God can work mightily through them. The church continues to penetrate the city through both chapels and extension locations. Seven chapels are owned by the mother church and are jointly supported by the chapels and the mother church. Each chapel has its own building and meets twice each week. Average attendance in Sunday school is approximately sixty for each chapel. Worship attendance averages seventy-five at each location.

---

1. Elmer L. Towns, "Trends in Sunday School Growth," *Christian Life* 6 (October 1976): 38–101.

The closest chapel to the mother church is two miles away and the most distant is thirty-five miles away.

In addition to the chapels, the mother church coordinates thirty-five extension classes. These meetings are a combined worship service and Sunday school that gather in parks, in yards of homes, or under trees. Unlike chapels, extension classes do not have their own buildings. They function more like gatherings and seed groups. Extension classes developed in 1972 from the Good News Clubs conducted since 1964.

Sunday school classes at the main location contain approximately fifty students. Sixteen teachers lead an average of fifty adult pupils at the main location on Sunday. At the other end of the age spectrum, preschool teachers each care for fifteen children.

Since English is a common language in the Philippines, the King James Version is used in the church.

The Ministry Team

Dr. Bob Hughes, the founding pastor, served as pastor and missionary for eighteen years, 1957–1975. His assistant, Dr. Armie Jesalva, became pastor in 1969.

Dr. Jesalva was raised in a Catholic home and was converted September 14, 1956, during an evangelistic crusade at his college. He received his Bachelor of Arts degree in 1956 from Central Philippine University, and his Doctor of Medicine degree from Southwestern University in Cebu City.

He taught his first Sunday school lesson in 1965. It was about the three wise men and the birth of Jesus. Dr. Jesalva began to assist Dr. Hughes in the preaching ministries of the church only three years after his public profession of faith and baptism. In 1967, Jesalva became aware that God was directing him from the medical practice into the preaching ministry. Five years later he officially resigned his practice for the ministry.

In 1969, Dr. Hughes recommended to the church that they call Dr.

Table 13

	Main Location	7 Chapels	35 Extension Classes	Total
Sunday School Attendance	1,800	420	8,000	10,220
Worship Service Attendance	2,500	525		3,025

Jesalva as pastor. Dr. Hughes remained as missionary until 1975 when he had to return to the United States for treatment of his cancer. He never returned. He joined his Lord in heaven in August, 1976.

Pastor Jesalva estimates that three hundred members participate in and support the Saturday visitation and evangelistic activities of the church. Approximately 60 percent, or 1,080 of the 1,800 members of the main church, are estimated to be active soul-winners. Among the 4,000 professions last year, 495 were baptized. Converts are baptized immediately.

New members are oriented into the life of the congregation through immediate follow-up, home Bible studies, and Sunday school.

Without hesitation, Pastor Jesalva identifies the three secrets of his church's growth as (1) soul-winning visitation, (2) the usefulness of the committed soul-winner by the Holy Spirit, and (3) the willing and trainable spirit of the people.

Goals of the church point to continuted growth. The pastor's personal goal is to win and baptize at least two souls a day. The church's priority for 1984 and beyond is to saturate Cebu Province, composed of forty-nine towns and five major cities, with the gospel. By 1988 he envisions a total of one hundred extension classes and seventeen chapels. Bible Baptist Church has the goal of making Jesus "King" of the islands. Only total involvement of church members, however, can make this goal a reality.

Churches of Africa

8

Africa's Miracle Center—
Miracle Center
Benin City, Nigeria

Benin City is located west of Lagos, the capital city of Nigeria. As a center of idolatry and human sacrifice, Benin City was known as the "city of blood." Islam and tribal religions are widespread in Nigeria; even witchcraft is common.

Benson Idahosa, a member of the Benin tribe, accepted Christ as his Savior in 1968. Benson's father was the prince of juju worship for the Idahosa clan.

Soon after his conversion, Benson began a Bible study group for other new Christian converts. He located a storefront building where his group could meet and paid for the first month's rent with his own money. This was the first Pentecostal congregation in that section of Benin City. His group advertised the Bible studies offered several nights each week.

By 1970 the group had grown to forty members. A major growth decision was made that year when the small congregation bought a parcel of land. This was a miracle for a group whose regular monthly offering averaged less than twenty dollars. Less than a week was required to raise the six hundred dollar purchase price. Construction began immediately on the foundation for a building.

Ruthanne Garlock writes,

> The venture in faith seemed to be well under way when four of the five elders of the group called on Benson to protest the size of the building he had laid out. "Your eyes are too big," they said. "We feel the new church should seat fifty people, and the building you have in mind will seat five hundred. We cannot have a hand in such a foolish project."
>
> Benson listened to their argument, but he told the contractor to continue laying blocks for the foundation.[1]

Idahosa's group experienced the leadership and financial struggles common to most young congregations. However, several victories over challenges resulted in renewed determination to grow and witness boldly. As the church grew, the decision was made to become an independent rather than a denominational congregation.

After an interrupted academic opportunity as the first foreign student enrolled at Christ for the Nations in Dallas, Texas, Idahosa returned to Nigeria in 1971. The church had grown to 250 members when a decision was made that Benson should be ordained.

Crusade Evangelism

After he returned to Nigeria Benson tried to organize other pastors to evangelize Benin City. This effort proved fruitless. Refusing to be discouraged, he led his congregation of 250 to attempt the impossible. He reserved the 60,000-seat Ogbe Soccer Stadium for a five-day evangelistic crusade.

The February, 1972, crusade began with a crowd of 5,000 and finished with 10,000 on the final night. Each night concluded with prayer and healing for the sick. Hundreds were born again and many miracles of healing were attributed to the power of God during the week.

After the crusade the sanctuary, with its capacity of 500, was inundated with worshipers. Overflow crowds gathered outside the entrance and windows. The five-hour Sunday morning praise services soon moved to the nearby tennis courts of the local university.

Continued membership growth brought accusations of "sheep stealing" from neighboring pastors. The newspaper repeatedly tried to dis-

---

1. Ruthanne Garlock, *Fire in His Bones* (Plainfield, NJ: Logos International, 1981), p. 90.

credit the ministry of the pastor and church. The reports only led to increased growth.

In 1973 a special praise rally was held to show gratitude for God's blessings. At this meeting Pastor Idahosa asked for several specific gifts including land for expansion of the church. God provided a large parcel of land near the airport. Once completed, the Miracle Center would accommodate nearly 6,000 people. The $300,000 sanctuary was almost debt-free by the November, 1975, dedication date.

An opportunity to broadcast by television occurred when the first television station in Benin City began operating. Money for the first program on the government station came from the pastor's personal banking account.

What had begun as a small Bible study group had grown to a large congregation. The body was planning to sponsor six crusades a year in various parts of the country and to establish branch churches, and the Bible study program was expanding to a one-year Bible college with a British missionary appointed as principal. It seemed wise that they should register with the government, so in 1974 the leaders incorporated under the name of Church of God Mission, International. At the time Benson and his co-workers were planning a few crusades in other nearby African countries. . . .[2]

Growth Through Satellite "Branches"

As the church grew, three causes led to the formation of satellite branches. First, the total saturation of the old 500-seat sanctuary with a regular weekly attendance of 2,000 people. The new sanctuary would not be complete until 1975, two years away.

Second, Pastor Idahosa had been conducting evangelistic crusades long before the opportunity for television appeared. The greater harvest of souls generated through these crusades created a proportionate concern for follow-up in an established church.

The creation of satellite groups by the church seemed a sure method of follow-up. Through the Bible school operated by the church, a constant flow of "branch" pastors for these new missions became available. On the evening before the present sanctuary was dedicated in 1975, the first Bible school commencement service provided forty-three graduates. All

2. Ibid., p. 128.

Myriads of motorcycles stand parked outside the Miracle Center in Benin City, Nigeria.

Table 14 Growth of the Miracle Center

	1983	1980	1975	1973	1972	1971	1970
Worship Attendance	10,000	6,000		2,000	700	250	40
Membership	10,000	6,000					
Satellite Branches in Benin City	30	17		3			
Total Branches	600		300	103			

From interview with Pastor Idahosa and Ruthanne Garlock, *Fire in His Bones* (Plainfield, NJ: Logos International, 1981).

pastors of the branch chapels are personally ordained and appointed by the pastor of the mother church.

Third, as explosive growth occurred at the Miracle Center, people continued to come from greater distances. These extension or satellite chapels provide immediate contact with the center for witness, ministry, and follow-up.

Evangelism is the main focus of the congregation and its branch chapels. Campus evangelism has led to the creation of a small army of approximately four hundred student evangelists. Several university campus centers are involved.

In addition to crusade and television evangelism, the students participate in two other evangelism strategies. After graduation from a university, the government of Nigeria requires ten months of government service. Graduates who are members of the Miracle Center network usually welcome the experience as a missionary opportunity at government expense.

Also, an estimated 50,000 university students spend their vacations in camps structured as schools of evangelism. Prisons, schools, and hospitals often receive special attention by this evangelistic task force.[3]

The Miracle Center baptizes 800–1,000 new converts each year. The twenty-eight branches in Benin City will baptize nearly 2,000 new converts annually. All persons baptized become members of the Miracle Center.

The ministry of the center and local branches is conducted by eight pastoral staff members, sixteen elders, and eighty deacons and deaconnesses.

The branch closest to the mother church is only ten minutes away and has 2,000 in attendance. The most distant is forty-five minutes away and

3. Ibid., pp. 152–54.

averages twenty-five present. The largest branch is the Iyaro branch, with an attendance of 3,000–4,000 each Sunday.

Monthly, many of the branches participate in the Sunday evening service at the Miracle Center. Pastors of the branch chapels may receive financial assistance for six to eighteen months, as needed. Monthly progress reports are expected of all branches.

The curriculum used by the church varies from material produced by Kenneth Hagin, Kenneth Copelin, T. L. Osborn, Harrison House of Tulsa, Christ For the Nations of Dallas, and Evangel Temple in Washington, D.C. These resources aid Bible study at the church, but the sole text for the classes each Sunday is the King James Version of the Bible. Separate classes are provided for men and women.

The Leadership Factor

How does the congregation make decisions? Is policy made by action of the pastor, deacons, or congregation? Members are quick to express their foremost recognition of Bishop Benson Idahosa as the voice of God for them.

When asked about the growth of the church, the church's leaders indicated:

1. Magnifying the authority and power of the Word of God as energized by His Holy Spirit.
2. The Miracle Center and branches set goals and work to increase their attendance every year. Both groups work hard and trust God for this increase through continuous evangelism.
3. The new-member classes meet each Sunday and receive books from

Table 15 Sunday School Attendance at Miracle Center

	Sunday School Attendance		Teachers at Miracle Center	Teacher/ Pupil Ratio at Miracle Center
	Center	*28 Branches*		
Preschool	300	4,000	10	1:30
Grades 1–12	1,000	5,000	12	1:83
Adults	3,000	10,000	30	1:100
Sub-total	4,300	19,000		
Total	23,300		52	Average = 1:71

their pastor. These classes in turn become new Sunday school classes.

In March, 1981, more than three hundred pastors participated in the consecration of Benson Idahosa as Bishop of the Church of God Mission, International. More than 15,000 participants and observers attended the event. The government television station broadcast the occasion during the Sunday evening news.

Jim Bakker, international host for the PTL television network accepted Bishop Idahosa's offer in 1976 to assume the responsibility of expenses for the Nigerian "PTL Redemption Hour" hosted by Idahosa.

On March 30, 1984, Oral Roberts University, Tulsa, Ohlahoma, conferred an honorary Doctor of Law degree on Bishop Idahosa and Doctor of Philosophy degree on his wife, Margaret. Bishop Idahosa is the contact person for Oral Roberts University Healing Teams that will go into African nations to teach and evangelize.

Ministry Matters

Ministries of the church include clothing and food distribution. The eight doctors and nurses in the church provide medical assistance to members. An attorney aids members with legal matters. An active jail ministry attends to the needs of a branch church composed of 200 prisoners.

Sixty members of the church constitute a group known as the Soldiers of Christ. This military-related group is committed to group and personal evangelism. They regularly use platform evangelism, signs, tracts, and films to aid them in their witness.

Benson Idahosa has ministered to more than sixty nations of the world. "More than a thousand churches have already been raised up under his leadership. . . . His International Bible School attracts upper-class people from eighteen African nations."[4]

4. Ibid., p. 195.

Churches of North America

9

First Baptist Church
Hammond, Indiana

Dr. Jack Hyles, pastor of the world's third largest Christian congregation, candidly assesses his church, "You either love or hate First Baptist Church. Not everybody likes our church, but everybody knows about us." He introduces his church as "the church with a heart."

Dr. Jack Hyles—God's Patriot

Hyles's mother was a Methodist, but his father was an alcoholic. Hyles was converted at age eleven in Dallas, Texas. His father died in 1950 before being converted. Dr. Elmer Towns notes one of Hyles's darkest hours:

One night my Dad said he would go to church. I called the pastor and said, "Would you preach on the Second Coming; my Dad's coming to Church?" (That was what had always scared me and I thought it would move my Dad.) When we got to church, they had a choir cantata. I cried all the way through. Daddy wouldn't come back. That was the only church service my Daddy ever attended.

101

Hyles went on to conclude, "I said if I ever pastored a church, I would preach Sunday morning and Sunday night. Folks expect the preaching of the Word."[1]

In 1947, at age nineteen, Hyles preached his first sermon. Stuttering was a severe affliction during those early years. Hyles humorously describes the struggle of that first sermon, "Elijah blushed and Heaven's flag flew at half-mast for three days." God would radically transform this problem into a powerful weapon against the powers of hell.

Hyles completed degree requirements at East Texas Baptist College and Southwestern Baptist Theological Seminary. Following Seminary, Hyles became pastor of the Miller Road Baptist Church in the Dallas area. He recounts those early years:

> As a young preacher starting out many years ago, I read the Book of Acts over and over again. I went to my knees and asked God to let me have a ministry and build churches that would be akin to the Book of Acts. When this was settled before God, my little country church in East Texas became a hotbed of soul-winning, even though we were ten miles out in the country. God gave us souls every week and a perennial revival spirit. . . .
>
> For seven years we labored in the Miller Road Baptist Church, Garland, Texas . . . the Lord led us and used us and used our people to grow a church from 44 members to 4,128 members in six and a half years.[2]

In 1959 Hyles became pastor of First Baptist Church in Hammond, Indiana. He has committed twenty-five years, nearly one-half of his life, to the growth of this one congregation.

Every winter thousands of pastors and church leaders attend the annual Pastor's School to both hear and observe how the church operates. Almost 5,000 curious inquirers attended the twentieth annual school in March, 1983. The Pastor's School is a major annual event begun in 1963 to introduce the "how" of what the church does, and why it does it to inquirers around the world. Five thousand guest pastors, church leaders, and interested registrants attended the 1983 Pastor's School.

Dr. Hyles insists that loyalty to God's Word and soul-winning are the top priorities for his congregation. This commitment led him to withdraw First Baptist from the American Baptist Convention during his first year as pastor.

1. Elmer Towns, *The Ten Largest Sunday Schools* (Grand Rapids: Baker, 1969), p. 54.
2. Jack Hyles, *Let's Build an Evangelistic Church* (Murfreesboro, TN: Sword of the Lord, 1962), p. 5.

Table 16   Growth of First Baptist Church, Hammond, Indiana

	1982	1980	1975	1970	1965	1960
Church Membership	74,373	59,598	35,954	13,041	5,866	3,045
*Worship Attendance**						
Sunday School Attendance	18,504	12,881	4,337	2,096	1,009	715
Baptisms	8,020	7,734	7,816	2,078	1,966	313
Professions of Faith	20,681			5,000		

* Estimated to be same as Sunday school.

Early in his ministry at First Baptist, he and his family experienced threatening telephone calls in the night. For Sale signs were regularly placed in his lawn during the cover of darkness, and a petition asking him to resign as pastor was circulated. In June, 1964, opposition became so intense that an arsonist burned the newly-built church auditorium to the ground during the early morning hours.

Hyles believes that the mark of obedience to God's Word is being a personal soul-winner. Without exception, the only persons allowed to sing or speak from the pulpit or choir are born-again, practicing soul-winners.

> At First Baptist Church, we require every staff member to be a soul-winner and spend at least four hours a week in personal soul-winning. We would not want someone leading our choir in "Send the Light," "Rescue the Perishing," "Where He Leads Me I Will Follow," and other great songs who is not a soul-winner. I would not want anyone typing my letters who was not a soul-winner.[3]

Dr. Hyles, affectionately called pastor, preacher, or Brother Hyles, is unapologetic about the priority of soul-winning as he teaches his leaders and members. New members are invited to a special reception where they receive a copy of *Let's Go Soul-Winning*, written by the pastor.

> This gives them a step-by-step set of instructions as to how to win a soul to Christ. The following Sunday night they are taught how to win souls. This is the first thing that our new members learn. . . . It is not unusual for a person to be winning souls to Christ within the first week or two after he

3. Jack Hyles, *Let's Baptize More Converts* (Murfreesboro, TN: Sword of the Lord, 1967), pp. 18–19.

is saved and many of our converts will win a dozen or more in the first month. This is the New Testament pattern.[4]

The rewards for soul-winning can be more than spiritual at First Baptist. Dr. Elmer Towns writes, "One elderly woman won a trip to the Holy Land by bringing 976 persons to Sunday School at the First Baptist Church, Hammond, Ind., during a contest."[5]

Some critics suggest that the church misplaces its priorities by focusing on numbers rather than needs. Outsiders are surprised to discover that every Sunday school absentee is required to be visited every week.

This kind of expectation and commitment by the pastor explains how the congregation's army of soul-winners was able to gather over 170,000 for their all-time record "high day" for Sunday school in May, 1976.

Dr. Jack Hyles shares his greatest ambition in life:

> I don't have many numerical goals, even though we would like to average 10,000 in Sunday School every Sunday. . . . The fundamentalist church is the only hope of America. I want to build an influential New Testament church that can be reproduced all over America, to help save our nation.[6]

He has worked most of his life trying to achieve this goal. More than a hundred young men have committed their lives to Jesus Christ under his leadership. These "preacher boys" are scattered across America.

Hyles is the author of thirty-four books and pamphlets with eight million copies in print. Annually he speaks in almost every state of the nation challenging preachers to stand for God in the cities where they serve. He set a Sunday school attendance goal of 10,000 weekly. He now reaches 18,000 regularly.

One of the most influential ministries of the church is the system of Christian schools located at nearby Shererville, Indiana. Known as Baptist City, the twenty-eight-acre campus of Hammond Baptist Schools and Hyles-Anderson College enrolls almost 4,000 students. The college alone had a 1982 enrollment of more than 2,000 students.

Ten years after becoming pastor of First Baptist Church, Hyles made three major decisions. Dr. Elmer Towns writes,

4. Ibid.

5. Elmer Towns, "50 Largest Sunday Schools in the U.S. Today," *Christian Life* 6 (October 1969): 31–46.

6. Elmer L. Towns, *World's Largest Sunday School* (Nashville: Thomas Nelson, 1974), p. 171.

It's "the church with a heart," says Pastor Jack Hyles, when talking about First Baptist Church of Hammond, Indiana. First Baptist has the largest Sunday school in the world.

He had 22 invitations on his desk to conduct city-wide revivals. In addition, he had an invitation to become president of a college and of a seminary. He realized he couldn't do everything, so to find the will of God for his life, he fasted and prayed for an entire day. He determined God wanted him to use the rest of his life: (1) pastoring the First Baptist Church to make it one of the most effective churches in America, (2) writing books to help preachers become more effective in their ministry, and (3) preaching to ministers to motivate them to go back and build great churches.[7]

He is a man of great compassion, conviction, and courage. Many Saturday nights he walks among the empty pews in the church auditorium and prays for those he visualizes sitting in those very seats the next day. In faith he claims the harvest of souls being reached by his army of soul-winners and the power of the Holy Spirit.

Sunday School: God's Net

First Baptist Church has the largest Sunday school in the world. On March 20, 1983, more than 33,000 attended Sunday school on a special high attendance day. The Sunday school's average weekly attendance for 1982 was 18,504.

More than 800 teachers lead the 804 Sunday school classes at the church. Dr. Hyles assumes personal responsibility for motivating, reproving, and teaching his teachers. Meetings are weekly and intensely motivational.

Organizational structure is simple. This allows maximum mobility, communication, and effectiveness. Even the departmental record card asks for minimal information and concludes with a request for "Visits Made," and "Souls Won."

The blueprint for Sunday school workers at First Baptist Church since 1969 is *The Hyles Sunday School Manual.* Since the Bible is the textbook, only the Bible is used by each teacher. The only version used is the King James Version. Teachers are instructed to leave all quarterlies at home, to invite limited involvement of class members, to avoid making pupils read or talk, to use visual aids, and to invite members to receive Christ as their personal Savior.

The seven requirements of all Sunday school teachers are (1) faithful attendance at all the public services of the church, (2) strict adherence to the church's policy concerning separation from the world (no drinking,

7. Ibid., pp. 167–68.

dancing, smoking, etc.), (3) giving the tithe as commanded in the Scriptures, (4) loyalty to the entire program of the First Baptist Church, (5) faithful attendance in Sunday school, (6) faithful attendance at the Wednesday evening teachers' meeting, and (7) a weekly time of visitation on behalf of the Sunday school.[8]

> It is explained to every prospective teacher that one of his duties is to visit the absentees in his class. The most important absentee to visit is the one who was absent last Sunday for the first time. . . We feel that a visit for the first absence might prevent the second absence.[9]

The Hyles Church Manual, also written by the pastor, explains basic church administration and ministry.

A major tool for evangelism and follow-up used by the church is the church bus. The blue Sunday school buses of First Baptist Church saturate the metro-Chicago area. During the winter and summer months, 125 buses are in operation. This increases to 175 in both fall and spring when the church conducts its two major Sunday school promotional-enlistment campaigns. The buses bring in a weekly average of 6,200 riders. The church used 62 buses in 1969 and as many as 230 in 1975.

All boys, beginning in the first grade, are taught by men. Men are to be examples of godly strength and women are to be the picture of godly grace and beauty.

The church has six separate Sunday schools. They meet from 9:30 until mid-afternoon. The earliest Sunday school is almost entirely families of the area. Only 1,500 people come by church bus. The eleven o'clock Sunday school pupils are brought by church buses from Chicago. This Sunday school is organized to ensure an overall average of one teacher for every twenty pupils. Only four classes exceed one hundred in attendance. The largest group is the Pastor's Class, with approximately 2,500 attending weekly. This class meets in the $2 million auditorium. It was built in 1975 to seat 5,000, and now seats over 6,500 attendants. The other three large classes average 100 to 250 in weekly attendance.

The congregation ministers to four hundred deaf members through three Sunday school departments. Approximately twenty-five blind students are taught through the church. Over two hundred retarded persons receive care and are active in the Sunbeam, (ages 4 to 12), and the

---

8. Jack Hyles, *The Hyles Sunday School Manual* (Murfreesboro, TN: Sword of the Lord, 1969), p. 94.

9. Ibid., p. 91.

Pathfinder, (age 18 and older), departments. The church provides twelve departments that reach more than one thousand Spanish speaking members. Overall Sunday school attendance averages 40 percent adults and 60 percent children.

Evangelism and Ministry

Four hundred men, women, boys, and girls made personal public professions each week of 1982 through members of First Baptist Church. Approximately 40 percent are baptized at the same time. Among the remaining 60 percent, some join other churches; others are baptized later. During 1982 the church reported 8,020 baptisms, more than 150 baptisms each week. Baptisms are also conducted during the Wednesday night services.

Evangelistic activities of the congregation usually involve only other fundamentalist churches. The pastor and church strongly oppose the ecumenical movement, the National Council of Churches, and the World Council of Churches.

The church reports that all new members baptized during the past year were new believers. Also, there are an estimated 4,000 soul-winners active in the congregation. Forty percent of all persons attending the church are adults. This means that approximately one-half of all adults are practicing soul-winners.

Extensive outreach occurs through the various channels of ministry used by First Baptist Church. Many are won through the rescue mission operated by the church. Each weekend several busloads of teenagers witness in inner-city neighborhoods.

Ministries offered by the church include clothing and food distribution, counseling and referral services, care for alcoholics and their families, outreach to university and international groups, the deaf ministry, witness and assistance to ex-prisoners and their families, convalescent homes, the jail ministry, and bus evangelism.

One national executive with a major hotel chain was asked to relocate. His life and family were so committed to First Baptist Church that he offered to resign rather than to relocate. He was not relocated. He became vice-president of his company and for years has served on a bus route inviting thousands of children, young people, and adults to attend the Sunday school of First Baptist Church, the church with a heart for souls.

10

Highland Park Baptist Church
Chattanooga, Tennessee

Although Highland Park Baptist Church of Chattanooga is the second largest church in North America, critics often protest, "That's the church with all the chapels. You can't really consider the church as being only one church." Even though the chapel concept is not as common in the U.S., churches with numerous chapels occur frequently outside the nation's borders.

Highland Park is known as The Church of the Green Light. The promise verse of the congregation is John 20:21, "As my Father hath sent me, even so send I you." It also is known as The South's Most Visited Church. Every issue of the church newspaper, *The Evangelist,* lists states and foreign countries from which visitors came.

The Highland Park Baptist Church has the fifth largest composite membership in the world. Composite membership represents an average of total adult membership, weekly Sunday school attendance, and weekly Sunday morning worship attendance.

Bootcamp for Soul-Winners
Highland Park Baptist Church, organized on October 26, 1890, was first known as the Orchard Knob Baptist Church. Only twelve people met that day on Ivey Street. Today there are 57,322 members.

Dr. Lee Roberson, pastor of the church from 1942 to 1983, shares these four goals of the congregation:

> *First,* we want to see many saved.
> *Second,* we want to set new Sunday School attendance records, both for the main church and our chapels.
> *Third,* we want to see new attendance records for the Training Union.
> *Fourth,* we want to reach new heights in our missionary giving.[1]

The church set a goal of saturating Chattanooga, house-by-house, during 1969. Every effort was made to contact all 322,000 people living in the metro area.

In 1976, the pastor and his staff gave a new challenge to the church.

> "The Big 10,000 Sunday School Campaign," was a three-month strategy to reach for the 10,000 mark in attendance "Sunday after Sunday." The plan was further, "to endeavor to contact personally 10,000 homes in our city. We will be mailing out 10,000 personal invitations. We are setting a goal of making 10,000 telephone calls. . . . At the end of our "10,000 Campaign," ten outstanding teachers of our Sunday School will be recognized."[2]

In 1982, the church selected twenty-five men and women to serve as leaders of evangelism teams. These twenty-five soul-winning groups were each composed of ten members. Each member committed to an intensive witnessing campaign to reach Chattanooga. Team leaders received training each Wednesday evening after the weekly prayer service. They met with their teams on Thursday night for the weekly visitation supper at the church.

Since 1939, the major mission strategy for Chattanooga has been the network of chapels. When Dr. Roberson came to Highland Park Baptist Church in 1942, the church supported only one chapel, the Central Avenue Mission, which opened in 1939.

The church now operates sixty chapels located as far as seventy miles from the main church. Many chapels average one hundred in attendance. The two largest have 250 to 300 attending each week. The chapels are led by students and faculty of Tennessee Temple University.

Many chapels are owned and operated by Highland Park Baptist

---

1. Lee Roberson, "The Day Before," *Evangelist,* December 29, 1982, p. 1. This is a sermon preached from Joshua 3:5.

2. "The Big 10,000 Sunday School Campaign," *Evangelist,* October 13, 1976, p. 1.

Church. During the first thirty years of the chapel ministry, approximately fifteen have become self-supporting, autonomous congregations. The church previously set a goal of one hundred chapels.[3]

Dr. J. R. Faulkner, pastor of Highland Park Baptist Church since 1983, served as co-pastor with Dr. Lee Roberson from 1949–1983. Faulkner, a former student of Charlotte Bible Institute in Charlotte, North Carolina, and Bob Jones College in Cleveland, Tennessee, has been a major decision-maker in the years of growth at Highland Park.

Buses at the Chattanooga church bring in more than 1,400 riders to Sunday school each week. These riders range from preschool-age children to adults and come from homes among the forty-five bus routes. Regular bus attendance has reached 2,000 riders on special high attendance Sundays.

It was under the leadership of Brother M. J. Parker that the bus ministry of the church was begun in 1949. Even though busy enough to be the number-one-salesman with the National Linen Supply Company in our city, Brother Parker found time to visit Chattanooga homes almost every day of the week to invite folk to church and Sunday School. He inspired thousands of folk to ride the buses. This resulted in many hundreds of people being brought to a saving knowledge of our Lord Jesus Christ.[4]

Most churches in the U.S. with aggressively evangelistic bus ministries can trace what they know from years of experience at Highland Park. Graduates of Tennessee Temple Schools, who have been trained in bus evangelism at Highland Park, began their own bus ministries as they relocated to other cities. Many have developed this type of ministry based on the Highland Park model.

Gospel tract leaflets are distributed through members of the mother church and satellite chapels by the thousands each year. Many are given to multitudes on the streets of the city. Tracts are considered to be a normal tool to be used during the regular church-wide visitation nights. Highland Park Baptist Church recently hosted the International Tract Convention.

Another essential key to training soul winners within the congregation is the rescue mission operated by the church. Organized in 1950, and

3. J. B. Collins, *Get a Glimpse of the World's Largest Church* (Chattanooga: privately published, 1973), p. 50.

4. "M. J. Parker Recognized as Nations's 'Greatest' Bus Director," *Evangelist*, September 7, 1977, p. 3.

Table 17   Chapel Ministry

	1939	1970	1975	1978	1983
Chapels	1	43	73	70	60

relocated in 1981 due to urban renewal, the seating capacity of the Union Gospel Mission is approximately one hundred. Dormitory space can accommodate fifty to sixty men at the mission. The church also established a rescue mission at Dalton, Georgia.

A report of activities at the Chattanooga ministry is impressive.[5]

Tennessee Temple University was founded by the church in 1946. It started with only eleven faculty and 109 students. The university now has more than 3,500 students enrolled. Students come from all fifty states and twenty-eight foreign countries. The church also operates an elementary school with a 1982–83 enrollment of 591, and a high school with 359 students.

An opportunity to reach children between the ages of nine and fourteen is Camp Joy. Camp Joy was begun in 1946, the year that Joy Caroline, Dr. and Mrs. Roberson's nine-week-old baby, died.

Dr. Roberson attended a TVA land auction and bought the land for $3,000. Today the camp covers ninety-two acres and is operated ten weeks each year. Each week involves forty-five counselors and over three hundred children. Activities include horseback riding, baseball, swimming, scripture memory, and special speakers. Results of the 1982 camp include: 3,021 attendants, 498 professions of faith, 625 baptisms, 310 rededications, and 16 commitments to full-time Christian vocational service.

The Annual Winter Youth Retreat occurs each December and attracts young people from several states. The 1981 retreat attracted 1,100 young people from forty-nine churches in fourteen states.

Circulation of *The Evangelist*, the church newspaper, has grown from 23,000 in 1968, to 67,000 in 1982. The paper is mailed at the church's expense to readers in all fifty states, sixty-two foreign countries, and twenty islands. Every issue lists a five-point outline with Bible verses on how the reader can become a born-again Christian by receiving Jesus Christ. The final point of the outline is a written prayer to help each person word his/her prayer of commitment.

Highland Park Baptist Church also claims to have the "longest running

5. "Union Gospel Mission Reports Great Year," *Evangelist*, December 1, 1982, p. 2.

Known as "The Church with the Green Light" and "The South's Most Visited Church," Highland Park Baptist Church of Chattanooga, Tennessee, also operates sixty chapels located up to seventy miles from the main church. Dr. J. R. Faulkner serves as pastor.

Table 18

	1982	Since 1950
Attendance	25,824	828,879
Professions of Faith	491	21,213
Baptisms	180	4,093
Rededications	231	16,956
Sunday School Attendance	3,049	44,646
Meals Served	37,102	1,425,069
Beds for Men	13,313	627,548
Pieces of Clothing Distributed	35,266	1,200,812
Bags of Groceries	1,114	31,236
Shoes Given	2,029	39,792

live radio program of its type in the nation." The first broadcast on December 13, 1942, was called "Call to Consecration." The program title was later changed to "Gospel Dynamite." In addition to its broadcast on the church-owned 66,000-watt station WDYN-FM, "Gospel Dynamite" also is broadcast Monday through Saturday on WFLI-AM. Daily, at 8:30 each morning, the opening words of the broadcast echo, "For I am not ashamed of the gospel of Christ; for it is the power of God unto salvation to every one that believeth; to the Jew first, and also to the Greek" (Rom. 1:16).

Organized to Evangelize

The major evangelistic organization used by Highland Park Baptist Church is the Sunday school. One staff leader writes:

In hundreds of meetings across the nation, I have said to Sunday School workers, the way to grow is to "pray, plan, and promote!" . . . Praying and planning can be done standing in one place, or sitting in one place, but to promote there must be action. The Sunday School is for the teaching of the Word of God, we must adhere to this with all diligence.

But, the main emphasis of every campaign of our church is the winning of the lost! We want to see people brought to the Savior. Without the winning of poor, lost, helpless souls, our work is nothing.[6]

6. "Highland Park Baptist Church to Conduct Four-Month Sunday School Campaign," *Evangelist,* January 26, 1983, p. 1.

A record Sunday school attendance of 14,384 was reached on Sunday, September 5, 1982. The goal for that Sunday was 13,000 attendants. Included in the record attendance were 5,500 in the satellite chapels. The chapels also had a record attendance.

> Thinking people will always ask, "Why this constant reaching for greater numbers?" The answer is simple: We want men and women, boys and girls to hear the message of our redeeming Christ. We have discovered that all peace and joy comes from Him.[7]

Each month different members of the church, all men, are enlisted to direct the Sunday school. In cooperation with the church staff, the monthly campaign is designed and built around weekly thrusts and slogans. Each Sunday has a special name and goal: Stretch Your Heart Sunday, President's Sunday, Fill Your Car Sunday, Power Sunday, Family Sunday, Baby Day, and many others.

Attendance in Sunday school has grown from 470 in 1942, when Dr. Roberson came as pastor, to an average weekly attendance of 9,026 in 1982. The mother church averages 4,847 and the satellite chapels report 4,179 on an average Sunday. More than 450 volunteer staff members teach and visit for the Sunday school.

The largest class at Highland Park is the Tabernacle Class with an attendance of over 800 members and visitors. Taught for many years by Dr. J. R. Faulkner, the class is organized into vice-presidents, who in turn lead division leaders. They in turn, lead group leaders.

To ensure the effective assimilation of present and future members, small worker-pupil ratios are maintained. For example, while one teacher may teach fifty pupils, group leaders usually lead only ten or less. Members in grades 1 to 6 usually have only five to ten children for every worker. Youth and adult classes are grouped to ensure one worker for every eight to ten members. Seven of the thirty-six youth classes exceed one hundred in attendance. Most of the youth attend smaller groups.

Three weekly classes are provided for deaf members of the church. The classes with their average attendance: Hands of Praise (60), Helping Hands (90), and the Deaf Married Class (40).

Other weekly gatherings are also well attended. The church has one of the nation's largest mid-week prayer meetings with over 3,000 present.

7. "The Secret of Steady Growth: Building a Great Sunday School," *Evangelist*, February 10, 1982, p. 1.

Table 19   Sunday School Attendance, 1942–1982

	1942	1970*	1975*	1982
Attendance	470	4,935	7,453	9,026
Church Membership	1,344			57,322

* The 1970 and 1975 figures come from the annual survey by Dr. Elmer Towns in *Christian Life* magazine.

Table 20   Missionary Support

	1948	1976	1977	1978	1982	1983
Missionaries	4	352	384	414	532	544

Sunday night Training Union classes meet for special studies during the hour preceding the worship service. On Sunday, September 5, 1982, 6,453 attended these classes, a record attendance.

Over one hundred ushers care for the needs of the people who gather each Sunday in the recently built 6,000-seat auditorium. Approximately ninety deacons attend to the ministry needs of the congregation.

As of 1983, the church also supported over five hundred foreign missionaries. After serving as pastor of the church for only six years, Dr. Lee Roberson led the church to launch World Wide Faith Missions. This organization gathers and channels funds to many missionary ministries. In recent years, over 50 percent of the church's receipts were designated for this cause.[8]

An annual missionary conference is sponsored by the church during the first week of November. As many as one hundred missionaries representing over thirty mission boards attend the event.

Although Highland Park Baptist Church and Tennessee Temple University occupy more than one hundred buildings, the secret to their success is the passion for reaching new souls for Jesus Christ in this generation.

8. "Dr. Roberson Honored at Reception for 50 Years of Preaching Ministry," *Evangelist*, September 6, 1978, p. 2.

11

Thomas Road Baptist Church
Lynchburg, Virginia

Thomas Road Baptist Church is becoming a popular tourist stop not only because of its 19,000 member congregation, but also because of its famous pastor, Jerry Falwell. Falwell, a Moral Majority leader, shares:

> I have often preached that the greatest church since Pentecost is yet to be built. . . . The Jerusalem church members saturated their own community and were accused, ". . . ye have filled Jerusalem with your doctrine." (Acts 5:28)[1]

Since its beginning in 1956, the church has grown from thirty-five adults meeting in Mountain View Elementary School to the present 19,000 that meet in today's 4,000-seat sanctuary.

The charter members moved almost immediately to a larger facility.

Dr. Elmer L. Towns, dean of the School of Religion, Liberty Baptist Seminary, Lynchburg, Virginia, gathered major research data for this chapter.

1. Jerry Falwell and Elmer Towns, *Capturing a Town for Christ* (Old Tappan, NJ: Revell, 1973), pp. 5, 7.

Church membership grew to over 800 members that first year. A record attendance was registered on the church's sixteenth anniversary in 1972 when 18,019 people attended. This also was the first year for the annual pastor's conference led by the church with 5,000 present.

Once again, on July 4, 1976, a record crowd gathered on top of the 2,800-acre Liberty Mountain to celebrate the church's twentieth anniversary. Liberty Mountain became the new home for the church–owned Liberty Baptist Schools.

The four schools include: the college with 3,341 students; the seminary with 247 students; the Bible institute with 107 students; and the academy with 1,369 students. The combined enrollment of the schools exceeds 5,000 students. Nineteen buildings were built and occupied debt-free within two years of the ground breaking ceremony. A master ten-year plan targets 10,000 students before the end of the 1980s, and 50,000 by the end of the century.

The Liberty Home Bible Institute is a home correspondence Bible course with an enrollment that exceeds 12,000.

Causes of Growth at Thomas Road

Two national factors prompted explosive growth of the church: media coverage and identification with the Moral Majority.

Dr. Elmer L. Towns, co-founder of the present Liberty Baptist College and dean of the School of Religion, traces the path of growth followed by the church in a 1982 report:

The church first gained national prominence when it was listed ninth in *Christian Life* magazine's annual listing of *The Ten Largest Sunday Schools.* Next, the best selling book, *Church Aflame,* (approximately 100,000 copies) told the story of the principles that caused spectacular growth. These led to national pastor's conferences which approximately 5,000 pastors and Christian workers attended in 1972 and 1973. *Newsweek* and various Christian magazines carried articles on the outstanding growth of the church. This national attention motivated families to move to Lynchburg to attend the church or enroll their children in the church's academy. . . .[2]

The Moral Majority was an effective evangelical political force in the 1980 national election. However, the post-election effect actually provided minimal growth for the church.

2. Elmer L. Towns, *An Accurate Picture of the Thomas Road Baptist Church.* An unpublished research study for Fuller Theological Seminary, Pasedena, California, 1982, p. 2.

Local residents of the area who join the church tend to be middle-class families. Sprinkled among the multitudes are a few millionaires and approximately one hundred members with doctorate degrees (mostly college faculty).

The worship services, however, simply reflect the needs of the multitudes.

As the nationally telecast morning worship service "The Old Time Gospel Hour" suggests, the music consists of gospel songs and contemporary special music. It is broadcast weekly on 297 television stations and approximately 500 radio stations.

Since Thomas Road Baptist Church is an Independent Baptist Church, with the Baptist Bible Fellowship, it is not accountable to written denominational guidelines. Dr. Towns reports that in 1976,

> The Missions Board of the Baptist Bible Fellowship voted to begin accepting the graduates of Liberty Baptist College for overseas assignment. . . . This constituted a national recognition or acceptance of the College. This action reversed the attitude of many pastors to the church and school, hence affecting church growth.[3]

One journalist noted in 1974, "The church has a core of approximately 200 separated Christians who carry Scofield Bibles, win souls, teach Sunday school and go visiting each week to boost attendance."[4]

In 1968 an important event occurred in Falwell's life. He received an honorary doctorate from Tennessee Temple College, owned and operated by Highland Park Baptist Church, Chattanooga, Tennessee. At that time Thomas Road averaged 2,640 in Sunday school attendance. Highland Park reported 2,400 in the 1968 *Christian Life* magazine listing of the "10 Largest Sunday Schools in the U.S. Today." Falwell left Chattanooga motivated to increase the membership of Thomas Road.

> Beginning in 1968 through 1973, indicates the Towns report, "Falwell emphasized saturation evangelism, using every available means, to reach every available person, at every available time." Also, he used the phrase "Super aggressive local church." This theological perspective was the foundation for growth from 2,640 in attendance in 1968, to 5,844 in 1974, a 390 percent decadal growth rate over five years.[5]

3. Ibid., p. 3.
4. Ibid.
5. Ibid., p. 4.

The Thomas Road Baptist Church in Lynchburg, Virginia, is known for its pastor, Jerry Falwell—a Moral Majority leader—as well as for its 19,000-member congregation.

Then came the Arab oil crisis of 1973–74. A significant shift in strategy was made from bus evangelism to building the college. The annual listing of the one hundred largest churches in *Christian Life* magazine indicates a decrease in the number of buses used from sixty-five in 1972 to forty-one in 1975. Today, twenty-six are operated.

The present 3,200-seat auditorium was built in 1970. Almost a decade later, in 1981, an additional 800 seats were added, for a total of 4,000. Even before 1970, the previous 1,200-seat auditorium was being used for adults only. The young people had their own worship service. Today Sunday school and worship attendance each average 11,000.

The church had only one morning worship service until 1979, when an earlier service was added. Three years later an earlier evening worship service also was added. As a result of these two changes, attendance on Sunday has increased by approximately 1,000 each week.

Dr. Elmer L. Towns, resident church-growth authority at Thomas Road, identifies six principles that God has used to multiply the church's membership, ministry, and missionary outreach:

1. *Continuous Evangelism*, with a focus on everyone reaching others for Christ.
2. *Web-Evangelism*, or growth through existing kinship and friendship relationships.
3. *Homogeneous Units*, or people with similar cultural interests. Thomas Road Baptist Church is basically a church of blue-collar workers reaching other workers like themselves.
4. *Special Days*. Annually, the two special times when maximum attendance is a goal are:
   (1) *Harvest Days* at Thanksgiving and
   (2) *Homecoming*, the final Sunday of June.
5. *Synergistic Principle* of multiple ministries. The power of any ministry is multiplied as other ministries are added. This mix of ministries produces a traffic flow difference similar to the difference between a quick-shop grocery on the corner and a shopping mall. Key ministries in this mix at Thomas Road include: television, radio, the Elam Home for Alcoholics, the Treasure Island Camp, the Hope Aglow prison ministry, and the printing ministry.
6. *Saturation Evangelism*. Since the church's earliest days mass mailings, radio, and television have been used to saturate the masses. Media selected have been those that continue to communicate even while the members sleep in their homes at night.

Today, as a result of cooperating with God in the application of these principles, one-third of the Lynchburg population holds membership in Thomas Road Baptist Church. It should be little surprise that the church refers to itself as the Church Aflame.

The pastoral staff alone consists of sixty-four people. A total staff of 1,300 leads the multitude of ministries at the church. Forty-four deacons assist the staff.

Missions Strategy

Thomas Road Baptist church has ministered to the black population for more than a decade. The church baptized its first black member in 1971. An average of 200–300 black worshipers attend regularly.

In addition to black members of the mother church, the Towns report indicates:

> There are approximately 400 children and adults who attend Sunday School at the inner-city services (90 percent black). This mission is conducted by the staff of the church away from its facilities, because the economically poor are more comfortable worshipping among themselves.[6]

Through its own Strategic Baptist Missions the congregation supports thirty foreign missionaries.

As graduates of the college and the seminary have planted new congregations across the nation, the Liberty Baptist Fellowship has been organized. This network of 185 new churches is part of a master national missions strategy to begin 5,000 new churches by the end of the century.

Sunday School Aflame

The adult attendance at Thomas Road Baptist Church averages 60 percent of the total Sunday attendance. This is almost 20 percent above the national average. One important reason why 3,600 adults attend is the pastor's Bible Class. This class was taught by Falwell for twenty-six years. Recently another staff member has assumed this key responsibility.

Rather than adopting the traditional departmental structure, Thomas Road uses the larger group master-teacher approach. The average children's Sunday school class has thirty in attendance. Public school-size classrooms are used. Each room will have four to five teachers.

There are seven adult classes at the main church with another at the

6. Ibid.

Table 21   Profile of Thomas Road Baptist Church

	1981	1980	1975	1971	1969
Total Membership	19,000	18,000	15,000	10,000	5,000
Sunday School Attendance	8,000	8,000	5,566	4,857	2,640
Adult Sunday School	5,604	6,014	3,745		1,300
Youth Sunday School	1,051	703	877		480
Children Sunday School	1,347	1,283	944		860
Buses	27	27	36	41	15
Bus Riders	798	651	1,043	1,152	33
College Enrollment	3,341	2,930	1,244	153	
College Faculty	154	133	75	1	

inner-city location. While adult classes mix men and women, the boys and girls meet in separate classes.

Young people have three age groups for Sunday school with over 300 in each. An estimated 80–100 young people actively participate in the visitation and evangelistic activities of the church each week.

Teacher-pupil ratio figures by the various age groups, except for youth, are not available.

The children's classes use curricula published by David C. Cook, Baptist Publications, Scripture Press, and Child Evangelism Fellowship. All youth and adult classes use the Bible only as their text in the classroom. Weekly teachers meetings provide additional help for the teachers.

Versions of the Bible used include the King James and the·New King James Version.

New members seeking baptism usually are new Christians. Baptisms average 200 annually. During the peak of the bus ministry, under Dr. Jim Vineyard's leadership, 500 baptisms each year was normal.

Looking Ahead

Major strategies are being developed by the church as it plans for the future. The saturated facilities have been carefully studied and projections have already been made to the year A.D. 2000.

The future looks bright under the super-aggressive leadership of Dr. Jerry Falwell, Dr. Elmer Towns, and other gifted members of the staff and congregational team. The church's goals are to fill the nation with doctrine (Acts 5:28) and to turn this world right-side-up in this generation.

12

First Baptist Church
Dallas, Texas

A deacon of First Baptist Church offers a series of motivational classes for unemployed workers in Dallas. One of the wealthiest men in the nation offers investment and financial counsel to his church. A world-famous evangelist has been a member of First Baptist Church since 1953. The deacon is Zig Ziglar, the financier is H. L. Hunt, and the evangelist is Dr. Billy Graham.

On July 30, 1868, First Baptist Church organized with eleven members: three men and eight women. Dallas, a city of muddy streets, boardwalks, and pot holes, had Methodist and Cumberland Presbyterian churches but no Baptist church. Evangelist W. W. "Spurgeon" Harris had been invited to lead a revival meeting the same year. The church was organized as a result of that summer's meeting.

Almost thirty years later First Baptist Church called its tenth pastor, George W. Truett. When he arrived in this city of 40,000 people, the church had 715 members, a Sunday school enrollment of 250, and three mission Sunday schools with 180 members.[1]

Leon McBeth's book, *The First Baptist Church of Dallas* (©1968, Zondervan) provided invaluable background material for this chapter. The quotations are used by permission.

1. Leon McBeth, *The First Baptist Church of Dallas* (Grand Rapids: Zondervan, 1968), p. 124.

Truett served as pastor until his death in 1944. In his forty-seven years at First Baptist, membership grew to 7,804.

Three months later, the thirty-four-year-old Dr. W. A. Criswell, from First Baptist Church of Muskogee, Oklahoma, became pastor of the Dallas church.

In an amazing dream God prepared Criswell for the move to Dallas:

> Criswell said that after Truett's death, but before he had in any way been contacted by the church, he dreamed that he attended the Dallas church. Vast throngs of people were streaming in. Criswell entered between two other men and took a seat in the balcony, slightly to the right of the pulpit. The church was banked with flowers, and a great casket rested at the front. Criswell asked the man on his right what this meant, and was told that the great pastor Dr. Truett, had died. People all around were weeping.
>
> In a few moments the man on Criswell's left pressed his knee and said, "You must go down and preach to my people." He turned; and it was Dr. Truett, dignified as ever, and speaking in his matchless voice.[2]

Under Criswell's leadership the church has continued in the spirit of the revival meeting that gave it its birth. Approximately 4,000 households make up First Baptist. Undesignated offerings during the 1982–1983 year totaled $5,788,528.

Criswell's first sermon as pastor of the Dallas congregation challenged his people, "We'll go on and up with our various works. We'll give to missions more money than ever before. We'll have a Sunday school with 5,000 in attendance every Sunday."[3] At that time, the church averaged less than 2,000 in Sunday school attendance. It now exceeds 6,000 each week.

Eager to lead his church, Criswell envisioned three great goals: (1) a week-day ministry to the total family, (2) a parking building to bring people from the suburbs to the inner city, and (3) adequate educational buildings to house a congregation growing through a soul-winning Sunday school. Today, all three goals have been reached. Continued growth requires constant alertness to future expansion needs. The evangelism goal for 1982 was 1,000 baptisms. The church baptized 1,034.

W. A. Criswell: A Baptist Legend

W. A. Criswell was the son of the town barber who also led congregational singing regularly. As a young boy he grew up in New Mexico. At

2. Ibid., pp. 227–28.
3. Ibid., p. 233.

Table 22 Profile of First Baptist Church, Dallas

	1982	1980	1970	1960	1950	1944
Total Membership	22,732	21,793	15,919	12,108	9,128	7,804
Sunday School Attendance	6,248	6,627	5,050	4,354	2,536	1,753
Baptisms	1,084	630	381	256	270	84

age six he had visions of being a preacher and was converted at age ten during a revival service.

Criswell was an excellent student. He received his Ph.D. with high honors, from Southern Baptist Theological Seminary, in Louisville, Kentucky, in New Testament Interpretation. Three churches called him as their pastor after seminary. During this period he met Betty Marie Harris and married her in 1935.

While he was pastor at the First Baptist Church of Muskogee, Oklahoma, he was recommended to the pulpit committee of First Baptist Church of Dallas. At first he refused to even consider following the popular Dr. George W. Truett. Less than four months after the funeral of Truett, however, Dr. W. A. Criswell, the unknown preacher from Oklahoma, was preaching his first sermon as pastor of the Dallas church.

Early in his ministry he made it clear to all that he was not another Truett. Criswell's aim was to build the church through the Sunday school. Under his direction Sunday school attendance grew from 1,753 in 1944, to its present 6,000.

Criswell, a past president of the Southern Baptist Convention, directs his 23,000-member congregation through his deacons. All major recommendations come through them and go to the congregation for final approval. Approximately three hundred active deacons serve the church.

Criswell preaches without notes from the pulpit. He has written more than thirty books. Most are the product of his verse-by-verse sermons from Genesis through Revelation. From 1946 to 1962 Dr. Criswell preached through the Bible.

In the spirit of biblical obedience, First Baptist Church has led the 35,000 Southern Baptist Churches in world mission gifts. Missions is not something foreign to First Baptist Church since they already teach within their congregation weekly the Word of God in Chinese, Spanish, Korean, Japanese, Portugese and Laotian.

Dr. Billy Graham says, "The open Bible in Dr. Criswell's hand is more

First Baptist Church in Dallas, Texas, occupies six city blocks in downtown Dallas. Dr. W. A. Criswell serves as pastor.

than decoration. He explains it and proclaims it. In his hand the Word of God comes alive."[4]

Growth Through Sunday School

Prior to Criswell's term as pastor, large Sunday school classes were popular. One men's class at First Baptist Church, the Baraca Class, began meeting in a local theater during church remodeling. Attendance reached over 1,000, with an average attendance of 641 in 1921.

Sunday school enrollment reached more than 6,000 at the church during the 1920s but gradually declined during the Great Depression. Three decades later, the 6,000-mark was achieved under the leadership of Dr. Criswell. Enrollment is now in its fourth continuous decade of growth under his leadership. The Sunday school now has 10,000 enrolled, with 6,000 attending weekly. The sizes of the classes, however, have changed radically.

First Baptist Church was predominantly a church of adults in 1944. An elderly deacon disagreed with the pastor's plans to reorganize the Sunday school into smaller groups, for all age groups. Criswell, however, refused to be satisfied that the church was doomed to remain a declining, inner-city church, maintaining a limited ministry to older adults.

Two major obstacles challenged his goal. First, the large adult Sunday school classes had become independent. McBeth describes the seriousness of the problem:

> For decades First Baptist Church adults had been grouped into large, semi-independent Bible classes without regard to age. These classes elected their own teachers, received and disbursed their own funds, and often met downtown at some site removed from the church. Some of them, like the Cranfill Class, conducted their own radio broadcast. Others, like the Baraca Class, had their own major benevolent project, which often raised more than $10,000.00 each Christmas for the Buckner Children's Home.[5]

Problems associated with the existing class structure included:

1. Oversight of these classes by the church became impractical.
2. The church was no longer able to select teachers for these classes.
3. Class projects became totally selected and perpetuated by the various classes, without approval of the church.

4. Ibid., p. 335.
5. Ibid., p. 254.

4. The class leaders refused to introduce newer and better teaching methods and resources to their members.
5. A unified calendar of activities among the classes could not be either developed or coordinated.
6. Some class projects conflicted with the emphases of the total church.[6]

Through major efforts in 1953 the members were taught basic church growth principles and restructuring followed. This reorganization of large classes into smaller classes and the grouping of these classes into departments was made possible by the renovation of existing buildings and by new buildings.

By 1968, the centennial year of the church, there were very few large classes. This was not accomplished without opposition.

The strategy of growth still centers around the nature and structure of the Sunday school. Today, their Sunday school reaches and teaches through its 356 teaching-units at the main church alone.

Today, the main church occupies six city blocks in downtown Dallas valued by one estimate at $200 million. In addition to the priority of the Sunday school for growth of First Baptist Church, the pastor attributes the increase to four other factors: (1) prayer, (2) visitation and personal soul-winning, (3) meeting felt needs, and (4) preaching the Bible as the Word of God.

Criswell identifies Isaiah 40:8 ("The grass withereth, the flower fadeth: but the word of our God shall stand for ever") as the promise verse for his congregation.

Through Dr. Criswell's leadership, the Sunday school has become the cutting edge for church growth at First Baptist Church of Dallas.

> Anyone and everyone can belong to the Sunday School, and should. This is the great reaching arm of the church. This is our primary instrument of visitation, soul-winning, and Bible teaching. I have often thought that God gave us the Sunday School to cope with the secular difficulties of reaching people for Christ during these present days. A pastor cannot stress the importance of the Sunday School too much. . . .
>
> There is a reason why so many of our churches are small and, in many instances, getting smaller. They do not build tremendously meaningful Sunday Schools. They do not enlist people, go after people, win people, teach people. They are spiritually dormant. . . . By the grace of God, the

---

6. Ibid., (adapted).

Table 23   1982 Sunday School Attendance

	Approximate Attendance	Age of Groupings	Total Teachers	Teacher/Pupil Ratio	Percentage of Total Attendance
Preschool	500	Birth–5	140	1:3	10
Children	660	6–12	146	1:5	11
Youth	620	12–18	50	1:12	11
Adults	4,420	18–up	136	1:33	68
Total	6,200		472	1:13	

church can expand, it can grow, and it can do it through the Sunday School.[7]

Approximately 250 members participate in the weekly structured visitation and evangelistic activities of the church. An estimated 70 percent of all baptisms represent the conversion of new believers. Soulwinners are trained through a variety of evangelism methods. Most training is done through the Sunday school and through the Church Training Organization. These methods include: marked New Testaments; Evangelism Explosion; CWT—Continuous Witness Training; and WIN—Witness Involvement Now. The last two are Southern Baptist methods.

The Church Staff and Growth

First Baptist has 450 staff members, including 200 part-time employees. The total ministry staff, including secretaries, is eighty. Eleven assistant pastors join with the senior pastor in caring for the membership of the First Baptist Church.

As senior pastor, Dr. Criswell views the ratio of staff members to church membership as a key to church growth or decline. He believes that a pastor can care effectively for a limited number of people. At that critical point, decline occurs even though new members are being added.

Each staff member added can himself reach and hold a certain number of people. The size of the number depends upon his ability and dedication. Around every staff member will be a cluster of people added to the whole.[8]

7. W. A. Criswell, *Criswell's Guidebook for Pastors* (Nashville: Broadman Press, 1980), p. 176.
8. Ibid., p. 82.

Assuming that a pastor is able to enlist and employ staff members who are willing to "visit, pray, witness, testify, cultivate, and love the lost," Criswell teaches that any staff member can pay for himself.

All a staff member has to do to pay for his salary and upkeep is to win and hold twelve new families to the church. That will do it. Ten of the tithing families will pay his salary on whatever economic level the congregation lives (one hundred twenty dollars a year in Uganda, twenty thousand dollars a year in Dallas). The tithe of the other two families will pay the light bill and the janitor bill for his service.[9]

Satellite Chapels

Mission chapels are nothing new to First Baptist Church of Dallas. Dr. George W. Truett inherited three mission Sunday schools when he became pastor in 1897. At that time, the satellite Sunday schools had 180 members while the main Sunday school reported 250 members. Forty percent of the Sunday school membership attended the mission chapels.

Eight decades later, the church administers seventeen mission chapels as well as ten other preaching points. Attendance in the chapels averages approximately 1,500, or one-quarter of the total Sunday school attendance.

Two types of mission chapels are operated by the main church. Some chapels are able to become independent, self-supporting congregations. Others, because of poverty or social and community conditions, can best function with support from a mother church.

Several chapels have achieved the status of self-supporting, self-governing churches. Others have attempted, but have not been as effective in their efforts, and have requested continued support. Chapels of First Baptist Church usually meet in their own facilities provided by the mother church. Each has its own pastor provided by the mother church. The by-laws of First Baptist Church state:

Meetings of Missions. No meeting of the members of a Mission or Missions of the Church shall ever constitute either a regular or special conference meeting of the Church for any purpose. No vote on any matter pertaining to any of the affairs of the Church shall ever be taken at any meeting of the members of a Mission or Missions of the Church other than their vote on the admission of a member to the Church as herein before provided. A member of a Mission of the Church, being a member of the Church, shall

9. Ibid., p. 83.

have the right to attend and vote at any regular or special conference held by the Church in accordance with these By-Laws.[10]

This description of the procedure is standard for most Baptist churches. Further provision is made for chapels proving their ability and desire to become autonomous. The largest chapel of the church has 225 members. The most distant satellite chapel is twenty miles from the main church.

Satellite chapels are the church's major channel for meeting benevolence needs throughout the Dallas area. Food, clothing, medical, and other help is provided through seventeen outreach ministries.

As early as the mid-1950s, the church sponsored eight missions. They reported a combined enrollment of 1,851 while winning and baptizing 245 persons.[11]

Each mission chapel has its own budget. However, First Baptist Church provides needed funds through its own budget or special offerings.

As of 1956, the Missions Committee of the Church targeted new chapels in areas of the city where a stronger economy made autonomy probable. This effort has been in addition to the location of chapels in less prosperous areas.

Other Ministries of Concern

Each member is asked to complete an extensive questionnaire to aid the church in its ministry. The results are computerized to insure accurate information.

The W. A. Criswell Foundation has been established as a corporation separate from the church. Its basic purpose is to provide financial support to the church, the Criswell Center for Biblical Studies, and the Criswell Academy.

The Criswell Center for Biblical Studies is a school for training pastors in biblical exposition, research, and other needed ministry skills. The Criswell Academy is a private elementary and secondary school with an enrollment of approximately 1,000 students.

As the largest of the more than 36,000 Southern Baptist Churches in North America, First Baptist Church continues to cast a long and visible shadow of influence as a model for growth potential.

10. See the *By-Laws of the First Baptist Church*, Dallas, TX, p. 3.
11. Adapted from McBeth, *The First Baptist Church of Dallas*, p. 280.

13

First Baptist Church
Houston, Texas

Houston is the home of one of the world's largest and wealthiest congregations, First Baptist Church. First Baptist was organized on April 10, 1841, in the home of Mrs. Piety Hadley. There were twenty charter members, four of whom were black. James M. Huckins, organizer and first pastor of the church, would be astonished to view the change his once small flock has experienced.

Dr. John Bisagno, the thirtieth pastor to serve the church, has led the congregation since February, 1970. Explosive growth occurred during the early 1970s, years of political, social, and religious unrest.

The entire congregation moved from the inadequate buildings at Lamar and Fannin to the present location near Katy Freeway on April 3, 1977. Each Sunday school department mobilized its own members to pack and move its furniture and supplies to the new location. Immediately after the move, more space was needed as enrollment continued to grow. By May, 1980, a new three-story children's wing had been built.

Less than one year later, Bisagno used an issue of the church newsletter, *The Orbit,* to present his new goal. The headline was "A Challenge We Cannot Ignore." Almost immediately he began:

During the decade of the seventies, the blessings of God upon our church and subsequent growth have been unprecedented. The church membership has grown by about 12% a year: from 2,800 to nearly 14,000. The average Sunday School attendance has grown 13% a year: from around 600 to 3,400. Our evangelism output is nearly incalculable. In 1969, we baptized only 50 people. During the seventies, we won between 15,000 and 20,000 to Christ with nearly half being baptized into the fellowship of our church. Stewardship has increased 24% a year, with total giving moving from $300,000 to over $5 million annually. . . . Sunday School departments have more people in the hallways trying to get in than can be accommodated in the classrooms. A small task force of policemen directs the traffic, turn-away crowds attend the services, over $1 million is now given annually to missions, and a pressing need for increased land and buildings is obvious.[1]

This issue also contained future growth projections. He reduced the 12, 13, and 24 percent figures for the sake of estimating conservative increases.

The statistics are staggering at the even slower 10% rate of continued growth to 1990. We will average 8,400 in Sunday School, have 33,400 church members, win tens of thousands to Christ, and give nearly $15 million a year to the work of the Lord.

He detailed a plan to raise $10 million for new buildings to meet the immediate growth crisis. Rather than borrow the funds at 15 percent interest and lose $21.6 million in interest, church families were given an awesome invitation: a double tithe, or 20 percent offerings, for two years. This would allow the church to occupy the new space debt-free.

I am challenging every member of our beloved church . . . to commit in faith through thick and thin; for better or worse . . . if hell freezes over; to suck it up; gut it out; to bite the bullet; pay the price. We must make the sacrifice to get an extra job, to pass up a vacation, to sell an extra car—to do whatever it takes—to give 20% of our income to our Lord through First Baptist Church for the next two years for this program. That's the plan. Two tithes for two years . . . we are not talking about just buildings and programs . . . we are talking about souls—hundreds, thousands, and millions of them—to be won, not only by the direct ministry of this church,

---

1. "A Challenge We Cannot Ignore," *Orbit* 8 (February 20, 1981): 11-1.

but by the influence and impact this step will make on the Kingdom of God through thousands of sister churches because we dared.[2]

Total membership of the church in March, 1983, was 15,263. This represents 7,228 households.

Training for Eternity

The team of seventy full-time and seventy-five part-time employees of First Baptist Church was coordinated by Dr. Harry Piland, administrative pastor since January, 1983. He previously served as leader of the aggressive Sunday school department of the Southern Baptist Convention in Nashville. He now is back in Nashville.

In addition to the staff of 145 at First Baptist, the organizational key is the volunteer Sunday school staff of 487 men and women.

The King James Version is the primary textbook of the Sunday school, although other versions are used.

Youth and adult members study every chapter and verse of the Bible every eight years through the Southern Baptist "Bible Book" curriculum.

Youth meet in separate boys and girls classes. As they become young adults they are given the choice of men's, women's, and couples' classes. Children's groups are all mixed groups. The church provides special classes for the deaf. These groups are for all ages. They have an attendance of about fifty with ten teachers. The Christian Hebrew class, another special class, has two teachers and an average attendance of twenty-five members. The Sunday school averages more than 600 single adults each week with twenty-six teachers and workers.

The teacher training class of the church provides a constant flow of new teachers each season. Graduates number fifteen or twenty at a time. This training class is an essential ingredient for a church with educational space for 6,000 to 7,000 in Sunday school. In the 1981 challenge the pastor said:

And, be sure of this. We have the teachers, the enrollment, this spirit, the momentum; everything to divide and doubly multiply every one of our 70 Sunday School departments except two or three.[3]

2. Ibid., p. 2.
3. Ibid.

Dr. John Bisagno, pastor of First Baptist Church in Houston, Texas, in 1981 challenged members of his congregation to a double tithe as part of an expansion and outreach project.

Table 24 Profile of First Baptist Church, Houston

	1982	1981	1980	1975	1970	1960
Church Membership	14,897	13,872	13,104	8,496	3,905	3,508
Worship Attendance*	6,000					
Average Sunday School Attendance	3,754	3,317	3,042	1,603	869	1,172
Sunday School Enrollment	8,248	7,445	6,727	3,378	2,167	2,279
Total Offerings (M = Millions)	$10.8M	$7.6M	$4.2M	$3.5M	$429,609	$371,752
Baptisms†	646	480	605	250	231	77

* Attendance in two morning services. Sanctuary capacity is 4,000.
† Baptisms totaled 1,669 in 1971 and 1,022 in 1972.

Many other classes, seminars, and retreats are provided to equip members. Sunday evening church training classes are targeted to specific interest groups. Topics offered include: God's Principles of Handling Wealth; Family Budgeting Workshop; an Entrepreneur's Workshop; Evidence of Our Faith; Estate Planning Seminars; the Lost Art of Disciple Making; Equipping the Church to Pray; and Sign Language Training.

During the week, the church has had retreats for newlyweds and the newly-engaged. Other offerings include Prison Witness Training.

Ministry and Missions

In addition to the 145 staff members and the 487 volunteer Sunday school teachers church members elect a deacon ministry corps of 225 men. Some deacons also serve in the Sunday school organization. They serve as both a ministry and policy suggestion group pending final approval by the congregation. Deacons are elected by the congregation.

The television ministry of the church makes it possible to touch tens of thousands of the three million people of Houston. Twice each Sunday, worship services are telecast on a local channel. Both services are broadcast live each week by radio. The choir and orchestra Easter presentation, "Living Pictures," has been televised nationally by cable television. "Tel-Evangelism" counselors are trained to assist approximately fifty television viewers who call weekly with questions and personal needs.

The first annual Houston Crusade was conducted by First Baptist Church in July, 1978. The fifth summer Houston Crusade was preceded

Table 25   Sunday School at First Baptist Church, Houston

	Attendance	Total Teachers	Teacher/Pupil Ratio
Preschool	468	102	1:5
Grades 1–5	513	118	1:4
Grades 6–12	458	79	1:6
Adults	2,561	208	1:12
Total	4,000	487	1:7

These figures do not include the satellite missions averaging 213 in Sunday school attendance.

by a men's prayer breakfast, a field house prayer meeting each night of the crusade, and a day of prayer and fasting on Saturday before the eventful week. During the crusade, two hundred adults served as crusade counselors. Hundreds of singles participated in the "World's Largest Single Adult Choir" on Friday night of the meeting.

Reports in *The Orbit* for July 16, 1982, gave the following summary of the week at nearby Delmar Stadium:

> Our 5th Annual Houston Crusade was no doubt the most blessed and fruitful we have ever had! A total of 603 responded to the invitations. Of this number, there were 244 making a decision for recommitment and 359 making first time professions of faith.[4]

During the 1981 Crusade 555 public decisions were made. Nearly 400 of these decisions were professions of faith in Christ. Dr. John Bisagno is the evangelist each year.

The church averages over five hundred guests in Sunday school and worship services each Sunday. How are they followed up? The First Baptist solution is no mystery:

> Church growth seldom just happens, but is the result of an aggressive outreach/visitation program. We are now ready to begin such a program.
>
> Each member of our church has been keyed into the computer by visit areas. Every prospect who visits our Sunday School or worship service has also been keyed by visit areas. This enables us to assign prospects to members who live in the same neighborhood.[5]

4. "God Did It Again," *Orbit* (July 16, 1982): 12–1.
5. "New Visitation Program Launched," *Orbit* 47 (November 21, 1980); 10–2.

The church reported 1,915 new members in 1979–1980, 40 percent of whom were from non-Baptist backgrounds. There were an average of 377 visitors weekly for an annual total of 19,227. They were followed up by the 530 church-elected Sunday school teachers.

> We enroll *one* person in Sunday School when we have *ten* visitors.
> Our church baptizes *one* person every time we enroll *three* people in Sunday School.
> We have averaged 47% of our enrollment in attendance for the past ten years.
> Sunday School enrollment is our best evangelistic indicator.[6]

There is no structured weekly visitation program where members gather at the church to receive prospect assignment cards. Lifestyle Evangelism is the present method of outreach. Many members, however, have had witness and counselor training for the annual crusade and various mission trips.

Since the church receives 40 percent of all its new members from non-Baptist backgrounds, effective new member orientation is essential. Approximately 90 percent of all persons being baptized come by conversion. Orientation is expected, but not required, of all new members. A five-week orientation class meets on Sunday evenings.

Missions is another word for love at First Baptist. Much more is involved than giving financially. However, the church gave $404,799.69 to specific mission causes in February, 1981.

Missions education plays an important role in making missions possible. The church's weekly newsletter prints detailed information on the five ways a member can serve the Home Mission Board and the nine opportunities for service on the Southern Baptist Foreign Mission Board.

November is Missions Month at the church. The major offerings taken during this time are usually designated: 70 percent to foreign missions, 15 percent to home missions, 10 percent to Texas mission needs, and 5 percent to mission needs among Southern Baptist-supported missions in the Houston Metro area.

Members are informed of mission needs. Twelve members publicly committed their lives to full-time missions service in November, 1977. The special missions speaker that year was Dr. Nilson Fanini from Brazil, pastor of the largest Baptist congregation in South America.

6. "200th Anniversary of Sunday Schools," *Orbit* 40 (October 3, 1980): 10–1.

The Master Builder ministry is a bold new ministry composed of one hundred men and women of the church. Master Builders are men and women with varying skills who offer themselves to the physical development of buildings and properties to be used in God's work. They are involved in mission projects in an ongoing ministry whenever and wherever needed.

Numerous opportunities for direct involvement in both home and foreign missions are provided through the church. One channel of ministry in Houston is the church's cooperation with the Houston International Seaman's Center which ministers to one out of every eight men who come through the Port of Houston. Also, hundreds of boxes of food are distributed to families in the Houston area annually. There is an annual Hebrew Christian Passover Banquet. The church operates Bethel Chapel, a mission among mostly Mexican-American families.

A Vietnamese family was sponsored by the church in 1975. In 1980, the 180-voice "Singing Texans" choir spent two weeks on a mission trip to England and Scotland. Again in 1981, 183 members participated in a mission trip to Tokyo, Hong Kong, and Hawaii. Other members have involved themselves in mission related trips to Haiti, the "river ministry" in Big Bend of the Rio Grande River area, Spain, South Africa, Zambia, Mexico and Kenya. Regular classes are provided at the church during Church Training time on Sunday evenings. This allows members who have recently returned from a mission trip to share with other interested members of the church. A Laotian ministry is operated in the church each Sunday with an average attendance of fifty.

Another reason for growth at First Baptist Church is the vision of the pastor to involve the total city in the ministry of the church. This began in the 1970s during the Richard Hogue Crusade. Each Wednesday noon a Bible study is led by the pastor. A luncheon is served and 300-500 businessmen and others attend. Dr. Bisagno leads this study.

The annual musical Christmas pageant is a sell-out. Ten performances are given in early December with 4,000 tickets sold for each presentation. National CBN Cable Television Network also telecasts the event.

One of the exciting ministries of First Baptist Church is its school, Northwest Academy. The congregation accepted this new ministry in March, 1980.

The church inherited a 14.7 acre site; nearly 300 students; 65,000 square feet of poorly maintained buildings; a long-term indebtedness of $775,000; a few good faculty members; and a lot of potential. Since June of 1980, enrollment now exceeds 1,000 students with more than eighty faculty members. . . . By actual count of parents, teachers, and students, more than 500 individuals have united with First Baptist Church after having some association with the school. There have been 60 or more individual conversions within the school in one-to-one sessions by teachers and administrators.[7]

Dr. Charles Allen, pastor of Houston's First Methodist Church, the largest Methodist church in the nation, echoes all that has been said: "The ministry of Dr. John R. Bisagno and the witness of First Baptist Church has lifted the Christian influence of every church in Houston. I love you both."[8]

7. "Northwest Academy Day at FBC," *Orbit* 19 (May 13, 1983): 13–1.
8. "A Challenge We Cannot Ignore," p. 2.

14

First Baptist Church
Jacksonville, Florida

The city of Jacksonville, Florida, is world famous for its eight miles of public beaches. To the Christian world, the significance of First Baptist Church eclipses even the annual roar of football fans at the Gator Bowl.

Founded in July, 1839, as Bethel Baptist Church, the first congregation was a mix of black and white members. For six decades the church grew. In 1901, the church buildings, along with 2,368 other buildings, were destroyed by fire. Ten thousand souls were left homeless in Jacksonville.

After rebuilding, tragedy struck again when the Great Depression of the 1920s and 1930s found many churches and businesses financially overextended.

First Baptist Church "became bankrupt in the thirties, losing all of its property and its good name in the community."[1] Dr. Homer G. Lindsay, Sr., who served as pastor from 1940 to 1969, then co-pastor and Pastor Emeritus until his death in 1981, recalls:

1. Homer G. Lindsay, Jr., *How We're Building a New Testament Church* (Decatur, GA: The Southern Baptist Journal, 1975), p. 137.

The church, in a depressed spiritual state, was allowed to buy back the House of Worship but completely lost all educational buildings. The Sunday School shrank from an enrollment of 1,800 to 700 in 1940. The pastor resigned and . . . The church called me from Chattanooga to become their Pastor, and thus began a long ministry of paying debts, restoring confidence, and rebuilding the walls that had fallen down.[2]

Tithers were enlisted by the hundreds, baptisms jumped from 35 to 200 annually, and Sunday school attendance grew from seven hundred to over one thousand. Since then, the church has built a new educational building every ten years.

Dr. Lindsay announced that he would retire on his sixty-sixth birthday, February 2, 1969. The church invited his son, Homer Lindsay, Jr., to become the new pastor. He agreed with the terms that his father continue as co-pastor for a four-year transition period. Under both father and son the church grew. During the years that Dr. Homer G. Lindsay, Sr., led the church, more than 5,000 new Christians were baptized.

Prior to becoming pastor of the Jacksonville church Homer Lindsay, Jr., led a new mission church in Miami. During his sixteen years in Miami, from 1956–1969, the Northwest Baptist Church grew from 42 to 3,280 members.

Dr. Homer G. Lindsay, Sr., writes that with the coming of his son,

everything has been centered around outreach: house-to-house and telephone religious surveys . . . Visitation program through the Sunday school; lay witnessing institutes . . . follow-up enlistment and bus ministry that began with two buses in 1969 and has grown to seventeen buses (1975) bringing an average of 700 riders.

Looking back from the vantage point of his eighth anniversary as pastor of First Baptist Church of Jacksonville, Dr. Homer Lindsay, Jr., comments:

As my wife and I were reflecting over these eight years, we marvel. . . . It all began in February of 1969 when I preached on a Sunday night from the 22nd chapter of Ezekiel about the city and brought a challenge to some six hundred people present for that Sunday evening service. Seventy-eight people walked the aisle as a response to that challenge. In that service was born the Bus Ministry and the Door-to-Door Ministry. By the end of 1969,

2. Ibid., p. 137.

Table 26   Profile, First Baptist Church, Jacksonville, Florida

	1983	1982	1980	1970	1968	1960	1950
Church Membership	13,833	13,249	11,460	3,959	3,522	2,612	3,179
Worship Attendance	6,000	6,000					
Sunday School Enrollment	12,203	12,203	10,970	4,140	2,835	2,595	1,810
Sunday School Attendance	5,227	4,747	3,979	1,764	1,324	1,140	1,100
Baptisms	641*	968	1,067	334	142	101	229
Buses†				9			
Bus Riders				300			
Total Households		6,500					

* Figure is for only the first half of the 1982–83 church year.
† The bus ministry began in February, 1969 with 2 buses and 38 riders. Limited space led to its discontinuation in 1978. In 1975 there were 750 weekly riders on 16 bus routes.

our Sunday school attendance had increased about three hundred. God has been so good during these eight years. Our Sunday school attendance has tripled and our church membership has tripled. We have seen our annual offerings go from $368,000 to $1,600,000. . . .

In 1973 we led the entire Southern Baptist Convention in baptisms.[3]

Though the bus ministry was phased out in 1978, due to already crowded building space, the Door-to-Door Ministry is stronger than ever. Baptisms, as indicated below, reveal that evangelism is the main goal of this Florida congregation:

1968—142	1971—434	1974—638	1977—609	1980—1067
1969—182	1972—427	1975—913	1978—915	1981—928
1970—331	1973—636	1976—723	1979—938	1982—968

An important transitional year for the church was 1976, when the new 3,600-seat auditorium was completed. The trend of multiplication growth after 1969 has not decreased. During the 1970s church membership doubled and Sunday school attendance almost doubled.

3. Homer G. Lindsay, Jr., "This Sunday, I Begin My Ninth Year As Your Pastor," *Evangel* 1 (January 2, 1977): 34–1.

The Four Basics

Throughout his ministry, Dr. Homer Lindsay, Jr., has taught his people four growth essentials: (1) faithfulness to the Word of God, (2) the church as a witnessing, soul-winning fellowship, (3) fellowship, and (4) tithing as God's plan of finance for His church. The church's pastoral leaders are confident that, with careful planning, Sunday school attendance can grow from 6,000 to 7,000 each week.

The biblical priority, or faithfulness to the Word of God, is serious business at First Baptist Church of Jacksonville. Dr. Homer Lindsay, Jr., and his co-pastor, Dr. Jerry Vines, are Bible expositors by conviction and practice. Dr. Vines joined the church staff in July, 1982.

In September, 1981, Dr. Lindsay began studies in three new books. He led members through the Gospel of John each Sunday morning, the Epistle to the Romans on Sunday night, and the Book of Revelation on Wednesday night. Dr. Vine preaches through other books of the Bible. Dr. Lindsay writes:

> My method of teaching the Bible is to take a book of the Bible, begin in the first chapter and go through verse by verse. . . . My teaching is primarily in the New Testament. . . . I try to have one of the three in the Old Testament, and the other two in the New Testament.[4]

Both pastors are unapologetic in their insistence that the Word of God is reliable when the best of men prove to be untrustworthy.

> In no uncertain terms, sounding no uncertain note, the Bible declares itself to be the Word of God. . . . It is my firm conviction that the first priority of any pastor's life must be the Word of God.[5]

The second priority essential for growth is outreach through evangelism, or soul-winning. Each pastor ought to be an example as a personal soul-winner. He will be ineffective if he fails to train and equip the members of his church to win and build others to Christ.

4. Lindsay, *How We're Building a New Testament Church*, pp. 20–21.
5. Ibid., pp. 18–19.

First Baptist Church of Jacksonville, Florida, overcame trials and tragedies on its way to becoming a vital influence in the community.

Commenting on the importance of organized visitation for training new and mature believers, Dr. Lindsay writes:

> The organized visitation program is essential. It is not enough to just train your people and commit them and let them go on their own. Most people need more direction, more guidance, and more encouragement than this. The organized visitation program gives the individual the encouragement he needs.
>
> It is necessary to focus our thinking on six key items:
>
> 1. We need to train our people.
> 2. We need a program to secure prospects.
> 3. We need an up-to-date prospect file.
> 4. We need good visitation folders.
> 5. We need an organized visitation program, held on visitation days at a specified time.
> 6. Using the Sunday school fixes definite responsibility.[6]

An estimated 1,000 members actively participate in the church's visitation and evangelistic activities each week; approximately 400 are soulwinners. A total of 2,800 members made commitments to win one person each month in 1982–83. One-half of all new members coming into the church, by estimation, are receiving soul-winning training: 500 to 800 new trainees each year.

Each Sunday morning, for twelve weeks, a class is taught in lifestyle evangelism. The church's young people are asked to commit the fall months to a door-to-door witness survey. During the third week in August approximately two hundred young people are trained by the pastor.

Putting learning into practice begins the first Saturday after the camp. The young people are divided into sixty visitation teams who visit fifty to sixty houses. After lunch, the teams are taken out for recreational activities. During these surveys, information is taken only on those families indicating nonattendance or at least a high degree of irregularity.

> Through these different methods of securing prospects our prospect file contains the names and addresses of more than 12,000 people. These are the people that our Sunday School seeks to reach.[7]

6. Ibid., pp. 23–24.
7. Ibid., p. 32.

The May 10, 1981, issue of *The Evangel* gave the year's summary of the Door-to-Door Teen Visitation. This survey ministry is a year-round effort. Twelve weeks each fall are set aside for the intensive youth survey work. Every household in Jacksonville is contacted annually.

In the winter and spring months, major thrusts are made by the Sunday school classes to enroll the prospects discovered in the fall surveys. This enrollment campaign is called Operation Andrew. Each class is given a goal of new people to be enrolled during the four-month period. A total of 1,749 new members were enrolled in Sunday school during the 1981 Operation Andrew campaign.

The summer camp ministry trains young people to accomplish the outreach strategy of the church. In 1979 the decision was made to divide the teenage camp into separate camps for junior and senior high students. This decision allowed the camp to reach its maximum saturation capacity in August, 1981. Among the highlights of the camp are the many rehearsals of the youth orchestra. The senior high orchestra alone has fifty instruments.

During the week more than thirty young people invited Jesus Christ to become their personal Savior and Lord. Another 200 rededicated their lives to the Lord through the week.

More than three hundred young people gathered at the edge of Lake Yale near Eustis, Florida, to see nineteen of their friends baptized in a concluding celebration service.

Every Tuesday morning as many as two hundred women visit throughout the city. A day camp is scheduled for the summer months to provide child care during this time.

The men of the church visit each Tuesday night. They have dinner together with music and testimonies. By 6:30 P.M., the men leave the church and return by 9 P.M. At least two hundred are active in this weekly meeting. Men unable to attend the Tuesday night visitation can go to the

Table 27   **Results of Teen Visitation, Fall, 1980**

327	Youth Visiting*
5,000	Unchurched Prospects Discovered
1,600	New Families Discovered

* 227 Junior High Visitors, 110 Senior High Visitors.

Men's Soul-Winning Club on Monday nights. This is a training session for men who want to be effective soul-winners. Soul-winning visits are simulated before the group followed by question-answer sessions. Each man receives a tape to aid him as a soul-winner. In addition to the weekly tapes, reading assignments about great men of the faith are made monthly.

Another exciting evangelistic strategy was shared by Dr. Homer Lindsay, Jr., in July, 1981. He enlisted twenty young adults as missionaries for the Door-to-Door Ministry. They would be full-time staff members for an indefinite period of time.

Each afternoon is designed for Bible study, prayer, and reports. Five hours, from 4:00–9:00, have been scheduled for uninterrupted door-to-door, soul-winning visitation. When a person makes a profession of faith, the soul-winner calls a special "Hot Line" list. A volunteer living in the same neighborhood is contacted for immediate follow-up. Each new convert, when contacted by his neighbor, is encouraged to make a public profession of faith at First Baptist Church the next Sunday. Whether or not the convert attends, he or she is automatically assigned to a specific Sunday school class for additional follow-up. A network of more than 170 department and class outreach leaders lead the Married Adult Division in outreach.

A third priority of the church is fellowship. An important part of the youth visitation is the youth cell groups. Designed for senior high school students,

> cells are an informal time of sharing, prayer and discussion. It's a time when a young person can express some of the problems he is facing at school, home or wherever. It's a time adults listen and guide the young people to Biblical answers for their questions.[8]

Anyone can attend the cells. Young people are encouraged to attend the Monday night meeting. They may attend a group composed of students from their own school or one of the other groups.

When the newest buildings were constructed and others were renovated, provision was made for a 1,500-seat dining hall. These plans included rooms for small groups to have banquets or dinners.

Finally, the church designed its Sunday school organization to ensure maximum fellowship potential by neighborhoods. Every member and

8. "Sr. High Cells Are Off to a Great Start," *The Evangel* (October 4, 1981): 38–2.

every Sunday visitor living in the Jacksonville area is automatically enrolled in a department and class according to age and zip code. Both
fellowship and follow-up are assured.

The fourth priority is tithing as God's plan of finance for all believers.
Tithing is still considered biblical—the only way to build God's church.

The front page headline of *The Evangel* for November 4, 1979, read,
"Pastor Is Praying for 5,000 Tithers." Eighteen months later, in March,
1981, Dr. Lindsay could report, "There are some 4,000 tithers in this
fellowship at the present time and some 2,000 of the 4,000 are giving love
offerings over and above their tithe to the building fund."[9]

First Baptist members gather on the first Sunday in November for a
most unusual observance. "For years," Dr. Homer Lindsay, Jr., notes, "the
First Baptist Church has been pledging their budget on one day. . . . There
is no sight on earth any more thrilling, nor is there any single service
more exciting than this annual *Chest of Joash Day.*"

Members are encouraged to arrive early on this Sunday morning.
Adults go directly to the main auditorium. Youth and children meet
across the street in another building. This service is a family event and is
one of the few services that is not televised live. A prerecorded service is
broadcast that Sunday. Each adult brings both the regular weekly tithes
and offerings in addition to a pledge card for the coming year's financial
gifts and places them into the chest located in front of the auditorium.
Dr. Lindsay shares the history of the chest:

> The Chest of Joash idea comes from the Old Testament where King Joash
> had a chest made and placed it in the temple. The people then placed their
> offering in the chest and the money was used to repair the temple. Years
> ago my dad had my brother build a chest. When I was a young boy, this
> chest was in my room and I kept my toys and different things in the chest.
> Once a year, dad would come in and empty this chest and carry it to the
> church where it would be used for this service. When the church was small
> the chest was large enough. Now the chest is filled many times and has to
> be emptied several times during the service.[10]

Building Through the Sunday School

First Baptist has a building capable of caring for 7,000 in worship
attendance and 6,000 in Sunday school by dual services and classes. The

9. Homer G. Lindsay, Jr., pastor's article in *Evangel* (March 1, 1981): 38–2.

10. Homer G. Lindsay, Jr., "Chest of Joash Day Scheduled for November 4," *Evangel* 9 (October
7, 1979): 36–1.

key lies in the 1,150 Sunday school teachers and 170 married adult department and class outreach leaders.

Unlike most churches, First Baptist Church structures its adult classes and departments by age, sex, and zip code. Both members and visitors are directed to groups whose members live in the same areas of the city. This is to reinforce fellowship and follow-up between members and visitors. Age structure within classes and departments is much like that found in most other churches. One major difference is the organization of both classes and departments into separate units for men and women. The only exceptions are the single-adult departments and the recently-formed newlywed class.

Among the children's groups, those in grades 3–6 meet during small-group time, men with boys and women with girls. Youth departments are organized by school, with mixed assemblies and separate small-group time for boys and girls.

A variety of curriculums are used by the church, including those issued by Scripture Press, Gospel Light, and the Southern Baptist Sunday School Board. In addition to the freedom to select varied curriculums, a special curriculum has been written to make certain that all members, especially adults, are thoroughly and regularly oriented and challenged in soul-winning. These special lessons are taught during one quarter of the teaching year.

The adult division of the Sunday school has nine women's departments with a total of fifty classes. The men have one department subdivided into twenty-nine classes. Care is taken to ensure that no class exceeds an attendance of fifty. A steady stream of teachers results from the annual six-month teacher training class which includes twenty-six hours of tape-viewing in addition to reading and written assignments.

Table 28   Sunday School Profile (1982–83)
                First Baptist Church, Jacksonville, Florida

	Sunday School Attendance	Age of Groups	No. of Teachers	Teacher/Pupil Ratio	Teaching Units	Unit–Pupil Ratio
Preschool	772	B–5	100	1:4		
Children	739	Gr. 1–6	150	1:5	105	1:7
Youth	596	Gr. 7–12	61	1:10	66	1:9
Adults	3560		148	1:24	134	1:26
Total	5667		559		305+	

The all-time record Sunday school attendance was 4,773 on Easter Sunday, 1980. Promotion day, September 7, had 4,768 in attendance. A new goal of 5,000 attending Sunday school was set for November 23. Attendance was 5,121. Six months later, on Easter Sunday, another goal was attained with 5,159 present for Sunday school. Again, just four months later, another record was set: 5,465 attended Sunday school for "Back to School Days."

Ministries and Missions

Music is everywhere at First Baptist Church. A total of four orchestras contain 156 members. Also, 70 percent of the 1,547 members of the fourteen choirs of the church are actively involved in the music ministry of the church. It is not unusual for some of the choirs to have a waiting list.

New member follow-up is important at this church. The new-member orientation has been directed for years by Mrs. Homer Lindsay. All of the pastors' wives are involved in this special ministry. All adults and youth are counseled through use of the Survival Kit produced by the Baptist Sunday School Board in Nashville. Twice each year a class is offered for children. Deacons and Sunday school teachers serve as counselors.

A team of sixty visitors regularly care for almost one hundred home-bound members. This ministry is directed by a retired couple.

Audio tapes receive world-wide distribution through the church. The Christian Life Foundation, a group of men who have incorporated a tape ministry, send more than 13,000 tapes each year. These tapes go to college students, servicemen in the military, shut-ins, and missionaries. Countries receiving tapes include Iceland, New Zealand, Australia, Mexico, Guatemala, Egypt, and several countries in Africa.

Television has been used by the church since 1977. The church broadcasts weekly on three stations. Each Sunday morning the service is broadcast to an estimated 42,000 people. A delayed telecast is beamed each Saturday night. Recently, the church began broadcasts on Monday, Wednesday, and Thursday nights. The total estimated viewing audience is 80,000. A power source at First Baptist Church is the army of more than 2,000 Prayer Warriors. Members involved in this strategic ministry commit themselves in writing and are listed in periodic issues of the church newsletter.

First Baptist Church grows through (1) involved members who take the Great Commission personally, (2) involved members who are trained "how to do it" and then do it, (3) deacons who also are committed visitors, (4) soul-winning leadership, (5) follow-ship by people who are willing to be led, and (6) the recognition of the power of unleashed prayer by the pastors, the leaders, and the multitude of committed Prayer Warriors.

15

North Phoenix Baptist Church
Phoenix, Arizona

In 1965 the prospering North Phoenix Baptist Church dedicated a new, $1-million auditorium. The church reported an average weekly Sunday school attendance of six hundred.

Two years later the congregation experienced hard times. North Phoenix had been unable to sell its former building and suffered financial difficulties, the church had no pastor for several months, and Sunday school attendance declined to four hundred.

Finally, the congregation received exciting news. Richard Jackson of First Baptist Church in Sulphur Springs, Texas, was coming as their new pastor. The pastor's first tasks were to improve the cash flow and to rearrange the priorities of the congregation. Once again there was hope and even excitement at North Phoenix.

In 1974, Dr. Eugene Skelton wrote:

At the end of the six years of Jackson's pastorate, the church has baptized more than 2,000 people with 70 percent of these being eighteen years of age or over. This is without a revival meeting and without a bus ministry. He feels both of these are good ministries; they just are not for his situation at the present time. During this period the church has had total additions of about 4,000; a net increase has been shown of some 3,000 people. This means that the church maintains a relationship of some kind to three out of four of those who are added to its membership.[1]

By Christmas, 1977, the congregation moved from the 1,600-seat auditorium to its newly-built 6,000-seat auditorium, constructed for $5.5 million. In 1981, the church built a new three-story educational building used by young adults and preschool children.

Sunday morning Bible study attendance, even in the summer months, approaches 5,000. Seven thousand worshipers pack the center to hear the pastor. On Wednesday, a crowd of 4,000 gathers for worship, celebration, and witness. During the Wednesday evening services up to fifty or sixty people confess Christ as their Savior and join the church. Mighty wonders of the Holy Spirit regularly testify to His presence.

The church was founded in 1948. Richard Jackson was the church's only pastoral staff member when he came in 1967. By 1983 he had gathered a ministry staff of sixty-five, including ordained staff members. The church employs 105 people.

Dr. Jackson, age forty-four, is a native Texan. He graduated from Howard Payne College in 1960 and Southwestern Baptist Theological Seminary in 1963.

He is a natural leader and has received three honorary degrees.

Magnificent Obsession: Soul-Winning

Our magnificent obsession at North Phoenix has been and always will be . . . soul-winning . . . New Testament evangelism . . . the making of disciples . . . the inducting or baptism of those disciples . . . and maturing of the saved. . . . This is not the decision of the pastor, nor is it the determination of some committee . . . it is the unquestioned command of Our Lord Jesus Christ.[2]

Among the hundreds baptized each year, 95 percent are new Christians who make a profession of faith to receive Jesus Christ as Lord and Savior.

The church reports more than two thousand trained soul-winners.

1. Eugene Skelton, *10 Fastest-Growing Southern Baptist Sunday Schools* Nashville: Broadman Press, 1974), p. 101.
2. Richard Jackson, "It's on My Heart," *The Word* (June 8, 1983): 23–1.

Table 29   Profile of North Phoenix Baptist Church, Phoenix, Arizona

	1983 (April)	1982	1981	1980	1970	1960
Total Church Membership	13,535	12,845	11,430	9,990	3,055	1,056
Worship Attendance	7,000	7,000	6,500	6,000	1,800	800
Average Sunday School Attendance	4,425	3,863	3,402	3,023	911	413
Sunday School Enrollment	9,453	9,342	8,173	7,411	2,097	904
Baptisms		1,286	1,193	1,033	365	64
Teaching Units, Total		600				
Total Offerings (M = Millions)		4.8M	3.8M	3.6M	400,000	93,000
Households in Church		7,105	5,869	4,911		

Continuous training is provided to equip new soul-winners. At least sixty to one hundred members are trained throughout the year in a twelve-week class.

Additional seminars and classes cover the methods of Campus Crusade and the Southern Baptists in their Witness Involvement Now materials.

An estimated seven hundred members are actively involved in the church's weekly visitation and evangelistic activities. More members are involved in lifestyle evangelism between Sundays.

What do you do to follow up on all those people who are being saved? The pastor's answer is two-fold: through the use of "Encouragers" and through involvement in the Sunday morning Bible study ministry.

One very important program is the one-to-one discipleship training in our Survivor-Encourager Program. This ministry was developed and is directed by Url Utterback, our Minister of Outreach. Every person baptized in our church is assigned a personal Encourager from his or her Bible Study Department to aid that one for eleven weeks. The Survival Kit from the Church Training Division of our Southern Baptist Convention is the major tool employed. . . . The desired result is to guide the convert to find his or her place in regular Bible Study attendance, worship attendance, and participation in personal witnessing. . . . The key to it all is regular involvement in our Sunday morning Bible Study ministry.[3]

3. Richard Jackson, "It's on My Heart," *The Word* (July 15, 1981): 21–1.

He concludes that those who "show up" also "grow up." Those who never get active in the Bible study classes seldom grow in Christ.

January of 1983 was Reclamation Month for the Bible study groups. There was a concerted attempt to reclaim all members who had not been involved in the church since October, 1982.

After one intensive search more than seven hundred prospects were discovered on Bible study rolls. These people, high school age through adults, are either unsaved, are members of a different denomination, or are affiliated with another Baptist church.

Outreach leaders were given a list of prospective members in their departments. Each leader was asked, throughout the month of June, to cultivate and lead each candidate to make a commitment for salvation or church membership.

North Phoenix Is Second Among 35,000 Churches

North Phoenix Baptist prefers to call its Sunday school simply Bible study. However, it is a Bible study mixed with a sharp cutting edge of soul-winning.

In 1982, research results were released by the Baptist Sunday School Board. During the last ten years North Phoenix Baptist Church's Sunday school was one of the fastest growing among the 35,000 Southern Baptist churches in the U.S. The church ranks second in two categories: enrollment increase and increase in the average weekly attendance.

Sunday school enrollment jumped from 2,867 in 1972 to 8,173 in 1981. This increase of 5,306 reflects an average of 590 new members each year. Average Sunday school attendance increased from 1,343 in 1972 to 3,402 in 1981. This increase of 2,059 reflects an annual increase of 229 souls. In the summer of 1983 attendance was close to 5,000.

> We're number two and we'll try harder . . . we know that with a little extra effort we could be number one. Some will say that only means we're in the numbers game, but to the faithful leadership of our church it means more people are being reached for Christ and matured as Christians. . . . We need to continue to do those things that we know will reach people.
>
> What does the future hold? If we would continue the same rate of growth during the next ten years as we have the past ten years, in 1990 our enrollment would be 13,479 with an average attendance of 5,461. However, we are already ahead of the yearly average.[4]

4. "North Phoenix Second Among 35,000 Churches," *The Word* (June 16, 1982):22–2.

When he arrived twenty years ago at North Phoenix Baptist Church in Phoenix, Arizona, one of Dr. Richard Jackson's first tasks was to deal with the church's difficult financial situation. Today, he leads his congregation in the investment of their souls in the work of God.

The two Bible study curriculums used by the church are produced by the Southern Baptist Sunday School Board. An estimated 80 percent of the congregation's young people and adults use the New American Standard Version of the Bible.

In 1982 enrollment in adult classes was kept under forty. Most of the sixteen single-adult departments average over one hundred in enrollment. Only five of the fifty-three adult departments have enrollments above one hundred. Among the 150 married-adult classes, only eight exceed thirty in enrollment.

Adult attendance usually averages one-half of the total class enrollment in Southern Baptist Churches. This means that adult classes probably average ten to fifteen attendants each week. Classes intentionally are kept small to ensure continuous and effective assimilation of new members. Also, each group is able to minister to the needs of existing members.

Classes for men, women, and couples are available at every age level. All young people's classes are separated into boys and girls groups. Children's classes, grades 1 to 6, are mixed.

The church provides two Bible study hours and two worship services every Sunday morning.

Thirty to fifty new teachers are trained constantly through the church's teacher training department. Training cycles are designed to last eight weeks.

Music used in both the Bible study groups and in the worship services consists mainly of great traditional hymns and arrangements. Examples include A Mighty Fortress Is Our God; Crown Him with Many Crowns; and All Hail the Power of Jesus' Name.

All of the pastor's sermons are expository. For three years Dr. Richard

Table 30   Teacher/Pupil Ratios of Classes at North Phoenix Baptist Church

	Attendance	Age of Groups	Teaching Units	Total Teachers	Teacher/Pupil Ratios
Preschool	730		44	200	1:4
Children	475	Gr. 1–5	32	100	1:5
Youth	576	Gr. 6–12	100	120	1:5
Adult	2,700		169	300	1:9
Total	4,481		345	720	1:6

126 newborn babies were enrolled in 1982–83.

Jackson's sermons have focused on three books of the Bible: Proverbs, the Gospel of John, and Acts. The church's pastor explains:

> I am not trying to say that there is no other form of legitimate Bible preaching than the verse-by-verse approach. . . . People do not need to hear what men have to say when they come to church. Folks need to hear from God. Through all these almost thirty years that I have been preaching, I have honestly sought to deliver God's Word. Never have I been more certain of that than since I made the commitment to verse-by-verse exposition.[5]

Ministries That Matter

Deacons. The 160 deacons of North Phoenix Baptist Church are viewed by the pastor and the congregation as a ministry team to families rather than a policy-making board.

A close bond of respect and love marks these men as true servants of God among their people. Dr. Jackson writes:

> The deacons are ministering servants in association with the pastor in giving spiritual direction to God's church. These men are willing workers who ask nothing but the privilege of service. It should be easily seen, therefore, that the ones who are selected by this ministering band to be their leaders are so chosen because they have distinguished themselves as servants.
>
> One does not become chairman or an officer in our deacon ministry through popularity or politics. Just as The Holy Spirit selects all of the deacons through prayerful participation of the church people, so He chooses His chairman and officers by the common consent of the servant body of ministering men.[6]

Each year, one-third of the deacons retire. More than fifty are elected by the congregation to replace them.

A Satellite Chapel. Phoenix, with its population of 1.2 million, has multitudes of people that have no interest in the city's churches. Others are receptive and waiting for direction on which church to attend. North Phoenix Baptist Church saw a need and began to fill it.

The church broke ground February 13, 1983, for a $500,000 building project on land purchased by the church for its satellite mission, Sun City West Baptist Chapel.

Sun City is a senior adult community. In 1983, the mission congrega-

---

5. Richard Jackson, "It's on My Heart," *The Word* (May 18, 1983): 23–1.
6. Richard Jackson, "It's on My Heart," *The Word* (December 15, 1982):22–1.

tion won and baptized many mature adults. Pastor Melvin Ratheal, a man with a successful record of building churches, is pastor of the chapel.

Since October 1, 1982, the Sun City West Chapel has averaged fifty attendants in Sunday morning Bible study, seventy-five in morning worship and forty-eight in Sunday evening worship. Thursday Bible study attracts an average of thirty-three attendants. By March, 1983, nearly one hundred attended the chapel's Sunday services.

A new facility is being built to seat 275 in worship service and 250 in its educational space. North Phoenix committed $1.2 million in 1982 to mission causes in its budget: one-fifth the total budget.

Television and Audio Tapes.   Since March, 1969, the gospel story has been televised from the auditorium of the North Phoenix Baptist Church. Ten years later the potential viewing audience was 1.5 million people.

On the twelfth anniversary of this ministry, a contract was signed with the Trinity Broadcasting Network of Santa Ana, California. The first coast-to-coast broadcast of the North Phoenix worship service was seen on April 4, 1981.

"Our two main purposes for wanting to go outside Phoenix and Arizona," commented Pastor Richard Jackson, "are to reach people for Christ and to encourage local church attendance." World Missions is the primary thrust of this ministry, which will be totally underwritten by the North Phoenix Baptist Church budget.

The program has the capability to reach 39 states, 4.2 million homes and approximately 20 million people.[7]

The service is broadcast each Sunday morning on a local channel. An edited version on video tape is then broadcast the following Sunday on the Trinity Network.

Church Growth Seminars.   Hundreds of requests come annually from individuals, pastors, church staff members, architects, contractors, consultants, denominational leaders, and others who want to visit and know more about the Arizona church.

They want to learn how the various programs work. As an attempt to share these principles with a maximum number of people and, at the same time, minimize the staff-time involved, the church conducted its

7. "Television Contract Signed!" *The Word* (April 1981): 9-4.

first Church Growth Seminar in the fall of 1980. The seminar is usually scheduled during October, with a registration fee of approximately $100 which includes most meals and the seminar notebook. Seminar alumni pay about one-half of the registration fee.

Other Ministries. Another means of outreach conducted by the church is its ministry to nearly 400 senior adults. Also, more than fifty deaf persons receive care from the church, as do alcoholics and their families, and inmates at the Arizona State Prison.

Causes of Growth at North Phoenix

The reasons for the growth of the church are noted by the pastor:

The Sovereignty of God. Dr. Richard Jackson, as Pastor, is often asked to explain just what makes North Phoenix a growing fellowship. He replies:

> The answer has its opening in the obvious . . . the Sovereignty of God. Surely Our Father has determined in His sovereign purpose to do a wonderful work in this place. It is also obvious in scripture and experience that God's sovereignty must meet with a people's willing response. Here at North Phoenix that ready responsiveness is indeed obvious.
> . . . The Sovereign God at work in a praying people at witness, a worshipping people gathered for service and a ministering people who care about others. That's what you will find here on the Lord's Day when The Father meets with His children.[8]

A People Sold Out to God. The spirit of this statement might best be expressed by the theme "Whatever it Takes!", used by the church in 1982. Writing in his weekly pastor's article, Jackson said:

> What a joy it is to be a part of a "Whatever it Takes" kind of people. It is easy to love folks who love the Lord and His church as you do. Being a part of North Phoenix is not convenient. It never has been. We constantly change. We challenge. We grow. As we do these things, the demands for commitment increase. Workers are needed. New schedules are necessary. Our giving must increase. To all of these challenges the faith family of North Phoenix says, "Whatever it takes, we will do."[9]

8. Richard Jackson, "It's on My Heart," *The Word* (June 16, 1982): 22–1.
9. Richard Jackson, "It's on My Heart, *The Word* (September 8, 1982): 22–1.

Commitment to Personal Evangelism.   When the pastor uses the word *evangelism,* he means soul-winning—evangelism that goes out with net in hand.

Quoting another Texan, Zig Ziglar, the pastor once described an optimist as one who goes after Moby Dick in a rowboat carrying tartar sauce with him.

> Our magnificent obsession . . . soul-winning! It always has been. It always will be. . . .
>
>   It is ours to introduce people to Jesus. . . . We have not been told to win the world to Jesus. Not everyone is going to believe. Not all are going to be saved. It is not yours or mine to determine who are the "elect" of God. It is ours to see to it that everyone learns of Jesus and His saving love. Thus our obsession is to introduce every person alive to Our Lord.[10]

Bold Conviction of the Bible as the Word and Power of God.   Simply stated, men must hear the Word of God rather than the opinions of mere men.

Belief in the Positive Power of Total Stewardship of Life and Possessions.   Quoting Dr. Jess Moody of First Baptist Church of Van Nuys, California, the pastor of North Phoenix challenges his own people:

> Throw a grenade into the stronghold of Satan. . . . When you put your tithe into the offering plate, you are pulling the plugs on grenades that will explode in one hundred nations (through our cooperative mission program). We can hit more targets at one time this way than by any other means. The battle is taken to the enemy every hour of the day and night, while awake and asleep. We are changing the world through grace, grit, and greenbacks. God furnishes the grace; we furnish the grit and greenbacks. Pull the pins! Over the top! Run, Satan, run.[11]

The 1982 budget of the North Phoenix Baptist Church was an unapologetic six million dollars. What a grenade!

Courage to Structure for Growth.   Untold hardships have been endured with joy as the members of North Phoenix have followed the leadership of their pastor and staff. To ensure the effective winning,

10. Richard Jackson, "It's on My Heart," *The Word* (June 8, 1983): 23–1.
11. Richard Jackson, "It's on My Heart," *The Word* (February 9, 1983): 23–1.

Courage to Structure for Growth. Untold hardships have been endured with joy as the members of North Phoenix have followed the leadership of their pastor and staff. To ensure the effective winning, reaching, teaching, and building of souls with God, classes constantly are created and new teachers are trained to prevent existing classes from becoming too large. The priority is a fellowship built around the Great Commission.

The Leadership of the Pastor. The heart of Dr. Richard Jackson runs red, deep red, for souls. He loves his Lord, his church, and his family. He has all the marks of a militant warrior for God. He is uniquely gifted to make it clear where the battleline is and he knows how to direct his influence and troops in that direction.

He obviously has a deep passion both for God's Word and for winning souls. He is a godly optimist who believes and has led his people to believe that "the best is yet to come." That vision is the major impetus in his congregation's willingness to invest their souls so that the "Valley of the Sun" might become the "Valley of the Son" in this generation.

16

First Southern Baptist Church
Del City, Oklahoma

The Southern Baptist Convention is the largest evangelical denomination in the U.S. More than 36,000 congregations with fourteen million members make up the convention.

Dr. Bailey Smith is the youngest man elected president of the Southern Baptist Convention. Since 1973 he has been the pastor of First Southern Baptist Church in Del City, Oklahoma, a suburb of Oklahoma City.

First Southern leads the Southern Baptist Convention in many ways. The church was the first Southern Baptist church to baptize 2,000 in one year. Over 1,000 have been baptized each year for the last twelve years, another first for the convention.

In 1983, the church registered another landmark. A decision was made to build a 7,000-seat auditorium on 80 acres. This building will be the second largest Southern Baptist auditorium in the world.

Rev. Wilson Beardsley, assistant to the pastor of First Southern Baptist Church of Del City, Oklahoma, gathered major research for this chapter. Appreciation also is expressed to the pastor, Dr. Bill Bryan, and other staff members who assisted Rev. Beardsley.

A Glimpse of Greatness

First Southern has developed a reputation as being a growing church even when it is without a pastor. It is the world's tenth largest church in total membership. In 1982 the church had 17,240 members; a worship attendance of 3,200; an average Sunday school attendance of 3,239; 1,060 baptisms; 4,925 households; and 426 teaching units located at the main facility. Total offerings for 1982 amounted to $3,863.536.

Dr. Bailey Smith is the sixth pastor of First Southern Baptist Church. He is the son of a Baptist minister. He was converted at age ten and began preaching at age eighteen. Smith is a graduate of Ouachita Baptist University in Arkansas and Southwestern Baptist Theological Seminary in Texas.

He has been the pastor of First Southern for over ten years.

First Southern originated in 1946 when Dr. Guy Bellamy, an associational missionary, discussed the possibility of a new church in Del City.

Construction of the satellite chapel was undertaken by First Baptist Church of Oklahoma City in 1948. The name First Southern Baptist Church was chosen because the neighboring First Baptist Church was an Independent Baptist congregation.

The move to the church's present site occurred in 1952 with the construction of a 300-seat sanctuary and adjoining educational space. More educational space was built six years later. A 1,200-seat auditorium, built in 1962, provided relief to the church. More than 500 attended services in space designed to seat only 300 people. Four years later, in

Table 31   Profile of First Southern Baptist Church

	1982	1981	1980	1970	1960	1950
Total Membership	17,240	16,204	15,539	4,596	1,050	432
Average Sunday School Attendance	3,239	2,902	2,712	1,519	487	80
Baptisms	1,060	1,164	2,028	341	37	41
Total Teaching Units	426	404	380	287	103	50
Total Offerings M = Million	$3.8M	$3.9M	$3.7M	456,444	58,887	18,582
Households in Church (estimate)	4,925	4,630	4,439	1,313	300	135
Sanctuary Capacity*	2,200 in pews; 2,800 with chairs					
Worship Attendance	1,000 in Early Service; 2,200 in Regular Service.					

* Construction of the new 7,000 seat sanctuary began in 1982.

1966, educational space to accommodate one thousand more Sunday school students was added. Another two-story educational building followed in 1969. Finally, in 1972 the present 3,000-seat auditorium was built for $1,350,000. The existing facilities were remodeled in 1973–74 and 1978.

Growth in facilities has been matched by additions to the church staff. Today, thirteen pastors serve the congregation. They serve, sometimes in dual roles, the ministries of evangelism, college students, single adults, the blind, and prison outreach. The church also has elected 103 deacons to assist in the ministry needs.

Classes, Classes, and More Classes

More than 400 Sunday school classes with 456 teachers reach, teach, win, and develop the 3,239 members and visitors that attend each week.

Dr. Bill C. Bryan, church administrator and minister of education, comments:

> We have never had a large auditorium emphasis, or have a personality come in . . . and call it Sunday School. . . . The Leadership becomes discouraged and disenchanted if goals can be reached by simply having a personality come in. We believe Sunday School is those events that take place in the departments and classes. . . . Teachers and Officer's Meeting on Sunday nights are vital. We have 95% of our leadership coming to the meetings.[1]

The church uses two of the three Sunday school courses developed and used by most Southern Baptist churches, the Convention Uniform and Life and Work.

All children's and young people's classes are divided by sex and are age-graded. Adults have men's, women's, and couples' classes.

In the Spanish department, Spanish is used for any members or visitors who do not understand English. In the deaf and the blind departments, sign language and braille are offered.

Smith preaches energetic, expository sermons to guide his army of Sunday school teachers. Evangelism through the Word of God and weekly visitation by Sunday school class members are the church's objectives.

---

1. "Education, Church Administration," *School of Ministry Notebook*, (Del City, OK: First Baptist Church, 1980), p. 3.

At First Southern
Baptist Church in Del City, Oklahoma,
more than 1,000 individuals have been
baptized each year for the last twelve
years—just one of many ways in which
the church, pastored by Dr. Bailey Smith,
leads the Southern Baptist Convention.

Table 32

Age Groups	Approximate Attendance	Pupils Per Teacher	Total Teacher Staff	Teacher/Pupil Ratio
Preschool	345	5–7	77	1:5
Grades 1–6	448	5–7	140	1:3
Youth (13–21)	969	7–9	136	1:7
Adult (22–up)	1252	12–15	103	1:12
Total	3014		456	1:7

Evangelism Explosion

In 1974, one pastor and five laymen became involved in Evangelism Explosion as a method of sharing Jesus Christ. The 3,000-seat auditorium had been in use less than two years. Sunday school attendance increased from 1,400 to 1,600.

By the fall of 1978, four hundred people were involved in soul-winning training and outreach. Earlier that year, in February, the first Evangelism Explosion clinic held in the church attracted people from as far as California.

Wilson Beardsley, assistant to the pastor at Del City, evaluates the focus on evangelism:

The focus is on evangelism. Evangelism feeds the other organizations of the church and the main organization is the Sunday School. Music is probably the third most distinctive element of the church. Music's function is to teach and train in evangelistic music which moves the heart, whose words are understood, and whose message is direct. We have graded choirs and an orchestra. The Sunday School involves 150-175 choir members and the orchestra involves twenty-five others.

A satellite mission is operated by the church. This daughter chapel averages fifty in Sunday school attendance each week. Members of the chapel meet weekly at their own building. It is located almost eight miles from the mother church.

Beardsley outlines the church's priorities:

1. To reach all men for Christ with a clear understanding of what it takes to be saved.
2. To grow in Christ-likeness so that they become effective church

members. This growth reaches maturity when they begin to win others. They never cease to mature in Christ.

Membership requirements are: (1) a clear salvation experience and baptism in a church of like-faith and order or baptism into First Southern Baptist Church of Del City; and (2) transfer of membership or statement of membership in another church of like-faith and order (interpreted as meaning Baptist). Personal questions are asked, even of those coming by transfer or statement.

The pastor wants to be convinced that they have had a genuine experience with the Lord before presenting them to the church for membership.

An estimated 400 to 600 members participate in the regularly scheduled visitation and evangelistic activities each week. The church estimates that 85 percent of all new members are new Christians.

New members attend a weekly orientation session which includes a slide presentation of the various ministries. At that time an information record is filled out for each new member. The church keeps computerized records.

The Sunday school is the follow-up organization of the church. The church clerks are trained in evangelism and make home visits to all who join the church. New members are baptized only after a trained counselor has gone over the plan of salvation with them and is convinced they are saved. If they desire to be baptized immediately, they are taken to the baptismal area where they are counseled again about the meaning of baptism and then they are baptized.

Six factors can be attributed to the growth of the church:

1. Evangelistic preaching and dynamic leadership.
2. A vigorous music program supported by a full orchestra.
3. A Sunday school membership determined to reach every un-churched person in the area.
4. Evangelism Explosion has been the program of sharing Christ with the lost for a decade. Three to four hundred people go out each week in the metropolitan area to witness for Jesus Christ and reach the lost.
5. The Starlite Revival each summer in the high school stadium. This two-week event has a nightly attendance of 4,000 to 5,000 people.
6. A people willing to pay the price of providing additional buildings. Adequate space and leadership can effectively continue to reach

and teach those whom God leads to the church. This reflects the faith of the people. Their willingness to evangelize indicates a teachable and obedient servant spirit.

Few Southern Baptist churches have ignited the bold vision of witness to the multitudes as First Southern Baptist Church has in Del City. The promise verse of the church is Romans 10:13. How appropriate that they refer to themselves as "God's Family Place."

This is a congregation with members that honor and follow the authority and loving leadership of their pastor, staff, and leaders. This congregation is willing to risk failure trying to work for the Master. This church is highly-structured, while free and informal, and excited about being filled with God's Holy Spirit. They are a people of faith willing to launch out into the deep. They look at God's resources rather than their own limited abilities. *Key!*

17

Bellevue Baptist Church
Memphis, Tennessee

One year after First Baptist Church of Dallas, Texas, called Dr. George W. Truett as pastor, a new church was organized in Memphis, Tennessee. In 1898, Mrs. Fannie Jobe left $1,000 in her will to Central Baptist Church. Her bequest provided funds to begin a new mission church "way out from the downtown area."

The same year, a committee of three men was chosen by Central Baptist Church to find a suitable location. The committee chairman rode a bicycle out four miles from downtown to look over a site at the corner of Bellevue and Erskine. The streets were still unpaved and the sidewalks and houses were still dreams in some contractor's mind.

Five years later a small stone church was built. Dedication was Sunday, July 12, 1903. The next month, the church's newly-installed pastor, Dr. H. P. Hurt, and thirty-two other charter members officially established the Bellevue Avenue Baptist Church. Eventually the Avenue would be dropped from the church name. By 1924 the original thirty-two members had multiplied to more than one thousand members.

Dr. R. G. Lee, known as the Prince of Preachers among Southern

Staff members of Bellevue Baptist Church contributed information about their specific ministries in articles appearing in their church's newsletter, *The Bellevue Messenger.*

Baptists, became pastor of the church in 1927. He was the fifth child of a share-cropper family in York County, South Carolina. During his thirty-two years as pastor he led the church to grow from 1,430 to over 9,000 members.

Lee served three terms as president of the Southern Baptist Convention while at Bellevue. During his ministry the present auditorium seating nearly 3,000 was built. He led the church to become one of the first churches in the world to own a fully-equipped television studio. He wrote many books and became world famous for his sermon, "Payday Some-day."

Dr. Ramsey Pollard was serving as president of the Southern Baptist Convention when he followed Dr. R. G. Lee as pastor in 1960. During his twelve years of ministry to the church many souls joined Bellevue. After he retired in 1972, Pollard entered an evangelistic ministry in addition to serving a second term as president of the Southern Baptist Convention. Dr. Pollard died in 1984. Dr. Adrian Rogers, seventh pastor of the congregation, joined Bellevue at age forty-one. Raised in a Baptist home with three brothers and sisters, he was converted at age fourteen and began preaching at age nineteen. Before his move to Memphis, he served the First Baptist Church of Merritt Island, Florida, for eight years. Under his leadership the 4,000-member congregation led the churches of the Southern Baptist Convention in baptisms.

The 9,000-member Bellevue Baptist Church experienced explosive growth. All previous attendance records have been broken.

As the eleventh largest Baptist congregation in the world, Bellevue also is the largest Southern Baptist Church east of the Mississippi River. The church's membership in 1982 was 13,249. Each week approximately 4,000 people attend Sunday school and an estimated 7,000 attend the morning worship services.

The church began a second worship service in 1977. In 1982, Bellevue began a second Sunday school and a third worship service.

Bellevue: Ministries in Motion

As preparation began for the presentation and adoption of the $4.8 million budget for the 1983–84 church year, Dr. Adrian Rogers wrote to the congregation:

Bold Bellevuers:

The prophet Daniel said, "The people who know their God shall do exploits." This budget is a 20th-century example of God's promise to the people called Bellevue who know their God.

The Promised Land of victory is before us. Bellevue is breaking through. Our Commander-in-Chief is Jesus. Our battle-ax is the Word of God. The banner over us is love.

The good hand of God has been upon us in the past, and the future is resplendent with hope.

We will meet and surpass this budget, because we love Him. We will give by faith, and we will give faithfully.[1]

In October, 1978, a major fund-raising campaign, "Together We Build," was conducted to raise funds to construct two multiministries buildings. Three goals were set. The "Hallelujah Goal" of $4 million would provide the new buildings and pay off all current debts of the church. The "Praise the Lord Goal" of $3.3 million would provide for the new buildings and reduce total debts by several hundred thousand dollars. The "Amen Goal" of $2.6 million would provide for the buildings and leave current debts at the same level.

During the intensive three-month program the church reserved the city's Cook Convention Center to accommodate the expected attendance of four thousand. More than three hundred hostesses made approximately four thousand telephone calls to ensure confirmed reservations for all children and adults.

A visitation team of two hundred workers visited approximately six hundred homes prior to the banquet to secure commitments. The church supplemented its own bus fleet with fifteen charter buses from the Memphis Transit Authority for shuttle service between the church parking lots and the convention center. Five years later, the two new buildings were complete.

Just one year before the building campaign, Dr. Rogers celebrated his fifth anniversary as pastor of Bellevue. The front page story of the church's newsletter, *The Bellevue Messenger*, sets the stage for understanding the growth of the church:

During these past five years the church has experienced unprecedented growth in every aspect. More than 5,100 have united with the church, of which, 1,865 were received by baptism. Sunday School has more than doubled. . . .

. . . Indeed in these accomplishments are the acquisition of thousands of dollars of property, vast expansion of parking provision, expansion of staff. . . .[2]

1. "1983–84 Budget: Ministries in Motion," *Bellevue Messenger* March 17, 1983, p. 2.
2. "Church and Pastor Observe Fifth Anniversary," *Bellevue Messenger* September 2, 1977, p. 1.

Bellevue has had many big and exciting days since Dr. Rogers became pastor. The "Feeding of the 5,000" in 1975 had over six thousand in attendance. His sermon that day was "The Lesson of the Loaves."

Tape Ministry. The tape ministry was started by the late Hugh Dyer shortly after Dr. Rogers' arrival at Bellevue in 1972. The ministry now produces 1,000 to 1,500 audio-cassette copies of the messages each week. About 150 customers are on a weekly mailing list.

The ministry began producing video tapes of the Sunday morning services and special seminars and presentations on a regular basis in 1975.

Television and Radio. When the morning worship service was telecast on January 5, 1958, Bellevue became one of the first churches in the United States to broadcast with its own equipment. In January 1983, the telecast of the Sunday morning worship service celebrated the 25th anniversary of the television ministry.

In November, 1970, nearly $120,000 of the church's annual love-offering purchased color television cameras. The church's two black-and-white cameras were given to the Foreign Mission Board to be used in Taiwan.

The 10:45 A.M. Sunday service continues to be telecast to parts of three states. Both Sunday services are broadcast on radio.

Printed Media. Six women operate the church's computer processing center. Contribution records, Operation Discovery, Hospital Visitation, Sunday school, church training, and church membership records are stored in the church's computer system.

In one recent month the processing center staff metered approximately 60,000 pieces of mail. With the exception of special brochures and the weekly *Messenger,* all printing for the church (more than 200,000 sheets monthly) is produced by the church's equipment.

Food Services. In a normal week, the church food service will provide meals for approximately 1,800 persons. On Monday, lunch is served to pastors from the 118 Southern Baptist churches in the Memphis area. On Tuesday, meals are served to the Baptist Women's group, Sunday school class meetings, and other groups. On Wednesday, the church-wide evening supper is provided for approximately six hundred members attend-

One of many ministries
at Bellevue Baptist Church in
Memphis, Tennessee, is a tape-
production ministry that produces
1,000 to 1,500 audio-cassette
copies of the messages each
week. Dr. Adrian Rogers is pastor.

ing the evening prayer service. Each Thursday, approximately five hundred of the city's businessmen gather for Bible study.

Music Ministries.   Dr. Tommy Lane was attending graduate school at the University of Southern California when God brought him to Bellevue. He had served three Oklahoma churches, including the 2,700-member First Baptist Church of Ponca City, before beginning his studies at USC.

Dr. R. G. Lee had met Dr. Lane several times, but it was not until December, 1947, that the musician was invited to pray about joining the Bellevue staff.

Dr. Lane, minister of adult music, led the adult Sanctuary choir to grow from forty members to a combined enrollment of approximately 250. Under the leadership of Dr. Lane and Rev. Jim Whitmire, minister of youth music since 1976, Bellevue's music ministry now includes approximately 1,500 adults and children in fifty choirs.

Each December the church choir sings George Frederick Handel's *Messiah.* The year 1985 marks the fiftieth presentation.

Jim Whitmire leads the youth choir in an annual presentation of "The Singing Christmas Tree." This one event attracts nearly 200,000 people to Bellevue. Today 170 young people sing from the tree as compared to 140 young people in 1976. The music is presented with a 51-piece orchestra.

A total of 412 people work to present the program. The tree is constructed with 7,500 pounds of steel and decorations. It has 5,500 bulbs in five colors synchronized by computer to flash on and off in predetermined patterns with the tempo of the music sung throughout the presentation. The tree stands forty-six feet from floor to star on top.

Approximately 42,000 persons attended the thirteen 1982 performances. At the conclusion of every presentation, Pastor Adrian Rogers presents a brief gospel invitation for attendants to register one of several decisions on a dual-purpose offering and decision envelope. In 1979, 351 people indicated that they received Jesus Christ as personal Savior and Lord as a result of the presentation. More than 1,146 such decisions were recorded in 1980. Another 837 decisions were reported in 1981. A record 1,768 conversions were registered during the 1982 presentation when Dr. Rogers led the sinner's prayer at the conclusion of each presentation.

Easter also is considered a crucial harvest time for reaching and changing lives at Bellevue. An estimated 21,000 persons attended the seven presentations of "Living Pictures" in 1982, directed by Rev. Jim Whitmire. During this dramatic musical depiction of the death and resurrection of Jesus Christ, 945 people indicated on their decision cards that they prayed to receive Christ. Many others asked for more information on the Christian life and for a visit from Bellevue members.

Youth Recreation. The recreational activities center is used heavily by adults, youth, and children at Bellevue. Their athletic teams are known throughout the city and the world.

In June, 1983, Bellevue was represented in the World Cup Youth Tournament in Stockholm, Sweden. A twelve-member team of twelve- and thirteen-year-old basketball players participated.

The team was selected to represent the United States in the 25-nation tournament on the basis of its AAU/Junior Olympic success in recent years. Bellevue has qualified for the national tournament in seven of the last eight years in the twelve-to thirteen-year-old division. They won the national title in 1976 and finished second in 1979.

Scripture Memory. A total of 227 boys and girls hid nearly 7,000 Bible verses in their hearts throughout 1982–83. An annual Scripture Searchers Memory Awards Banquet recognizes this commitment to personal spiritual growth. All of the boys and girls were in grades 4 to 6. The first awards banquet occurred in 1976.

Each child receives a beautiful certificate and a special award from the pastor, Dr. Adrian Rogers.

Three levels of memorization are recognized: "Discoverers" learn 52 verses; "Pathfinders" memorize at least 25 Bible verses plus the books and divisions of the Bible; and "Scouts" memorize between 4 and 25 verses.

Missions Involvement. In 1983 Bellevue members committed over $1,200,000 to missions. Sixty percent of the largest mission offering in the church's history was designated for denominational mission causes and 40 percent for local church mission projects. Of the 60 percent designated for denominational mission causes, 65 percent is assigned to foreign missions, 30 percent to national home missions in the U. S., and 5 percent to state missions.

During the 1982 Missions Conference, the church approved nine members for foreign mission service. Members of the congregation regularly are involved in short-term mission service to Africa, England, and Korea. Nearly 80 Bellevue members joined 1,600 Southern Baptists in Pittsburg for saturation evangelism. They witnessed house-to-house in cooperation with Southern Baptist Churches in that area.

A refugee school for fifty adult students from Laos, Cambodia, Korea, Vietnam, Thailand, and Cuba meets in the church each Monday. Three classes are taught in beginning English and one in advanced English.

Since 1977, high school students and young adults travel to minister on the Navajo Indian Reservation in northeastern Arizona. The fifteen-day trip covers almost 4,000 miles. Each participant receives sixteen hours of training for this rugged venture. Each team member also is required to complete two mission projects in Memphis before a mission trip.

It is estimated that only 5 percent of the 150,000 Navajos are professing Christians. During the ten years that Bellevue has sponsored teams to the reservation, approximately 300 different church members have participated. About 250 Indians have trusted Christ, three churches have been organized, and several Navajo pastors have emerged.

Evangelism Ministries. An estimated 500 soul-winners are actively involved in reaching multitudes in Memphis each year. Dr. Adrian Rogers, since 1973, has activated his thirteen-week, soul-winning training class twice each year. Known as "God's Invasion Army," this training has equipped approximately 500 to 1,000 members to share their faith with another person.

In 1979, Rev. Ken Babrick, one of the adult ministers at the church, introduced the "Laws of the Harvest" method of evangelizing. Today most evangelizing is lifestyle evangelism by those trained at the church.

This may be a transition that in the future will unite the strengths of both structured and lifestyle evangelism.

Men's and Women's Ministries. Velma Rhea Torbett became the women's ministries director for Bellevue in March, 1982. The church has invited national Christian Women's Conferences to meet at Bellevue, but it also has been aggressive in commanding the attention of women for God in the Southeast. In 1980 the Mid-Continent Christian Women's Concerns Conference was hosted by Bellevue. Specific strategies are regularly formulated and employed by this ministry of the church through city-wide conferences and seminars.

Since April 3, 1980, when eighty men met in the Bellevue dining room for the church's first men's luncheon, impressive growth has occurred. By 1983, more than six hundred men crowded the weekly time of fellowship and Bible study open to all men of the city. The luncheon meets each Thursday.

Dr. Adrian Rogers leads a Bible study. When he is traveling, Dr. Gray

Allison, president of Mid-America Baptist Theological Seminary, leads the study. About one-third of the men attending the luncheon are members of Bellevue.

Neighborhood Fellowship Ministry. Approximately six hundred Belle-vue members have become involved in the Bellevue Neighborhood Fellow-ship. It began as a pilot effort in 1982. Each month small groups of twelve to fourteen Bellevue members meet in homes, by neighborhood, for the purpose of fellowship. The groups are composed of new and mature Christians, sixteen years and older.

The meetings consist of a dinner, sharing, prayer, and a ten-minute devotional time that is centered around the concept of true Biblical fellowship. In addition to the monthly meeting, fellowship during the month by meeting practical needs is stressed.

Specific dates for the meetings are suggested by the staff coordinator, Rev. Paul Williams, to avoid scheduling difficulties. The church has groups meeting in approximately three-quarters of all neighborhoods.

Education/Service Ministries. In the fall of 1981, church members were surveyed during Sunday school and at home to discover specific areas of interest such as recreation, church leadership background, and special education background.

The "Operation Discovery" survey included approximately 460 areas of interest.

The information is stored in the church's computer center and is used by the church staff, deacons, Sunday school, and other ministry organi-zations.

The church has plans to survey each Bellevue member approximately every 36 months to ensure accurate information. For example, during one specific six-week period, the church resurveyed its members living within selected zip code areas of the city. New members age sixteen and older are surveyed every three months.

In a typical month, approximately 2,000 pieces of information are entered in the Operation Discovery files. As a result of Operation Discov-ery, approximately 2,150 Bellevue members were ministered to or con-tacted about serving in a specific area during a ten-month period.

As the congregation continues to grow in membership, the staff in-tends to be sure the needs of the people are met, if possible.

A total of 131 active deacons serve as both a ministry and policy

Table 33   Profile of Bellevue Baptist Church

	1982	1981	1980	1972	1960
Church Membership	13,370	12,484	11,657	8,739	9,480
Worship Attendance	7,000	6,200	5,000	2,000	
Average Weekly Sunday School Attendance	3,921	3,765	3,473	1,382	2,421
Sunday School Enrollment	7,951	7,263	6,343	2,731	4,236
Total Baptisms	703	701	567	162	226
Total Teaching Units	267				
Total Home Fellowship Groups*	27				
Total Member Households	5,800				

    * In 1983—52 groups with 676 attending.

Table 34   Teachers per Pupil in Sunday School at Bellevue

Age Group	Ages	Approximate Attendance	Total Teachers	Teacher/Pupil Ratio
Preschool	Birth–5	684	113	1:6
Children	Age 6–Gr. 6	633	42	1:15
Youth	Gr. 7–12	377	55	1:7
Adult		2,504	111	1:23
Total		4,198	321	1:13

making group. Members are elected by the congregation on a rotation basis.

Various versions of the Bible are used in the Sunday school but the King James Version is always used from the pulpit.

Throughout the Sunday school three types of adult classes are available: men's, women's and co-ed. In the younger classes, through grade six, boys and girls meet together.

Bellevue has 65 adult Sunday school classes. Only fifteen adult classes have an attendance above fifty. Of these fifteen classes, only five have over one hundred average weekly attendants.

Causes of Bellevue's Growth

Bellevue is a highly organized congregation but communicates an image of informality to those outside the church. The able, enthusiastic leadership of the pastor, gifted staff, and congregational leaders are a major reason for the church's growth.

Dr. Adrain Rogers attributes the following nine ingredients as the primary causes of growth at the Memphis church:

1. Expository preaching.
2. A reliance on the ministry of the Holy Spirit.
3. A spirit of warmth. Informal but dignified worship services.
4. A great music program.
5. Media outreach.
6. A lay leadership that creates the feeling of confidence in the financial structure.
7. A strong, multi-gifted staff.
8. Buildings and parking.
9. An evangelistic spirit.

Bellevue's Next Ten Years

In September, 1982, the proposed master strategy for the 1980s was formally presented to Bellevue members. The proposal came as a joint recommendation of the pastor and the long range planning committee.

On September 16, 1982, the front page of the church newsletter reported:

The goals and plans were not presented presumptuously or to put God into a corner. They were the outgrowth of approximately three years of praying and planning by the Pastor and the Long Range Planning Committee. "We are not trying to out-figure God," the Pastor said, "but with our diverse ministries and dynamic growth, it is absolutely mandatory that we establish guidelines to remain warm and personal to meet the needs of every Bellevue member and most of all to glorify God.

. . . We are asking God to give us at least 10,000 more baptisms in the next ten years.

. . . We are asking our Lord to multiply our missions ministry . . . and to permit us to give to His glory a total of $20,000,000 in the next 10 years.

. . . Bellevue Neighborhood Fellowship: Monthly meetings of small groups will be held all over the Memphis area to nurture . . . His own people.

. . . We anticipate that upon land (to be provided by the Lord) we will have to build a new worship center with a seating capacity of between 6,000 and 10,000, new educational buildings to accommodate an average attendance of 8,000 in Sunday School.

. . . A new parking garage.

. . . A new retreat center.

. . . More diversified counseling ministry, including premarital and all
family related consultation as well as the establishment of seminars,
retreats, and study curriculum to enhance the Christian family.

Dr. Rogers notes:

We are not in the business of raising money; we are not in the business of
building buildings. We are in the business of transforming lives and bringing people into a personal and saving relationship with Jesus Christ.[3]

On Sunday night, October 30, 1983, the congregation officially voted to
move their church from the center of Memphis to the eastern part of the
county. A study indicates that sixty percent of the church's members live
within a fifteen-minute drive of the new 265-acre site. A 10,000-seat
auditorium is under consideration at the new location. The church plans
to transport the elderly to the church. This new site invites continued
growth.

3. Michael Clark, "Bellevue Baptist Unveils Huge Project," *Commercial Appeal* September 14,
1982, pp. A–1, 12.

18

Calvary Chapel
Santa Ana, California

Santa Ana, California, is only fifteen minutes from the Pacific coastal waters. Neighboring Los Angeles County to the north harbors eighty-one cities with a population that exceeds seven million people. The five-county urban area is home to over eleven million people.

Many superchurches have sprung up in this densely populated area. Calvary Chapel is a superchurch that attracted young people and grew rapidly during the 1970s.

In 1978, Russell T. Hitt referred to this new center of rapidly growing Evangelical churches as "California's God Rush":

> Although only 33% of the area's population admits to church membership, this spiritual Death Valley sprouts super churches. . . . And only a few miles from . . . Garden Grove Community Church (i.e., Crystal Cathedral) stands Chuck Smith's Calvary Chapel in Santa Ana which has a membership of more than 9,400 but is named by 30,000 who regard it as their primary source of spiritual nurture. Now Calvary Chapel, dubbed "the institution-alized afterglow of the Jesus Movement," is proliferating by establishing 27 satellite chapels in Orange County.[1]

1. Russell T. Hitt, "California God Rush" *Eternity* (March, 1978), p. 31.

Since 1978, membership has increased to more than 15,000 with 35,000 that regard Calvary as their source of spiritual nurture. Calvary now has 300 chapels nationwide.

A First Visit to Calvary Chapel

Calvary Chapel cannot be seen from the nearby interstate. The church is not even visible until you are about one block away. Suddenly you see that the parking lots circling the one-story sanctuary are filled. Cars line the curbs on every side.

Since the worship service has already begun, several loops through the lots finally locates one lone parking space. Unlike other churches, ushers are not visible to give direction. As you approach what appears to be the main building, you begin to hear the voice of Pastor Chuck Smith through the outside speakers that surround the main auditorium courtyard.

The sanctuary doors are locked. California law requires locked doors once the seating capacity has been reached. Signs on the door direct visitors to the adjacent fellowship hall. You can see the open doors of an occupied building less than fifty feet from the 2,500-seat sanctuary.

Inside the open doors are six closed-circuit color television screens spaced along the north wall of a large room containing rows of metal chairs. Several hundred worshipers are meeting here. A chair is stacked with bulletins to guide the visitor through the service. Again, no ushers are visible.

You notice that some of the people are dressed in suits and ties; most are wearing casual clothes. The image of the pastor on the screen is lifesize. His conversational voice is easy to listen to and the three-piece vested suit would allow him to pass for an executive from any of the office towers nearby.

The Sunday bulletin in your hand reads, "This Week at Calvary." A full assortment of classes and fellowships is listed, with the word *fellowship* used frequently. The church offers a Sunday night study in Amos 6–9, a Monday night study in Exodus, and other Bible studies scattered throughout the week: men's groups, women's groups, and special interest groups.

Groups and fellowships are listed for young adults, young couples, singles, Spanish, Jewish/Gentile, musicians, working women, surfers, campers, men and women just out of jail (New Life Fellowship), problem drinkers (New Thirst Fellowship), Koreans, and others.

Three notes in the bulletin are of special interest. The first says, "Home Fellowships—See Bulletin Board in Courtyard." The second reads, "Nightly (10 P.M.–8 A.M.) Prayer Watch—Call Church for laymen to pray with you." The third announces, "Adult Bible Study . . . for Next Week Read Obadiah and Jonah." Obadiah and Jonah together have five chapters. This must be a church where you walk through the pages of the Bible, week-by-week.

The bulletin gives a simple statement of faith:

Our supreme desire is to know Christ and to be conformed to His image by the power of the Holy Spirit.

We are not a denominational church, nor are we opposed to denominations as such, only their over-emphasis of the doctrinal differences that have led to the division of the Body of Christ.

We believe that the only true basis of Christian fellowship is His (Agape) love, which is greater than any differences we possess and without which we have no right to claim ourselves Christians.

Echoes of the "Jesus People Movement"

Calvary Chapel began with twenty-five members in 1965 and grew rapidly during the restless years of the 1970s.

Before 1965, Chuck Smith attended junior college in Santa Ana and his wife Kay attended Los Angeles City College. After graduating from Life Bible School in Los Angeles, they began their ministry together among Four Square Gospel congregations.

Those early years led them to Prescott and Tucson, Arizona. The Lord relocated them to southern California: Corona, Huntington Beach, Los Seranos, and Costa Mesa.

Finally, after seventeen years of ministry, God led them to change the focus and direction of their service. They opened their home in Newport Beach to Bible study groups and soon had forty to fifty regular participants. Five other home groups began in Laguna Beach, Corona, Costa Mesa, Newport Beach, San Clemente, and West Covina.

As the groups multiplied, so did the responsibility for ministry. Smith now had groups meeting in various locations Monday through Friday evenings. He resigned his leadership position as pastor of his Costa Mesa Church in September, 1964.

After a series of successive moves that led to the formation of the Corona Christian Association, and later the Corona Christian Center, a small group of three couples grew to 150 in eighteen months. Chuck had been working at various jobs during this period as a construction worker and as a teacher.

Hugh Steven tells how prayers began to be answered, invitations came

Calvary Chapel is one of many superchurches that have sprung up in the southern California area. Located in Santa Ana, this church attracted young people and grew rapidly during the 1970s. Chuck Smith serves as pastor.

at just the right time, and miracles began to confirm the dreams of the Smith family:

> Chuck began his ministry at Calvary Chapel on a cold bright December morning in 1965. The Chapel, once the handsomest church building in Costa Mesa, was now one of the oldest and looked it. . . . It just seemed that no one cared about the little church. . . .[2]

Kay struggled with the wisdom of her husband's decision. She finally was able to accept his call to Costa Mesa as good for her, too. He had come as assistant pastor of a church with only twenty-five attending regularly. Soon the pastor resigned, and now Chuck was pastor.

Three years later, in March, 1968, a Lutheran church building became available as a temporary meeting place. One month later the Santa Ana School District notified Chuck that the Greenville School had been "declared surplus and . . . open for bid." Chuck, the church leadership, and the congregation moved quickly. God provided the $53,000 needed to purchase the property.

At this time a beach ministry opened and "hippie" youth began to receive Christ as Savior and Lord.

The "hot spot" for conversions was Tahquitz Canyon. Young people living in the canyon had great needs that Pastor Chuck Smith and his people were ready to address. Many were converted each week.

A judge in Riverside learned of the request for a commune from the church's youth. He allowed them to use an old motel rent-free. Within two weeks, sixty-five were baptized in the motel's fish pond. By the end of the summer, five hundred had been baptized. Soon, fifteen similar communes sprang up across California; eighty were organized in Oregon and Washington State.

Calvary Chapel experienced rapid expansion. Wall-to-wall people became a normal occurrence. A brief problem occurred when a sign appeared: "No Bare Feet Allowed in the Church." This proved to be more raw material for God to use for miracles at the chapel.

> The traffic . . . came not from the three hundred people the church was designed to hold, but from the hundreds that crowded into the chapel during the following months. Chuck designed the church to hold three hundred never dreaming it would ever be completely filled. He believed an

2. Chuck Smith and Hugh Steven, *The Reproducers* (Glendale, California: Regal Books, 1972), p. 21.

average attendance of approximately two hundred seventy was an ideal congregation.[3]

Within five weeks of the move into a 300-seat auditorium on the first Sunday in June, 1969, Pastor Chuck Smith decided to begin a second worship service. Capacity crowds by mid-1971 led to a third morning service. "To make sure everyone who came had a seat, the ushers regularly set up five hundred extra chairs on the outside patio."[4]

Audio tapes of Pastor Chuck Smith's messages began to be distributed across the nation, into home study groups in southern California, and even into prisons like San Quentin.

A major factor in the growth of Calvary Chapel is the music program. Singing groups whose members have been touched by Calvary Chapel's ministry include Children of the Day and Love Song. In early 1969, the church's group, the Maranatha Singers, participated in Christian rock concerts. Personal testimonies of deliverance from the drug culture became a regular part of these concerts. Tapes, records, posters, brochures, and tracts were scattered everywhere. The response was unbelievable.

Record albums released by groups like Love Song, Blessed Hope, and Children of the Day sold 25,000 copies within a matter of months.

> To handle the runaway record sales, concert bookings, voluminous follow-up mail and Bible correspondence courses, Calvary formed a subsidiary nonprofit organization called Maranatha Music/Publishing. . . .
>
> Each person who makes a profession of faith at a concert or at Calvary receives lesson one of a fourteen lesson course (Navigator Bible Correspondence Course). . . . This seems to be the easiest and most effective method to handle the ten to fifteen thousand yearly decisions and get them into a systematic study of the word.[5]

By November, 1971, the chapel bought eleven acres of land for $300,000. Immediately, a 90' x 180' tent was raised to accommodate the regular crowds of 1,400 people.

Before their present 2,500-seat sanctuary could be completed, the church again had to hold a second, and third, service. Worship services also are conducted in Korean and Spanish.

Negotiations are currently in progress with the city for the purchase of

3. Ibid., p. 62.
4. Ibid., p. 63.
5. Ibid., p. 81.

more land for parking lots. If approved, the church plans to proceed with the construction of a 6,000 seat-sanctuary. Pastor L. E. Romaine, who serves with Pastor Chuck Smith, indicates that the money is already in the bank.[6]

In addition to the four Sunday morning and evening services, the Bible study group meets each Thursday night. This meeting has approximately 2,300 regular attendants. The Lord's Supper is observed during this meeting.

The chapels begun by Calvary Chapel have a unique relationship to Calvary. Once a chapel is begun, the mother church expects the mission to be autonomous; totally independent of the mother church. Satellite chapels are not included in either the membership or attendance figures of the mother church.

The Functions of a Church

Ephesians 4 is recognized by the pastor as the purpose statement of the church's priorities and functions. Members of the pastoral staff indicate a very loose definition of the local church by most traditional standards.

The church does have a membership roll but it is viewed only as a way of satisfying legal requirements for incorporation by California law. It serves no other purpose. Many churches provide structured guidelines for visitation, evangelism, membership enlistment, and follow-up. These structures are deemed unnecessary by the church leaders and are best carried out through informal home and special ministry groups. Mature members are expected to care for the needs of new members.

The priesthood and responsibility of every believer is developed through pulpit and small-group communications. This appears to exclude the traditional understanding of the doctrine of the New Testament church as it relates to leadership and group expectation. Pastor Chuck Smith would strongly disagree in expected "body life" terms. He maintains:

The main emphasis of the church is not evangelism: the main emphasis is the ministry to the body, the result being that the healthy body reproduces, and that evangelism such as we have is the by-product of a healthy church,

6. F. Burleigh Willard, "An Accurate Picture of Calvary Chapel," An Unpublished Research Report for Fuller Theological Seminary, Pasadena, California, 1982, p. 10.

Table 35   Profile of Calvary Chapel

	1982	1975	1970	1969	1965
Membership	15,625	9,400	1,000	1,000	25
Worship Attendance	12,500*	9,400	1,000	1,000	25
Auditorium Capacity	2,400++†	2,400	800‡	300	—

   * This data is for adults above high school (omits 500 youth).
   † Two other assembly areas are equipped with closed-circuit television for overflow crowds. The Fellowship Hall seats 700 per service regularly. Another auditorium seats 550 and several hundred listen to the speakers outside on the grounds.
   ‡ Auditorium capacity was still 300, but ushers set up 500 extra chairs on the courtyard each week.

and not the goal or aim of the church . . . and evangelism such as we have never dreamed possible is a result.[7]

Teaching the Bible is seen as the primary function and cause of growth at Calvary Chapel. The only appearance of a formally structured teaching time occurs on Sunday and Thursday under Smith's leadership.

Approximately forty Sunday school classes are provided for children and young people each Sunday morning. Traditional classes for adults are not scheduled. Instruction is also provided on Sunday nights and Thursday nights for those below high school age.

Most instruction of adults, other than the Sunday and Thursday services, is provided through nearly sixty ministry, prayer, and Home Bible Fellowships. The church is best known for these Christian education fellowships.

Today the median age of adult members is approximately thirty. It was twenty-five a few years ago. Attendance and faithfulness almost constitutes membership at Calvary Chapel. While many opportunities to belong to ministry groups are available, each member is accountable only to God.

The only questions asked are two questions concerning salvation and the Lordship of Jesus Christ in your life. Public invitation is offered by the church for those who wish to respond in these two areas. Eleven pastoral staff members minister to the Calvary Chapel flock.

Financially, the Chapel indicates that

they spend $2.00 on outreach for every $1.00 spent at the Chapel. There was no formal statement as to what these outreach ministries were, but they obviously included some 115 radio programs and six television broadcasts, the production and distribution of tapes and music, the establish-

7. "How Did Calvary Chapel Do It?" *Eternity* (March, 1978), p. 32.

ment of new Chapels and support of mission groups such as Wycliff Bible Translators, Campus Crusade, Missionary Aviation Fellowship and others.[8]

The church donated $350,000 to Project Pearl, getting one million Bibles to Christians in China; $50,000 to Eastern European missions; $62,000 to evangelistic outreach in Central America; $30,000 to evangelism in Israel; and $50,000 to establish a school to train pastors in Africa. The total missions budget was $1,650,713.

Chuck Smith began his first day as pastor by asking each member to read ten chapters of the Bible each week. He began with Genesis 1–10. During the evening service he would review and analyze the same ten chapters covered in his Sunday morning sermon. He taught his people, "If we cover ten chapters each Sunday and fifteen chapters when we come to the Psalms we can go through the whole Bible in two years."[9]

When the Chapel began three services in 1971, this format was reduced to five chapters each week. This allowed him to spend more time as he began teaching the New Testament and to preserve each sermon on an hour-long cassette tape.

Calvary Chapel is not a conventional congregation. This church is heard across the nation through electronic media. Calvary Chapel continues to fill the city and land with its doctrine. An estimated one hundred new converts profess their faith each week.

8. Willard, "An Accurate Picture," p. 10.
9. Smith and Steven, *The Reproducers*, p. 24.

19

Melodyland Christian Center
Anaheim, California

One of the largest charismatic congregations in the nation meets several times each week in what was previously the largest bar in Orange County. George Cunningham reported:

> In fact, the Melodyland building itself was the site of the Celebrity Lounge, the largest bar in Orange County. The lounge operators still had twenty-five years to run. For months after the church group took over the theater, the Celebrity Lounge would open for a few hours each day, earning Melodyland the dubious distinction of being the only "church-with-a-bar-inside."[1]

In 1960, the Anaheim City Council was determined to prevent any church group from moving into the area of the Disneyland-Convention Center entertainment complex. The council feared a battle between bars and churches. In addition, Orange County consistently enforced its ordinance prohibiting bars and liquor stores from opening near churches.

1. George Cunningham, "Theatre-in-the-Round Center Stage for the Gospel," *Orange County Register* (March 12, 1978), p. 13.

Melodyland, however, posed a reverse problem. The council was faced with a church wanting to move into an area heavily populated with bars and liquor stores. Legal action was averted since Melodyland had previously adopted the title "Christian Center" and did not erect any crosses on their property. Their goal was to reach people rather than close bars.

Melodyland, an independent congregation, organized in 1960 with a mere twenty-seven people. The name Christian Center of Orange County was selected. Later that same year space problems occurred and the Woman's Assistance League Building became their new home. Still later, the center again experienced rapid growth and moved to E Street.

"The church started as an independent congregation, then affiliated with the Assemblies of God, and withdrew one year later in good standing," reports Pastor Wilkerson. At that time, the building held nearly six hundred and was filled in five weekly services.

The congregation held its first services in the present 3,750-seat auditorium on Easter Sunday, 1969. A decision had been made to disassociate with their denominational roots and become an independent congregation. The church's monthly Monday night meetings averaged 2,000 in attendance.

Melodyland Christian Center presents new members to the congregation in a regular monthly worship service. Approximately fifty new members come professing Jesus Christ as their personal Savior and receive water baptism each week. Baptisms are administered at the conclusion of the Sunday evening services and during the Thursday morning Prayer and Share Service.

The congregation's leader, Pastor Ralph Wilkerson, classifies the activities of the church as church ministries, special events, or affiliated ministries.

Church Ministries

The church ministries include Melodyland Middle and High Schools, Anaheim Christian College, American Christian Theological Seminary,

Table 36 Statistical Estimates, Melodyland

Total Church Members	Composite Membership*	Morning Worship Attendance	Sunday School Attendance	Total Baptisms	Total Offerings
20,000	11,000	10,000	3,000	2,600	$3,000,000

* Average of total church members, morning worship attendance, and Sunday morning Bible study groups (Sunday school).

Layman's School of the Bible, home group meetings called Care Groups, the Pastoral Counseling Center, women's ministries, service ministries, Overcomers' Classes for the developmentally disabled, Melodyland book and tape stores, musical concerts, men's ministries, and youth ministries.

An introductory booklet about the center, *Melodyland Today*, comments, "'Education from diapers to doctorate,' the visionary slogan of Chancellor Ralph Wilkerson, is nearing completion in Melodyland Schools and Colleges." The middle school has an enrollment of approximately two hundred and high school enrollment exceeds five hundred students. Christian College exceeds one hundred students and the graduate school enrolls nearly one hundred.

Accent on the center's teaching priority is reinforced by the schools during the week and by the Layman's School of the Bible on Sunday mornings and weekday evenings. The Sunday morning School of the Bible resembles a seminary classroom rather than a traditional Sunday school.

Noel Weiss, nationally recognized Jewish Christian, attracts five hundred to his classes on the Old Testament and Bible prophecy. Another large class, with an attendance over one hundred, is the Melodyland Married Class led by John Cairns.

Continued international attention is being given to the Care Group ministry directed by Karen Hurston, former editor of *World of Faith* magazine published by Church Growth International in Seoul, Korea. Karen coordinates church growth research and training through home centered Care Groups. Thirty-six of these groups meet throughout the Anaheim area at least twice each month.

Care group leaders are screened by the church and taught by Pastor Wilkerson in monthly leaders' meetings. Future expansion of Care Groups will offer an opportunity for each member of the Melodyland family to become involved.

Twelve pastors and approximately fifteen pastoral interns serve the counseling needs of the center. Interns are usually students enrolled in graduate school at Melodyland. They also assist in baptisms, teaching, and counseling ministries. Eight full-time counselors, including a Christian support-team of one psychiatrist and four psychologists, are available to the people of Melodyland.

When a child completes the Christian education curriculum provided by the church, he has studied the entire Bible three times. Competency among Sunday school teachers is ensured for both teachers and aides through a six-week training course and mandatory monthly teachers' meetings.

Among its service ministries the congregation maintains a twenty-four hour prayer chain served by prayer room counselors. Developmentally disabled persons above four years of age receive love and instruction each Sunday through the Overcomers' classes.

A wide variety of resources are available through the Melodyland bookstore and tape store. Tapes of each sermon are available immediately after each service.

Men's ministries include a six o'clock prayer meeting each Thursday morning. Employment counseling also is available on Thursdays to assist those who are unemployed or considering a career change.

Special Events

The Special Events directory of the church lists telecasts, Charismatic Celebrations, Church Growth Symposiums, musicals, and Tel-A-Round.

Television crews eagerly tape the 10:30 Sunday morning worship service. The service is telecast weekly.

Charismatic Celebrations, which began in 1968 as Charismatic Clinics, are an annual August event designed as an evangelistic Bible conference. The week-long event features biblical scholars and evangelists. Registrants attend from around the world. Nearly 5,000 attended in August, 1982.

Annual Church Growth Symposiums focus on topics of current interest to church leaders. The American Christian Theological Seminary sponsored the first conference in July, 1982. The topic was church growth through home groups. Speakers included Drs. Paul Yonggi Cho, Jack Hayford, C. M. Ward, Ralph Wilkerson, John Hurston, and others.

Music is a major event at Melodyland. Choir attendance averages more than one hundred. Participants swell to four hundred for the annual Easter Splendor celebration. Monthly musicals are produced by Richard Cook in cooperation with the Melodyland music department and its community choirs. Featured Christian performers replace the regular music events with major musical or stage play productions at Easter, Christmas, and a portion of the summer months.

Another event which has resulted in more than six thousand children making decisions to follow Christ is the Tel-A-Round. Designed for unchurched children, Tel-A-Round is composed of a corps of talented volunteers who regularly perform through musicals and puppets in city parks, convention centers, and fairs.

Affiliated Ministries

These ministries include ethnic language groups, the California Christian Institute, the Melodyland Church of the Deaf, and the famous Hotline Help Center.

Worshipers at Melodyland Christian Center in Anaheim, California, meet in what was previously the largest bar in Orange County. Ralph Wilkerson is pastor.

The ethnic diversity of Melodyland is seen in its ministry among Hispanic, Romanian, and Korean groups. Each Sunday afternoon almost four hundred Romanians gather for their weekly service. During this time the Hispanic group, of over one hundred members, gathers for the Spanish service, as do the Koreans. Each group maintains active separate agendas of mid-week activities and Bible studies.

Melodyland Church of the Deaf, for the deaf and hearing-impaired, assembles each Sunday evening in the multi-purpose building. Almost one hundred participants gather for the service conducted in American sign language. Several members are actively involved in the artistic Immanuel sign Language Choir.

California Christian Institute has a two-fold purpose: it provides access to a group of professional therapists skilled in the biblical principles of emotional and spiritual healing and it provides graduate degree training in Christian counseling, communication, and professional administrative skills. The Orange County Christian Psychiatric Center is affiliated with the institute and provided help for more than five thousand individuals in 1981.

The Hotline Help Center at Melodyland was started by Pastor Ralph Wilkerson in 1969. It was organized as a separate corporation and functions as an affiliate, independent of the church. The center is dedicated to crisis intervention, prevention, rehabilitation, and counseling for the whole person: body, soul, and spirit. This twenty-four hour Hotline, or personal counseling service, may be the oldest and largest service of its kind in the world.

In 1982 the center responded to approximately 127,000 calls; over 10,500 each month. Robin Hicks, hotline administrative assistant, says that "with our monthly statistics, we then assess the community's most pressing problems and adapt our programs and training to meet these needs."

Hotline Help Center's community services has a staff of over fifty trained volunteers and ten full-time employees. They provide twenty-four-hour crisis aid for drug and alcohol abuse, emergency food and housing, marriage and family problems, interpersonal relationships and loneliness.

Exit is a service for homosexuals who are searching for a way out. Literature is distributed worldwide and counseling is also available for discouraged parents and friends. Job placement counseling is offered for the unemployed. Opportunities with local businesses are listed for job seekers on a no-fee basis. New Wine for Problem Drinkers provides

Table 37 Melodyland's Growth in Membership

	1960	1970	1980	1983
Members	*27*	*5,000*	*15,000*	*20,000*

qualified counselors on a one-to-one relationship as well as weekly group meetings. A myriad of other ministries are available.

Conclusion

Pastor Ralph Wilkerson, son of an Assembly of God lay-preacher, was converted at age five and preached his first sermon at age fourteen. He grew up in Oklahoma and was the second of three sons. He is the father of two daughters.

Today, at age fifty-six, Wilkerson has led the Melodyland Christian Center from its original group of twenty-seven followers to its present membership of 20,000.

The center is diverse in its use of Scripture. Versions used within the congregation are the King James, New International Version, and the New American Standard Version.

Sunday School curriculum includes Gospel Light. Teachers are allowed much latitude to design their own curriculum.

Soul-winners are trained through counselor training each Sunday and the weekly Thursday night Witness Training Class which extends into Friday and Saturday. The annual Charismatic Celebrations encourage each member to develop a personal lifestyle ministry of evangelism.

Causes of growth for the center include: (1) the dynamic of the Holy Spirit, (2) the healing ministry of the church which is focused on the prayer service for the sick each Thursday, (3) "signs and wonders" as described in Scripture producing deliverance from substance abuse, and (4) the team-teaching ministry of the center by capable leaders like Pastor Ralph Wilkerson, Walter Martin, Noel Weiss, John and Karen Hurston, and John Cairns.

Melodyland Christian Center is known by its motto: "Melodyland, A Center for All Christians."

Churches of Latin
and South America

20

Jotabeche: Evangelism in the Streets— Jotabeche Methodist Pentecostal Church
Santiago, Chile

Street preaching is considered a relic of the past in many cities of the world. But, in the streets of Santiago, Chile, multitudes of small singing groups preach and march toward the 15,000-seat auditorium of the Jotabeche Methodist Pentecostal Church each Sunday. More than 100,000 residents of the capital city find refuge and purpose at Jotabeche Church.

Chile is approximately the same size as Texas. Nearly one-half of the nation's population is clustered around Santiago. Cradled in the seven-hundred-mile valley between the rugged Andes Mountains and the Pacific Ocean, Santiago is the commercial, industrial, and cultural center of Chile.

This country population is estimated to be 80 percent Catholic. Evan-

Dr. R. Frank Coy, president of Baptist Theological Seminary in Santiago, Chile, and missionary for the Southern Baptist Convention, gathered major research data on this chapter.

gelical churches contain two million souls and 90 percent are Pentecostals. One-third of all Pentecostals are identified with the Pentecostal Methodist Church.

The Jotabeche Church is the largest Pentecostal Methodist Church and the largest Christian church in Chile.

Visitors who attend the services at Jotabeche are impressed with the confidence and dignity of Pastor Javier Vasquez as he leads the thousands who gather several times each week. Just as memorable are the instrumental choir and the precision singing of the 150-voice polyphonic concert choir. The music that swells from the church saturates the ears, mind, and heart.

Statistics on Jotabeche Church are difficult to gather but those available command attention. Since Javier Vasquez at age forty became the church's second pastor on October 26, 1964, total membership has grown from 40,000 to 80,000. The pastor's estimate of 80,000 includes only full members, those age twelve and older.

Vinson Synan, assistant general superintendent of the Pentecostal-Holiness Church (U.S.) quotes 1980 data shared by Bishop Mamerto Mancilla, leader of Chile's Pentecostal Methodist churches: "Mancella reported that the church in Chile had a baptized membership, 12 and older, of 318,000. The total membership, however, exceeds 620,000."[1]

This information indicates that there are almost twice as many total members as baptized members throughout Chile. Therefore, a total membership exceeding 100,000 at Jotabeche is possible. Actual membership could total as much as 150,000 if the national average also holds true for the denomination's largest member church.

Throughout Chile, the Pentecostal Methodist church reports 176 churches and 3,800 mission chapels. Membership is approximately 650,000 according to the national secretary. Dr. Peter Wagner indicates that as of 1973, the membership was approximately 750,000.[2] Today, more than one in every six members of the national church body is a member of the Jotabeche congregation in Santiago.

Crowds enter the 15,000-seat auditorium on the north side of the temple. All of the church's property at this site is located on the same city block. Public transportation arteries surround the block. The subway

1. Vinson Synan, "Mission to Chile," *International Pentecostal Holiness Advocate* 6 (July 13, 1980): 64–4.

2. C. Peter Wagner, *Look Out! The Pentecostals Are Coming* (Carol Stream, IL: Creation House, 1973), p. 18.

system has a terminal at the front door of the church. In addition to the city buses that pass every few minutes, the intercity bus system is one block away and the railway station is two blocks to the east.

When Jose Javier Vasquez was named pastor of the Jotabeche Church he was also employed as a specialist in transportation estimates. He retired early from his government position to lead the church. His understanding of transportation is a valuable resource since the Jotabeche Church administers a network of forty temples (buildings with a capacity exceeding 600) and 60 preaching points called locales (buildings with a capacity of less than 600). These satellite locations extend ten miles from the main temple on Jotabeche Street.

Jotabeche: Through a Member's Eyes

A home visit with an active church member and worker living in one of the distant temple locations provides a sharper focus on how the church and its satellites function.

Mrs. Elsa Luna operates a clothing store and cuts hair in her home for a livelihood. She also is an active visitor and Sunday school teacher for the satellite temple located two blocks behind her house.

When she was eleven years old a family member died. While reading the words of a hymnal belonging to that relative, she was converted to Jesus Christ.

Approximately seven hundred local residents attend this temple each Sunday night, with three hundred fifty to four hundred attending Sunday school. Sunday school teachers usually rotate every three to six months to prevent feelings of possessiveness for a particular class or age group. This assures greater flexibility with little conflict in administering the congregation.

Elsa's admiration for her pastor and church is very evident. A distinguishing mark of all branch chapels in the Jotabeche system is a tilted cross. Pastor Vasquez explains that this unique symbolism distinguishes their buildings from Roman Catholic structures. It also reminds members that they, as believers and servants of the cross, are to carry its message and ministry into their neighborhoods.

Since automobiles are beyond the buying power of many families in Chile, most members attend services by bus. Pastor Vasquez's sons operate a fleet of eighteen inter-city buses which they purchased in Brazil. Each Sunday, almost thirty additional buses, rented from the city, transport members from the chapels to the mother church.

Elsa remembers the days back in 1953 when the government allowed

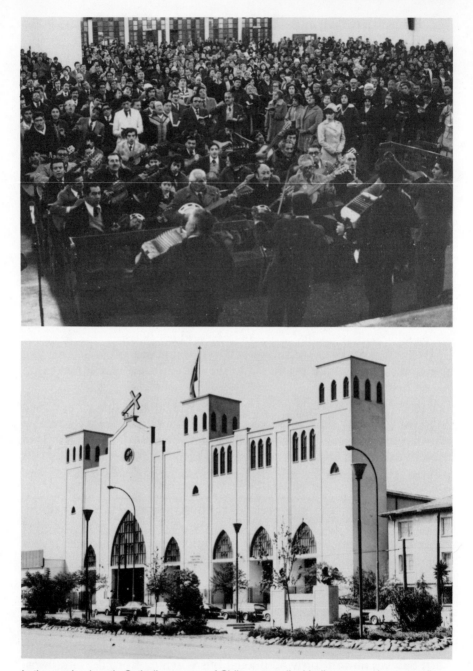

In the predominantly Catholic country of Chile, evangelical believers number two million. Many of these are identified with the Pentecostal Methodist Church, the largest of which is the Jotabeche Methodist Pentecostal Church in Santiago.

the development of houses in her neighborhood. Every Sunday morning men would come to her neighborhood on bicycles from their branch of the Jotabeche Church which was over five miles away. Groups of member-evangelists would gather early and visit the outlying areas.

The families of Elsa's area waited patiently for a pastor of their own but were unable to obtain one. Usually, the main temple would send out an ordained preacher for a one-year period. If his work progressed, he could remain for two or three years.

Elsa indicates that a sanctified separation as a Bible-based standard for Christian living is very important to members of her church. She explains that the term means, "what you do not do."

This standard of separation, in addition to conversion, is closely linked to leadership requirements in the congregations.

A group of twenty to thirty members serves as directors in the enlistment of leaders for Sunday school classes. Once the directors select and approve a name, the candidate's name is given to the pastor for final approval. To be selected for leadership a person must be pure in speech and abstain from dancing and the use of both tobacco and alcoholic drinks.

Elsa taught her first Sunday school lesson in 1960. Teachers attend a pastor's class each Saturday at the main temple. During the class the pastor announces the passage to be taught in each satellite location. The lesson is only two or three verses. Bible teachers are sometimes called *canuto* in derision. The name, however, is actually considered a compliment. It is the name of a well-known French evangelist.

Elsa's description of evangelistic visitation conducted by her church proved helpful:

> **Monday**—Morning and evening services at the local annex.
>
> **Tuesday**—Men's meeting: all men are invited to the temple for training in evangelism. Training is by groups.
>
> **Wednesday**—Women's meeting: about eighty women gather at Elsa's local chapel for an hour-long prayer service. They pray for their pastor, the nation's president, for all pastors, for unction of the Holy Spirit, for people in institutions, sick men, sick women, radio pastors, their own church, and countries at war.
>
> Elsa specified that only one woman prays during the hour, with a second woman by her side.
>
> **Thursday**—Worship service at the local annex.
>
> **Friday**—Evangelistic service: annexes assemble at the temple.

Saturday—Youth meetings: evangelistic caravans and street preaching with a choir.

In a tone of intense conviction and urgency, Elsa insists that the key to the growth of any church is faith and hard work with follow-up from the first day.

There is no doubt that this precious saint of the Jotabeche Church loves her Lord, her pastor, her church, and her ministry.

Pastoral Leadership

When asked why Jotabeche Church has prospered, Pastor Vasquez with a twinkle in his eye and a smile on his face replied, "I blame the Lord."

As the only full-time salaried pastor of the 80,000-member congregation, he has twenty-three assistants (*ayudantes* in Spanish) who donate their time to the church. The pastor feels that a church cannot exist with more than one pastor. "You can't have two heads to a body," he shares. The history of Jotabeche Church reinforces this view. Organized as a congregation in 1914, the Santiago church was the symbol of transition for Chilean Pentecostals. Pentecostals, as a movement in Chile, did not prosper during World War I. Valparaiso, a Pacific seaport located fifty miles east of Santiago, had previously been the struggling center of Pentecostal activity in the country.

After the First World War, Valparaiso started to become relatively less important, and the centre of gravity of the Pentecostal movement shifted increasingly to Santiago. In Santiago itself the First Church managed to establish a group in 1914, and in 1917 the main church moved to a large hall on a street called Jotabeche . . . within a few years a great revival did come. It was felt first in Concepcion in 1921 and then in Santiago the year after.

. . . By 1924 the First Church had 16 groups and the second church 8. Early in 1928 the First Church succeeded in acquiring a large property on the same street as the meeting hall they had used since 1917.

The Pentecostal movement grew up in Chile at a time that the trek from the countryside to the big cities had begun. Tremendous frustrations were building up in the lives and minds of the poorest inhabitants of these cities.[3]

3. J. B. A. Kessler, *A Study of the Older Protestant Missions and Churches in Peru and Chile* (Oosterbaan and le Cointre N.V., 1967), pp. 298-99.

The Pentecostal meetings touched the masses whose lives were in cultural transition. Roman Catholic church leaders had alienated them with a history of identifying with the land owning class.[4]

Earlier, in April of 1910, independent Methodist missionary Willis Hoover led Methodist churches in both Valparaiso and Santiago to separate from the Methodist Church in Chile. Four issues led to the eventual exodus: nationalism; an anti-missionary movement caused by liberal theology sweeping the U.S.; the withdrawal of missionaries, which allowed the lay ministry to fill the leadership vacuum; and Pentecostal doctrine imported by Hoover from America.[5]

The first Pentecostal church in Santiago, a splinter group of First Methodist Church, grew more rapidly than a second group that also broke away. Opposed to having pastors and superintendents, the work in Santiago prospered. During the first five years, seven new churches were organized. However, the need for pastors and superintendents became obvious.

Hoover publicly discouraged the study of books and theology among his pastors because of the widespread infiltration of liberalism in printed materials. His policy of complete isolation from other church groups proved to be his greatest strength and the source of his greatest grief.

Hoover asked Manuel Umana, an energetic man who had just moved to Santiago from Limache, to assume leadership of the nongrowing group that had separated from First Methodist Church. Umana, with no formal training, led the group in January, 1912, to occupy a better meeting hall. Within seven months the church organized five additional groups.

Hoover, as the founder of Pentecostalism in Chile, ordained Umana as a deacon in 1913 and as a full presbyter in 1916. Umana later became the leader of the opposition against Hoover. The opposition cited Hoover as being overly autocratic and questioned his morality. Extended struggles followed in both Pentecostal and civil courts over positions of leadership and property rights. When Hoover died in May 1936, Umana became the champion of Chilean Pentecostals. Under his leadership much of the present style of music at Jotabeche Church began.

On July 3, 1937, Manuel Umana became pastor of the Jotabeche congregation for life. At a controversial annual conference in 1941, he also became superintendent of the Methodist Pentecostal Church for life. Unrest followed. In 1963 he excluded 200 members who openly criticized

4. Ibid., p. 324.
5. Ibid., pp. 107–8, 128, 289, 290.

him. His leadership and church troubles also began to get widespread coverage in the major national Communist newspaper. Other expulsions continued until his death at age 82 in August, 1964. Umana served as pastor of the Jotabeche Church for fifty years from 1915 to 1964.

Learning from their mistakes, leaders of the Methodist Pentecostal Church determined that the pastor of the largest congregation should not serve simultaneously as bishop of the denomination.

Three months after the death of Manuel Umana, Javier Vasquez became the new pastor. Jotabeche Church was experiencing intense growth. As the assistant to Bishop Umana, Vasquez had served voluntarily without pay for several years. Pastoral assistants still receive no salary.

Pastor Vasquez shares:

> When I was sixteen years old God called me. One year later I organized a church. This all happened where there was no evangelical church, out in the country from one of the towns in southern Chile.
>
> At age seventeen, I had a growing, good-size congregation. Shortly after that I came to Santiago to study a profession, as an accountant, specializing in economics and transportation. I also worked in the railway system of the country. While I was doing this study, I became a helper of the first bishop, Manuel Umana, here in this church.

Six years after Vasquez became pastor of the church, Chile elected its first Communist president. Social conditions in the country deteriorated rapidly. November 11, 1973, President Allende was removed from office during a military coup. The new government soon met organized opposition from some of the major religious leaders. These leaders included the Catholic cardinal, the Lutheran bishop, the Methodist bishop, and the Jewish chief rabbi. On August 23, 1974, they sent General Pinochet, the president, a letter requesting less religious repression.

Meanwhile, in December of 1974, a full-page advertisement supporting

Table 38   Growth of Pentecostals in Chile

	1929*	1961*	1980†
Pentecostal Members in Chile	10,000	620,000	782,000
Percentage of Protestant Community	30	40	85
Pentecostal Increase		+610,000	+162,000

* J. B. A. Kessler, Jr., *A Study of the Older Protestant Missions and Churches in Chile and Peru* (Oosterbaan and le Cointre N.V., 1967), p. 322.

† P. J. Johnson, *Operation World* (Bromley, Kent, England: STL Publications, 1978), p. 248.

the new government appeared in the magazine *El Mercurio.* Over thirty evangelical churches had submitted the advertisement.[6] This action marks a significant chapter in the history of Chile's Pentecostal churches.

The same month Jotabeche Church was scheduled to officially dedicate its new 15,000-seat auditorium. For the first time in Chilean history the president of the country visited a non-Catholic church. Dr. R. O. Corvin writes:

> President Augusto Pinochet, with many other men in high positions of state, attended the Sunday morning dedication service. The President cut the red, white and blue ribbon which symbolized the first fully official worship service in the new auditorium. President Pinochet expressing himself said, "I am deeply moved. This has been a beautiful occasion, solemn, patriotic, and of much faith.[7]

Santiago newspapers reported an overflow crowd of 20,000 people at the Jotabeche Church dedication. Reporters also estimated an additional 100,000 people standing outside.

Dr. R. O. Corvin, a Pentecostal speaker from the United States, participated in the formal dedication and describes the leadership style of Jotabeche's pastor:

> Pastor Javier Vasquez is a wonder as he directs the worship of the thousands. . . . With eagle eyes . . . he observes the choir, the usherettes, the thousand member band and singers, and the multitude. With one raised hand he can quiet 5,000 shouting worshipers in half a minute. With one raised finger his ushers can take care of potential disturbances.
>
> This man has time for the poor. He sees to it that the hungry are fed and the widows with their children have proper care.[8]

The pastor is self-confident and communicates his convictions and sense of vocation to the ministry. After serving twenty-five years as secretary to the first pastor, Pastor Umana, he was no novice when he became pastor.

His dress is conservative: dark suits and white shirts. Javier Vasquez has the appearance of a corporate executive while, at the same time, radiating a warm and compassionate interest in those around him.

6. World Christian Encyclopedia, 1982 ed., s.v. "Chile: Church and State," by David B. Barrett.

7. R. O. Corvin, "Gloria a Dios: World's Largest Pentecostal Sanctuary Dedicated," *Pentecostal Holiness Advocate,* February 9, 1975, pp. 4–5.

8. Ibid.

His two libraries center almost exclusively around the Spanish Bible. He noted during an interview:*

> I am just the opposite of David. He was a shepherd of sheep and then he became an administrator. I was an administrator in secular work and later the Lord called me to shepherd sheep.
>
> Since I preach four times a week, I have little time to study. I have an office here in my home with lots of books and there is another office in the church where I have other books. But I don't have time to consult these books. I just stand by the scripture which says, " . . . take no thought beforehand what ye shall speak, neither do ye premeditate; but whatever shall be given you in that hour, that speak ye; for it is not ye that speak, but the Holy Ghost." (Mark 13:11)
>
> I go to the service completely empty, but confident that the Lord will give me the message for the service. So the Lord speaks through me in each service.

Pastor Vasquez celebrated his fifty-eighth birthday in 1983. His parents were converted at the same time as their son and are members of the same denomination. He is one of three children and has five sons and daughters.

He is highly regarded among the officials of the present government. His previous work in government offices helps him understand government officials and procedures. Several legal treatises still used by the government were written by him.

The Thunder of Praise

Sunday school at Jotabeche begins at 10:30 A.M. The church members communicate personal warmth and expectant excitement.

It is customary to kneel on the back benches for prayer before being seated. Ushers with identification badges help the people find seats. During the service these same men stand in the aisle approximately every five to ten benches apart.

Attendance during Sunday school is less than that of the morning worship service. The Sunday school on Jotabeche Street has an attendance of approximately 1,100 each week. When combined with the forty chapels, this figure swells to 10,000.

All classes at the cathedral meet in the auditorium with separate

---

* At Jotabeche Methodist Pentecostal Church, June 1981.

classes for men, women, boys, and girls. As the people enter the building they go immediately to their assigned areas in the large, open room.

The morning schedule allows the Sunday school to meet until noon. The meeting begins with the group singing a hymn. Nearly sixty guitars and mandolins lead the congregation. After singing, the congregation stands, raise their hands toward heaven, and with a thundering shout, cry out "glory to God" three times. The superintendent leads in prayer. Next comes the reading of the Sunday school text and the memory text.

By 10:45, the classes are in session. The teachers stand in intervals of about three benches and teach an average of ten people. The noise level is very intense.

In the women's group, nearly two hundred women are taught by nineteen teachers. Since there is no nursery, children under four years of age stay with their mothers.

The Bible is the sole textbook used in the classes. There also are no offering envelopes or class enrollment books. An offering is taken, however, at the conclusion of the lesson. Each teacher interprets the text and may spend much time encouraging the group and sharing his or her personal testimony of how God is at work in lives today. Class members are encouraged to speak at the conclusion of the lesson and share their testimonies.

At eleven o'clock a bell sounds and the offering is taken. The bell, at Jotabeche and other Pentecostal churches, is kept on the pulpit.

The significance of the bell would go unnoticed by most casual visitors.

The use of the bell was borrowed by Pentecostal churches from their Methodist ancestry. It is the symbol and final call for obedient silence during debate and excessive demonstrations of religious experiences during a worship service. So absolute is the authority of the bell that its use led a group of malcontents to leave Jotabeche in 1913 to form a new church called *Inglesia del Senor* (Church of the Lord).[9]

At 11:20 a second bell is sounded and the teachers sit down. The superintendent takes charge and asks each group to read the memory verse. The pastor takes his place on the platform.

As the classes conclude, announcements are made, two hymns are sung, and the children return to their parents. This final twenty to thirty minutes is the traditional time among most non-Catholic churches for the pastor to summarize the morning lesson. As Pastor Vasquez speaks

9. J. B. A. Kessler, *A Study of the Older Protestant Missions and Churches in Peru and Chile*, p. 296.

in his pleasant voice, he displays an unquestionable compassion for his people. Throughout the service, a trademark of the Jotabeche congregation is the thunder of singing and the three-fold "glory to God!"

After a final hymn, the people are dismissed. In a sign above the pulpit the words, *Dios es amor* (God is Love) are written in large letters for most of the congregation to see. That love is shown among the members of this church.

The most famous meeting at Jotabeche probably is the Sunday evening service. Before the 6:30 meeting, several hundred bands of about six members each converge on the main temple from every sidewalk leading to the church.

These street corner evangelists, all members of Jotabeche Church, have been saturating Santiago with the gospel for two hours. As they inch their way toward the temple, through the city streets, each group has conducted many meetings with a short sermon, testimonies, and music. These caravans of guitars, violins, and accordions have gathered many curious spectators along the way.

Policemen, dressed much like soldiers, stop traffic as more than one thousand street evangelists appear from all directions. The awesome thunder of their singing causes those praying and waiting inside the sanctuary to stand as they join in the choruses of praise.

The ushers at night are women dressed in pale blue uniforms with caps and white gloves. They are stationed every ten to fifteen pews in the aisles to help people to their seats. They also take up the offering. As they pass the cloth bag on the end of a long stick among the people they say, "God loves a cheerful giver."

On a typical night only one-fourth of the congregation's membership can attend the services at the main temple. The city is divided into four sections and each section attends the evening celebration once each month. Most of the people attend one of the seventy smaller temples scattered across the capital city.

The balcony, in the main sanctuary, has a capacity for 2,000 musicians. Imagine 1,000 guitars, mandolins, violins, and accordions joined by 1,000 voices in the people's choir.

A highlight of this service is the performances of the 150-voice polyphonic choir. In contrast to the other instrumental and choral choir, the polyphonic choir is a group with men and women dressed in formal wear with ties and long gowns. This group usually sings immediately before the pastor stands to preach.

While the hymns are sung and the orchestra plays, many of the church members shout "amen" or "glory to God" or raise and clap their hands. Some move to the aisle and dance in the Spirit.

Prayer is offered and is followed by intense singing and a concluding three-fold "glory to God." After announcements, the first offering is taken followed by a reading of the sermon text from the Bible and a song from the polyphonic choir. The sermon seldom lasts longer than thirty or forty minutes.

Preaching without notes, Pastor Vasquez speaks in a somewhat paternal and prophetic but not condescending manner. His vocabulary has a deliberate simplicity. He speaks with a conversational tone that has a calming effect. He is able to make members feel that he is speaking directly to them. His messages give assurance and stimulate hope in the believer. The messages often have no identifiable outline. *See p. 218*

Each service is usually concluded with prayer for salvation. Healing is offered to the thousands who indicate their needs by kneeling at their bench-like pews. Public invitations are difficult to offer since space does not allow it. Those making decisions are asked to kneel at their seat. Assistants then pray with all who kneel.

The layman who directs the service asks the people to stand as they raise hands into the air and spontaneously give three "glory to God" benedictions.

After the message, the second offering is usually taken. The band plays and the choir sings while the offering is collected. The polyphonic choir concludes the service.

Baptism at Jotabeche Church mainly is for infants. The pastor baptizes few adults. The children are asked for a certificate of baptism when enrolling for school. Pastor Vasquez does not dedicate or present babies publicly. He believes that this was a practice reserved for Old Testament times.

Later, when a child is older and is converted, he or she may request baptism, but this rarely happens. If a second baptism is administered, it is called consecration. When a person of another church requests membership, his original baptism is accepted.

The pastor is the only person authorized to baptize. When an adult is converted and asks for baptism, a required probation period is practiced. Six months after joining, a candidate for baptism and membership becomes a probationary member. After three years a probationary member becomes a full member and may participate in the Lord's Supper.

The major emphasis made at Jotabeche is repentance and the fruit of repentance. The new convert must give ample evidence of conversion

before being admitted into the membership. Requirements for membership are basically two: conversion and legal marriage. Divorce is not
permitted in Chile and a vast number of marriages separate with the
spouses living with another person. Many Protestant churches would
receive such persons for membership only after the former marriage is
annulled and the present relationship is legalized by lawful marriage.

At Jotabeche the Lord's Supper is observed only once every four to six
years. Some Methodist Pentecostal churches observe it twice a year. The
ordinance is open to believers present in the service. The pastor administers the Supper with the superintendent of the district.

The congregation recognizes the biblical doctrine of spiritual gifts and
gives prominence to the Holy Spirit. Pastor Vasquez feels that that Holy
Spirit is manifested through believers in many ways. He believes that
speaking in tongues is not the only evidence of the baptism of the Spirit.
He does not speak in tongues and has not danced in the Spirit. He believes
that the most important gift of the Spirit is "the correct interpretation of
the Bible." SEE p. 218, 221

The church is not interested in the ecumenical movement. The pastor
does love and respect other church groups but feels that "each church
should work in its own corral." He encourages and practices evangelism
but not proselytism.

Reasons for Growth

Street Evangelism. The biblical strategy for winning the millions in
both Santiago and Chile for Jesus Christ is not left to chance at Jotabeche.
The house-to-house strategy of Acts 20:20 is unapologetically taught and
practiced by members as meaning bold, aggressive confrontation of the
multitudes with the gospel of Jesus as Savior and Lord.

Approximately five hundred members participate in the visitation and
evangelistic activities of the church each week. These five hundred people
are assigned jobs such as hospital visitation, jails and prisons ministry,
and care for the sick. They meet every Tuesday for instruction and are
called volunteers. They are willing to do anything assigned by the pastor
or his officials.

Volunteers also preach in the streets in Santiago each Monday. Each
Wednesday, women preach in the streets. On Thursdays and Fridays, all
men and women again preach in the streets. The influence of the church
is multiplied hundreds and thousands of times in its contact with the
masses through street evangelism. Any church able to mobilize an army

of 2,000 street preachers surely demonstrates the power of a visible and bold evangelism.

Previously, the church's street evangelism activities were unorganized. Anyone could speak and say anything they wanted to say. This tended to allow bragging about past sins. After much criticism, steps were taken to correct this abuse.

Each Tuesday evening street preachers from the church and its satellite locations are taught the week's sermon. All groups present the same sermon. The speaker is designated before the teams go into the city.

Each Sunday afternoon the teams scatter in groups of six to nine members. In the smaller temples, the whole congregation may minister as a group in the streets. As these groups return to the main temple, they form a line of two members side-by-side along the sidewalk. Groups gathering outside the sanctuary usually extend three or four blocks away.

Ministries offered by the church include tutoring services, medical clinics, jail ministry, hospital ministry, church-type missions, and bus ministry. One of the daughter chapels ministers to former prisoners and their families.

Satellite Chapels.   These mini-congregations are scattered across Santiago. Those groups meeting in buildings with a capacity smaller than 600 are called locales. Groups with assembly halls accommodating crowds larger than 600 people are called temples. The main temple on Jotabeche Street is called the "cathedral."

All satellite temples and locales are administered by a volunteer ministry staff accountable directly to the pastor of Jotabeche Church. These men are not considered to be pastors of the smaller congregations.

The larger temples are called classes and the smaller units are referred to as annexes. Each class is responsible for several smaller annexes in its area of the city.

Among the classes of the satellite chapels, the largest has 3,000 members and the smallest has more than 600 members. The most distant class-temple is ten miles from the cathedral.

Jotabeche organizes approximately three new satellite chapels each year. Vasquez indicates that during his first seventeen years as pastor, ten men who ministered to the larger chapels were ordained. Their temples were released by the mother church and became independent congregations.

Attendance at the main temple will average 2,000 in Sunday school; the combined total for all locations is 11,000. As mentioned earlier,

Sunday night and mid-week services each attract 14,000 worshipers. Most members walk or ride the bus to church.

Pastor Vasquez cannot be accused of overestimating attendance and membership. It has been mentioned that he gives a low membership figure of 80,000, which omits children under age twelve. He indicates that 80 percent of his members regularly attend. The other 20 percent are required to work at secular jobs on Sunday. Vasquez shares that any others are not counted. Thirty city buses are rented to bring members to the cathedral each week.

A Sunday School Network.   Unlike most large churches in the United States, Sunday school takes a minor emphasis when compared to the pulpit ministry. The fact that Jotabeche gathers an average of 10,000 for Sunday school each week in its combined locations is significant.

Attendance will average 1,100 at the main location with another 8,900 in the satellite Sunday schools. The church divides the city into four sections: the south section with almost 3,000; the west section with almost 3,000; the east section with a little less than 2,000; and the northern section of the city and the cathedral with 1,000 to 2,000. A team of sixty teachers teach each Sunday at the central campus. Teacher-pupil ratios among the age groups reveals a low of one teacher for every sixteen pupils. This would be envied by teachers in many of the larger churches of the world. It allows close contact between the two groups.

Among the 1,100 attending Sunday school at the cathedral, 24 percent are preschool age, 10 percent are children ages four to twelve, 26 percent are classified as youth ages thirteen through twenty-five, and adults above age twenty-five constitute 40 percent of those in small group Bible study. Seven percent of Sunday's attendants are teachers.

Pastor Vasquez meets every Saturday morning with all Sunday school teachers. Some of the smaller groups receive their instruction through affiliated temples in their district. At the Saturday meeting he teaches the next Sunday's lesson to about 1,400 leaders. If the 7 percent rule for teachers follows for the 10,000 attending all the Sunday schools, this would give an estimated total of 700 teachers in the Jotabeche Sunday school network. The 1,400 leaders who are taught each week by the pastor must include a multitude of substitute teachers.

He has no special curriculum plan or program but uses themes he feels led by God to use. In all classes, even children's classes, only the Bible is used. Children's teachers adapt the text to a child's understanding

Table 39   Sunday School Class Structure at Jotabeche Church

	Approximate Attendance	Age by Groups	Pupils per Teacher	Number of Teachers	Teacher/Pupil Ratio
Preschool*					
Children	Boys—53	4–12	18	3	1:18
	Girls—55	4–12	18	3	1:18
Youth	Boys—169	13–25	12	14	1:12
	Girls—113	13–25	19	6	1:19
Adults	Men—226	26 up	14	16	1:14
	Women—217	26 up	12	18	1:12

*Infants stay with their mothers.

level. In about 60 percent of the other churches in the denomination, a booklet is used for the lesson. The pastor selects the passages to be studied. Study groups are separated into men's and women's classes. This same model also is applied in the younger age levels.

Principles Identified by the Pastor.   Seven reasons for the growth of the church are targeted by the pastor. In his order of priority the reasons include:

1. A tenacious belief and conviction that the Bible is the Word of God, word for word.
2. Ministry and preaching are directed to the daily experience of the people.
3. His deep love for the church and theirs for him.
4. Obedience to the pastor. He says that the members maintain unquestioned obedience toward him.
5. Utter dependence on God as the Director of the church.
6. A deep commitment of the members to love each other and the new converts. They will not quit visiting a weak convert or member.
7. A sense of forgiveness within the membership.

When Pastor Vasquez was asked to identify a key scripture verse chosen as the promise verse for his congregation, he replies, Psalm 23:1, "I shall not want." God will provide every need.

The motto for the church is *Chile Sea para Christo* (That Chile Might Be Won for Christ).

21

San Salvador's Evangelistic Center
San Salvador, El Salvador

One of the world's largest churches is located in one of the world's smallest countries. The Evangelistic Center of San Salvador, capital of El Salvador, inspires 18,000 people in weekly Bible study. El Salvador is a small country approximately the same size as Massachusetts.

San Salvador, with its population of 400,000, is located in Central America, approximately one thousand miles south of New Orleans. It is a city torn by strife in a country struggling with social and political revolution. It is also a haven for the poor from the interior provinces.

Since 1979, death threats to pastors, missionaries, and other church leaders have become prevalent. Pastors have been shot in their pulpits and over 30,000 citizens have been killed since that time. El Salvador, like other Central American nations, has been subject to Cuban and Soviet influences during these years of civil war.

Despite the adversity, the center continues to experience deliberate growth. Since 1980, almost 90 percent of those attending still come from a distance of up to seven miles. Before the war, many more came ten miles to attend services. The 200 branch Sunday schools and 280 cell groups, or out stations, have experienced continual growth.

The Evangelistic Center began after a 1956 crusade. The congregation met in temporary facilities for nearly four years before calling a young pastor from New York in 1960. The twenty-six-year-old Gilberto Marrero began with approximately fifty members and led them for almost eleven months. The new pastor, Juan Bueno, led ninety-nine members and 300 attendants at the center.

Born on May 2, 1938, to Assembly of God missionaries, Juan's earliest years were spent in Modesto, California. After years of missionary service in both Venezuela and Cuba, his parents moved to Santiago, Chile. His family would spend seven years in Chile. He was converted at age five, his first year in Chile.

Almost a decade later, Juan enrolled at Bethany Bible College in Santa Cruz, California. Bethany also awarded him a Doctor of Laws degree several years later. Bueno has served the church for twenty-one years as their second pastor. His only other church experience before coming to San Salvador was as an associate pastor in California from 1958–59.

The population of El Salvador is reported to be 95 percent Roman Catholic. Evangelicals constitute 4 percent of the 5 percent Protestant segment of the population. During the 1970s, the number of Evangelical Protestants increased by almost 5,700 annually. Dr. David B. Barrett writes:

> . . . the most spectacular gains have come in recent years among the Assemblies of God, who have built up a large following since their arrival in 1922. Pentecostalism represents the principal alternative to Catholic dominance in El Salvador at the present time.[1]

Barrett lists 352 Assembly of God churches. Over 80 percent of the 100,000 affiliated members are adults. Over one thousand foreign missionaries representing forty-six denominations serve in El Salvador. National religious leaders total 970 inside the country.

Agents of the Kingdom

In 1960, the year before Dr. Juan Bueno arrived in San Salvador, the first auditorium was built to accommodate a crowd of 900. This would be the first of eleven construction projects during the next twenty-two years. Construction projects are normal events to neighbors of the center.

As multitudes continue to come, the congregation continues to build.

1. *World Christian Encyclopedia*, 1982 ed., s.v. "El Salvador," (chart) by David B. Barrett.

Dr. Bueno led his people to begin a Christian school with eighty-one students in 1963. *Liceo Cristiano* was the name chosen for the school. The first building was constructed to care for 350 students in 1964. The school system now has 6,550 pupils enrolled in nine locations. The main school and branches provide training for kindergarten through grade twelve. A medical clinic provides special care and vaccinations for the school children. All children wear uniforms. As of 1983 the school buildings include an enlarged auditorium to seat 1,500; twenty-seven classrooms which accommodate twenty-five students with desks; a gymnasium-youth center; an administration building-medical clinic; and a three-story teachers' college. The college, built in 1982, is designed for an enrollment of 100 students. Today the church Pastor Bueno leads has a ministry staff of five men and four secretaries. The Christian school staff numbers one hundred. Included in this team are two co-pastors, an associate pastor, a youth pastor, and a minister of music.

The ministry responsibilities of the congregation are entrusted to fifty deacons and nine elders. Two of the elders are alternates to the seven active elders. Deacons are appointed for ministry-related service and elders are elected to care for administrative affairs. The church also appoints forty deaconesses. Their responsibilities include serving as home cell leaders, ushers, and overseers of the smaller satellite Sunday schools.

The curriculum used by the church is the Vida series. It is published in Spanish by the Assemblies of God Spanish Publishing House in Miami. The series is fully age-graded. Sunday school classes are separated by sex until junior high school. All classes above sixth grade are mixed.

Bueno has seen the church expand from a worship attendance of 300 in one service in 1961 to 5,500 in four services in 1983. During the 1960s the Sunday school tripled from 300 to 900. Attendance by 1980, in both weekday and Sunday meetings, had reached 15,000. Ten thousand met at the main campus and five thousand met in the 200 newly-formed branch locations.

By 1982, the main location had an attendance of 12,000. The 200 branch locations had 6,000 in attendance each week. The congregation had a 1983 attendance goal of 20,000 in all ministries, and actually reached 22,000.

Usually, the branch ministries come to the main church location twice a year. The two occasions are the New Year's Eve Prayer Vigil and the Church's Anniversary Celebration on the first Sunday in May.

Since 1970, twenty-five branch churches have been organized in San Salvador. From 1970–75, satellite congregations were not released from

In a country where death threats to pastors, missionaries, and other church leaders have become prevalent, The Evangelistic Center of San Salvador continues to grow. Many of the worshipers come from a distance of up to seven miles. Dr. Juan Bueno has served as pastor for over two decades.

the mother church. However, starting in 1975, two new churches are created each year and two established satellite churches are released as autonomous congregations.

In a letter, Pastor Bueno writes:

> We are turning two of our largest satellite churches over as "sovereign assemblies" in January (1983) which means we will need to increase about 2,000 in membership just to keep up with the loss of these two congregations. . . . They are still projecting a goal of 20,000 in attendance by the end of 1983. . . . We are also believing the Lord to allow us to start two new churches during the 1983 calendar year, one of which has already been selected as far as the area and future leadership.

The satellite (chapel) units may range from 3,000 attending with 500 members to 400 attending with about 75 members. Members attend the main church from as far as nine miles.

Membership guidelines require a person to be at least sixteen years old in order to be a full member of the congregation. All persons under sixteen years of age who have professed Jesus Christ as personal Savior are considered associate members.

Approximately one hundred persons are baptized each month for a total of between 1,000–1,200 each year.

According to church sources, there were only thirty to seventy branch Sunday schools from 1961–1980. By 1980 they totaled two hundred. In addition to the branch Sunday schools, all of which meet away from the main church campus, there are the out stations. Out stations are organized like the cell groups in Seoul's Central Church.

The Evangelistic Center began the use of out stations in 1979. As these cell groups mature and grow, Dr. Bueno compares them to the house churches of Acts and Colossians. They form a network of evangelistic outreach that makes it possible to reach people even ninety miles away.

After only one year the center had 200 out stations reaching 3,000 people. By the end of 1982, the second year, there were 280, with an attendance of approximately 4,200.

Few churches have the experience of building neighborhood centers, in homes, involving over 4,000 members and potential members. The goal is to saturate entire communities with the gospel through friendship and home-based evangelism.

Out stations come in a variety of types. From its first years, the church has organized separate cluster groups for women, men, young people, and prayer.

The 280 out stations are now coordinated by the congregation. Seventy groups are specifically for women and thirty are for young people. However, prayer groups are the most numerous. A total of 180, or 64 percent are prayer groups. For every ten groups, almost three are women's groups, one is a youth group, and six are prayer groups.

The number of households represented in the church can be estimated by using branch ministries attendance. The average family size in El Salvador is approximately five persons per household. If a figure of 18,000 Sunday school attendants is used, a base of 3,461 families can be estimated. However, the use of 5.2 as the average family size assumes that every member of the family attends. An estimate of four or five thousand households attending the church would be reasonable to assume.

Although present average weekly attendance is 18,000, not every member attends every week. The 1983 attendance goal of the congregation was 20,000. Since 18,000 are now regular attendants, at least 2,000 additional irregular participants attend services. These invisible attendants, when activated, will help ensure that annual goals are reached.

This challenge of potential growth offers an opportunity for believers in El Salvador and the world to pray for the saints of San Salvador. An acceleration of the civil war in El Salvador could radically affect future growth at the Evangelistic Center.

Because the church has thoroughly saturated the neighborhoods where members live, the prospect for church survival is excellent. House churches could continue the ministry of the church, along with the branch Sunday schools, if regular services were temporarily disrupted during war.

Excluding the 280 out stations or cell groups, there are 200 branch Sunday schools. Only one-sixth, or 17 percent, of all teaching units meet at the main location.

Celebrating Saints

The first of three Sunday morning multitudes converge on the pale blue Evangelistic Center (*Centro Evangelico*) before eight o'clock. A cross perched on the slender tower above one of the entrances welcomes worshipers several blocks away.

Located in the heart of downtown San Salvador, the center has services four times each Sunday. Morning activities include three Sunday schools. Worship services are in progress during these same periods. A concluding Sunday school and worship service meets at four o'clock.

Table 40   Sunday School Profile—Evangelistic Center (main location), 1982

	Approximate Attendance	Age of Groups	Teacher/Pupil Ratio	Number of Teachers
Preschool	3,000	Birth–Age 5	1:26*	38
Children†	3,400	Grades 1–6	1:21	160
Youth	600	Grade 7–College	1:12	48
Adults‡	5,000			
Total	12,000			

* This ratio is obtained due to same teachers serving in multiple Sunday schools.
  † Approximately 700 children attend branch Sunday schools each Sunday.
  ‡ Approximately 2,000 men and 3,000 women attend these worship services (adults do not meet for Sunday school).

Attendance among adults is greatest at the eight o'clock service. This first worship hour attracts an estimated 2,000 adults. The second and third periods regularly reach 1,400 each. The afternoon attendance includes approximately four hundred adult Bible students. Perhaps one-quarter of the afternoon congregation attended one of the earlier training and celebration events.

Among the several adult classes available each week are the New Doctrine Class, Advanced Doctrine, a class for young couples, and the Auditorium Class taught by one of the national pastors. The Auditorium Class is the most popular class, with almost 4,800 in attendance. The other three classes average under one hundred pupils. Another popular group is the New Doctrine Class. This thirteen-week orientation course is required for all baptismal candidates. The entire course must be completed before the ordinance will be administered.

Candidates for conversion attend in great number each Sunday. The one hundred baptisms each month reflect a congregation with a genuine passion for souls. Unlike growing churches in some parts of the world, all baptismal candidates are new believers. Growth by transfer is almost unknown to the people of Evangelistic Center of San Salvador.

Excitement and expectation blend with the swell of the organ and piano each Sunday. The first three services are almost standing-room-only crowds. The attendance shrinks during the four o'clock service when guitars replace the organ.

The fifty-five-voice choir sings praises only once each month in the morning services. Visitors and members, however, enjoy hearing the choir sing the sounds of heaven every Sunday evening.

Without hesitation, the pastor attributes the growth of the congregation to three definite principles. First, the priority given to Lordship Principles. The principles place a major focus on Jesus Christ and the joy of being His faithful servant to fellow-believers and non-believers.

Second, the pastor recognizes the total commitment of his members to the lordship of Jesus Christ over their lives and possessions. There is a visible willingness and joy in serving others in Jesus' name and for His glory. The response of the people to a series of sermons on Lordship Principles led to rapid growth at the center in 1970.

The third growth principle has been the church members' involvement, on a mass scale, in evangelism and ministry. This major key to growth for the congregation was the training of members in organizing and leading branch Sunday schools.

Bueno's prayer is that the Holy Spirit will continue to use the Evangelistic Center to encourage growth among the sixty other Assembly of God congregations in metropolitan San Salvador.

The pastor speaks highly of the staff God has given the church. Special gratitude is expressed for the ministries of the national pastor, Cristobal Ramirez; co-pastor Orlando Flores; pastor of juveniles, Lisandro Bojorquez; and missionary Jerry Smith. Other church leaders have literally invested their lives for the kingdom under the leadership of this dedicated staff.

When asked to name his favorite book of the Bible, Bueno points to the Gospel of John. First Corinthians 1:18, "For the preaching of the cross is to them that perish foolishness; but unto us who are saved it is the power of God" is his favorite verse.

He lists three personal goals: first, developing leaders to shape El Salvador through the new Teacher's College; second, an attendance of eighty in the night Bible school; and third, the development of a disciple staff for leading his people to continued growth in Christ-likeness.

His goals for the church include the creation of two new churches each year.

Ministries of the church, in addition to the school, include: literacy classes, preschool care, food distribution, free medical clinics, limited legal assistance, counseling service, jail ministry, and care for ex-prisoners and their families. Also, the church provides free preventive medical care and tuition for pupils enrolled in the satellite schools.

Juan Bueno, now forty-five years old, believes in the Lord of his church and the churches of the Lord more than ever before in his life. The staff and elders of San Salvador's Evangelistic Center continue to lead their people in bold evangelism during these uncertain days.

22

Brazil's Super Churches

Brazil is home to three of the world's largest churches. Sao Paulo is the evangelistic headquarters of both *Congregacao Crista* (Christian Congregation) and *Brasil para Crista* (Brazil for Christ). Rio de Janeiro, located two hundred miles northeast of Sao Paulo, is the evangelistic turf of the Madureira Assembly of God.

In this immense country there probably are several secluded, independent churches still unknown to the rest of the world. Continued research into the large churches of the country may bring them to light.

Congregacao Crista, Sao Paulo

Sao Paulo, the industrial capital of South America, is a city of approximately nine million people. The population of Sao Paulo almost doubled during the 1970s. This growth was the result of the migration each year

Perry Ellis, director of evangelism for Brazil and missionary for the Southern Baptist Convention, gathered major research data on *Congregacao Crista.*

Harold Renfrow, executive secretary of the Rio de Janeiro State Convention of Brazil for the Southern Baptist Convention, gathered major research data on Madureira Assembly of God.

Dr. Larry Keyes, director of Overseas Crusades of Santa Clara, California, coordinated the gathering of major research data on Brazil for Christ (*Brasil para Crista*).

Note: Gratitude is expressed to Perry Ellis for sharing his staff to aid in translation and for repeated efforts to set up interviews with the pastor of this church.

Table 41   Profile of Brazil's Super Churches

Church	City	Auditorium	Total	Composite
Congregacao Crista	Sao Paulo	3,500	67,600	23,640
Madureira Assembly	Rio de Janeiro	3,000	28,000	7,333
Brazil for Christ	Sao Paulo	25,000*	14,000	

* 10,000–15,000 seating and the rest is standing capacity (estimated).

of one-half million native Brazilians from the rural interior to the urban center.

David B. Barrett lists 3,500[1] *Congregacao Crista* congregations with 600,000 adults among its membership of one million. Fifty-three percent of the members live in Sao Paulo and an additional 30 percent reside in the neighboring state of Parana.[2] They stress a second experience. The two are conversion and the baptism of the Spirit. The first experience is Baptistic while both would generally be considered Pentecostal.

Congregacao Crista represents one of the more than one hundred indigenous church bodies in Brazil. The group adopted the model of the large "central church" with numerous sister chapels, a common Third World growth pattern. Many of the chapels grow large enough to become a "regional central church" that, in time, plants its own sister chapels.

In 1965, William Read wrote:

There are now many *Congregacao* church buildings . . . seating 5,000 or more people. . . . Such large, adequate buildings are to be found in Londrina, Parana, Maripora, Campinas, Sao Caetano, Vila Carrao, Agua Raza, Jundiai, Santana, Igarapava, Bom Retiro, Araraquara, Guarulhos, Santos, Curitiba, and other places. From the standpoint of buildings alone the *Congregacao* is an impressive member of the Evangelical church family in Brazil.[3]

The Central Church

The *Congregacao Crista* had its beginnings in Brazil in 1910. Louis Francescon, an American from Chicago, traveled to Sao Paulo by way of Argentina. After an extensive and unusual encounter prepared by the

1. Figure indicated by the church for 1983 was 6,400 congregations.
2. *World Christian Encyclopedia,* 1982 ed.
3. William R. Read, *New Patterns of Church Growth in Brazil* (Grand Rapids: Eerdmans, 1965), p. 34. Used by permission. The church indicates a seating capacity of 3,000 instead of 5,000.

Holy Spirit in the state of Parana, west of Sao Paulo, eleven people were confirmed by conversion, as well as by water and Spirit baptism.

Moving to Sao Paulo, Francescon initially joined a Presbyterian church in the Bras district of the city. His preaching soon caused a serious division with his new doctrinal position on the Holy Spirit. From that division in June, 1910, the *Congregacao* was born.

The church remained an Italian community congregation with sermons and music in Italian until about 1935. At that time, as William R. Read indicates, "Half of the hymns (1–329) were Italian and half (330–588) Portuguese."[4] The 1943 edition of the hymnal of the church was available in Portuguese only. The transition from a gathering of converted Italian immigrants to a fully-developed indigenous movement in Brazil was complete by that time.

The central church, located in the heart of Sao Paulo, reports 67,600 members. There also are an estimated 60,000 youngsters attending who are the children of these members.

Membership is measured by the total number of believers (140,000 in Sao Paulo and suburbs in 1983) partaking of the Lord's Supper. This classification is further defined as those participating who are at least twelve years of age. An exception to the age guideline is provided for younger children who by the Holy Spirit have spoken in tongues.

The *Congregacao* is a central church meeting under one roof several times per week with sister chapels that assemble on their own for worship services. In addition to the regular Sunday morning and evening services, the groups meet at the main facility each Tuesday, Wednesday, and Friday. All locations are led by lay leaders who receive no salary. None of the congregations have a paid ministry staff (pastors, directors of music, or Christian education leaders).

The central church in Sao Paulo, prior to the construction of its existing sanctuary in 1954, met in rented meeting halls. This temple was built at an expense of $1.5 million and seats approximately 3,500 people.

Approximately 360 sister chapels are owned by the central church. Over 200 of these are in the region, with an additional 157 in Sao Paulo. Within recent months the church has had an many as eighteen chapels under construction at a building cost of about $65,000 each. There is one central baptistry in each region. The largest sister church has approximately 800 members. The most distant chapel is twenty miles away.

Twice each month the construction committee meets to consider

4. Ibid., p. 24.

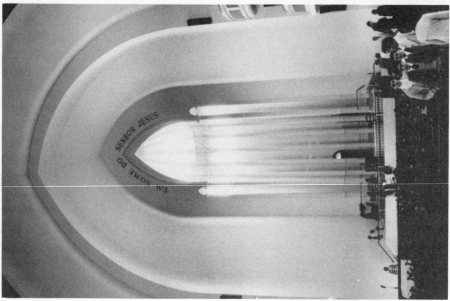

The central church of the Congregacao Crista (Christian Congregation) is located in the industrial capital of South America—Sao Paulo, Brazil. Whereas the main building seats 3,500 people, the mother church also owns approximately 360 sister chapels in the city and region.

future building projects and to discuss those already under construction. The committee is composed of engineers, architects, and merchants. All money collected in the sister churches is sent to the central church. Thirty brothers take care of the accounting responsibilities. The church does not use radio, television, or publications such as regular newsletters for mass mailings.

Each week between 300 and 700 leaders of the central church and chapels gather at the Bras location to transact business and make spiritual decisions. The representatives include the elders, the co-operators, and the deacons of these churches. The *Congregacao* does not have deaconesses. The central church has five active deacons whose primary service is the distribution of food and clothing to those in need. They are presented by the elders at the regional meetings in the churches.

Approximately 400 *anciaos* (elders) serve the mother church and its satellites. One *anciao* serves nine congregations in church buildings rented or owned by the *Congregacao*. New buildings are reported at the annual meeting during the Easter holiday week.

The *anciaos*, as elders of the church, function as pastors or mission pastors. They feed, lead, and oversee their flocks. Their responsibilities include presiding at worship services and administering both baptism and the Lord's supper. Every fifteen days the central church observes the ordinance of baptism.

During the early 1960s new administrative procedures were adopted in order to coordinate all sister churches. Geographical areas with *Congregacao* groups were divided into districts with nine-man commissions for administration of material matters.

Imagine . . . Thousands of Baptisms a Year

The central church is located on a relatively narrow street in the manufacturing section of the city. Once inside, the three overlapping cathedral-ceiling arches captivate the visitor. The center arch is bathed with a halo of brilliant sunlight that accents the ten, forty-foot columns beneath. Along the upper edge of this inner arch, in black letters, is the spiritual watch-word of the congregation, *"Em Nome Do Senhor Jesus"* (In the Name of the Lord Jesus). The same words are printed on the front of the pulpit in silver letters.

Two balconies gracefully curve above the heads of the congregation. The only furniture beneath the three arches is a traditional enclosed pulpit centered between two simple chairs. A rail separates the congregation from the pulpit area.

Immediately behind the pulpit area is a recessed baptistry. Baptismal candidates enter the baptistry pool through two visible doors. Men enter the pool from the door on the congregation's right and women through the door on the left.

It is a common event to see as many as two hundred to three hundred adults baptized during a single morning worship service. The ordinance is administered by one elder assisted by two deacons, all dressed in chest-high boots (waders). A constant stream of men and women dressed in gray robes alternately enter the water. During 1982, 18,686 of the 64,312 total baptisms administered by the *Congregacao*, were in Sao Paulo alone. In 1983 there were 71,510 baptisms of new believers in Brazil.

When a baptismal service begins, the presiding elder mentions guidelines for those coming to be baptized. The candidate must be twelve years of age, unless he has "received the gift of the Holy Ghost under that age," and his marital life must be legal and in order. The progression of this new spiritual life is seen as being conversion, baptism, and regeneration. Throughout the baptismal service the congregation in unison, and even individuals in the crowd, cry out intensely, "glory to God."

An eighty-piece orchestra, located immediately in front of the pulpit, leads the congregational singing during the worship service. Since 1932 there have been no guitars or drums used in the music of the church. One leader comments, "Our music is more sacred without them."

Requests for prayer are received and tabulated. The elder reads the summary of prayer requests and the congregation kneels for prayer.

All men are kneeling on the right side of the auditorium and all women are at prayer on the left side. The women members have their heads covered with white veils during the service. The unbaptized are easily recognized because of uncovered heads. Other hymns are sung throughout the one-and-one-half-hour worship service.

Babies who have been with their mothers in the women's section of the sanctuary begin to cry by the end of the service. When the service concludes, the men greet one another with a handshake and a "holy kiss." The women greet one another in a similar manner. Between men and women there is only the handshake. Every greeting begins with the words: "The peace of God." The greeting is acknowledged with an "Amen." According to William R. Read, the *Congregacao* has placed the largest order for Bibles the Brazilian Bible Society has received.

No official Sunday school curriculum is used by the church in the services for the children and young people. They meet to receive teaching from the Bible, sing hymns, and memorize scripture verses. The Bible is the only recognized literature of the church. Other literature is considered inappropriate. Young people's services are only for the unmarried.

Attendance, rather than enrollment, is emphasized at the Bras location. Enrollment rolls are not kept. Children, age twelve and under, assemble in one hall while the rest meet in another hall. *Auxilliars* (helpers) lead the children rather than teachers. The church reports approximately three hundred children attending with four *auxiliar* helpers in each of the two groups.

Each Sunday afternoon at three o'clock the single young people meet for a separate service next to the temple. The group is divided, with men on the right side and women on the left.

The pupils follow the leader in their own Bibles but do not take notes. They are encouraged to memorize verses from the text and repeat them at the next meeting. Each pupil uses his or her own personal hymnal which is available only to members.

Doctrines, Deacons and Decisions

What does *Congregacao Crista* believe about baptism, the Lord's Supper, conversion, church officers, priorities of the church, evangelism, and the orientation of new members?

Baptism is understood to be necessary for salvation. Baptism by immersion is practiced. The age of baptism is twelve or older, unless the candidate has already received the baptism of the Holy Spirit. It is a congregational act which the candidate participates in to be "obedient to the Scriptures." There is no baptism preparation class and only faith in Jesus Christ is required.

The Lord's Supper is administered only to members of the congregation. It is understood to be a memorial but gives a special blessing to those who participate in its observance.

In order to be converted, one must believe in Jesus Christ as Savior and live a life that demonstrates this claim. This decision implies a commitment to the church and its doctrines.

Three officers are recognized in *Congregacao Crista*. They are elders, deacons and co-operators. The elders are experienced in the ecclesiastical life of the church. They normally do not decide crucial issues in their congregation without the elders of the branch churches.

Decisions are made by all elders serving in the greater Sao Paulo area. They usually meet once each week and their decisions are final. They do not keep minutes of their meetings.

At the next level there are deacons whose major responsibility is to care for the poor. Their ministry is directed toward the distribution of food and clothing to church members and the community.

The co-operators function as elders and in the place of elders except for the functions of water baptism and the administration of the Holy Supper.

The congregation recognizes seven spiritual gifts. The gifts include speaking in tongues, interpretation, healing, prophecy, wisdom, discernment, and miracles.

Congregacao Crista does not keep records of organized visitation or of evangelistic activities. Many visit and evangelize but in an unstructured, day-to-day, lifestyle manner. Initially members usually assume a certain personal oversight for new converts evangelized by them.

Any estimate of the number of soul-winners in the church would be pure speculation. The church keeps no listing of its soul-winners. One church leader stated, "Soul-winners aren't trained by the church. They are trained by the Holy Spirit."

In the first half of the 1980s, the central church baptized an average of 300 new converts each week.

Once baptized, the new member is expected to follow the doctrinal and ethical practices of the church. Women wear the white veil, modest, street-length dresses, and uncut hair. Men usually wear ties and cannot have long hair. They greet one another by saying, "A Paz de Deus" (God's Peace be with you).

The exclusion of members is practiced only in the case of scandal, where the testimony of the church is involved.

Reasons For Growth of Congregacao Crista

Three reasons for growth are listed by elders of the church:

1. Growth is based on the direct action of the Holy Spirit in the fellowship of the church.
2. The congregation bases its work of faith and cooperation without regard to race, color, or social class.
3. Elders are not paid to guide congregations. The money is used to help the poor and to build new temples.

William R. Read adds the following factors:

1. The church began as an Italian people movement which, for the first twenty-five years of its history, reached Italian immigrants.

These earliest members spoke Italian, like their founders, and worked on farms and coffee plantations. Later they migrated to the industrial cities of Brazil, especially Sao Paulo. There were few cultural barriers to be crossed.[5]

2. About 1935, when Italian was replaced with Portugese in the hymns and preaching of the church, the church again experienced massive growth. Whereas the church began as an Italian people movement, it now reached many thousands as it became a Portugese Brazilian people movement.[6]

   A third wave of growth was experienced as northern relatives and friends of those members in the area around Sao Paulo also believed and moved south. Church planting became extensive.

3. The absence of several factors that often hinder the growth of other mission-type churches, subsidized from outside sources, allowed the congregation to focus its energies on growth.

   This indigenous climate was encouraged by the absence of "institutions, financial subsidies, pastoral support and mission policies from outside agencies. Such freedom allowed the major emphasis to be placed on the church planting characteristic of this church."[7]

Madureira Assembly of God, Rio de Janeiro

Rio de Janeiro is one of the world's most crowded cities with a population density of approximately 90,000 people per square mile. The city is second only to Sao Paulo in total population among Brazilian cities.

Surrounded by mountains, Rio is so large that it can be viewed in its entirety only from an airplane. Thousands of buildings are clustered along the beaches and villages of this urban giant.

Sugar Loaf Mountain, on one end of the city, rises more than 1,300 feet out of Guanabara Bay. Rising even higher over the millions of offices, homes, and slums below is the towering statue of Christ the Redeemer opposite Sugar Loaf Mountain. After the darkness of night has obscured Sugar Loaf, the lighted Christ stands symbolically with outstretched arms as guardian of the city.

Scattered throughout the Rio valley are 120 satellite chapels of the 28,000-member Madureira Assembly of God. The congregation has two hundred pastors.

5. Ibid., pp. 40–41.
6. Ibid., p. 41.
7. Ibid., p. 42.

Pastoral Leadership

Until his death on August 26, 1982, Paulo Leivas Macalao served for more than fifty years as the pastor of the Madureira Assembly of God Church. He organized the church on November 15, 1929. Pastor Paulo's wife, Zelia, served as co-pastor under her husband's leadership.

Paulo was the son of Brazilian army General Joao Maria Macalao. Following his birth in the city of Santana do Livramento, he enrolled in the Baptist school of the old Federal District.

After high school graduation he attended Realengo Military School. However, after he began his military training, he changed direction by dedicating himself to the service of God. Pastor Paulo vividly recalls, "While a student earlier, at the Baptist school, I envied the students who were studying to preach the Gospel of Jesus Christ."

Pastor Paulo shared in an interview before his death, "At the end of 1923, while looking for the truth, I found a tract of the Church of God known as the Church of the Orphanage. There I found some believers of the Assembly of God." On June 26, 1924, missionary Gunnar Vingren conducted his first baptisms on Caju Beach. "I was the second believer to be baptized in the waters." He had been converted three months earlier on April 5, 1924, at the age of thirty-one.

During the days that followed, the group of believers needed a preacher. The missionary went about his mission to win other new converts. Pastor Paulo, recounting the occasion leading to his first sermon at thirty-two years of age said, "Nobody wanted to preach. I went to the park and preached but nobody wanted to hear me preach. I learned to love preaching in the open air. To develop my voice, I would get alone and preach to a telephone pole as I imagined it to be my congregation."

Five months after his conversion and baptism he received his baptism of the Holy Spirit on November 3, 1924. Six years later, Gunnar Vingren took advantage of the visit of Swiss missionary Levi Pethrus to ordain the young Paulo to the ministry. Those early years were difficult and created many family problems as the young Paulo made the transition from military school to the ministry. After observing his unshakable faith, his parents became more supportive.

The first centers of his evangelistic meetings were the suburbs of Rio, including Realengo and Santa Cruz. Later, he included Niteroi and Petropolis as new, and sometimes large, churches were organized.

Pastor Macalao built his first temple in the Bangu area of Rio for the Assembly of God. This first site, still in use, had a seating capacity of 300

The Madureira Assembly of God Church in Rio de Janeiro has 28,000 members. Many of these are scattered throughout the Rio valley in 120 satellite chapels. The congregation has 200 pastors.

people. The structure was built in 1933. The mother church relocated in 1939 to the present site with its seating capacity of 1,000.

Much growth occurred in the Madureira section of the city. Twenty years after the 1,000-seat building was completed, it was expanded to hold 3,000 worshipers.

Pastor Macalao was for many years counselor of the Brazilian Bible Society and president of the Ebenezer Bible Institute with almost 300 students. Many students are preparing to become pastors. He has served as perpetual president of the Asssemblies of God Publishing House and president of the Fiscal Council of the Order of Evangelical Ministers of Brazil.

The shepherd of Madureira served only two churches before he came to Madureira. He began his work at Madureira in November, 1929.

The Structure of Strength

All members of the Brazilian Assembly of God churches are issued a personal identification card. Each card has its own serial number identifying, in sequence, when the member affiliated with the national body. The card carried by Pastor Paulo is number 0001. All cards issued to members of chapels of Madureira Assembly identify the carriers as members of the mother church.

Most growth today is concentrated in the chapels located away from the main campus of the mother church. While the mother church lists fifty-five teaching units at the main facility, both the morning and evening services will average between 1,500 and 3,000 in attendance. Pastor Macalao indicated an average weekly Sunday school attendance of approximately 1,500 at the main location. Attendance climbs, according to observers, when the pastor is at home, preaching in his own pulpit.

Madureira Assembly of God is a mother church with daughter chapels called "ministries." Approximately two or three new "ministries" are organized each year. The main church and satellites meet each month to discuss plans and to receive instruction and Bible teaching. The ministry

Table 42   Profile of Madureira Assembly

	1980	1975	1970	1965	1960	1955
Church Membership	18,520	15,300	8,095	5,532	3,771	
Sunday School Enrollment	1,100	800	650	500	400	320
Baptisms	586	636	541	338	307	242

meeting is regularly scheduled for the first Tuesday of each month. The pastor of the mother church is president for life and presides as moderator over this joint meeting of all general workers, pastors, and deacons. Each May all of the church's leaders convene. The constitution and by-laws of the church govern these meetings.

The property of each ministry is owned by deed in the name of each local chapel, with the mother church having final and actual ownership. Consent of the mother church's pastor and his council of pastors is required for all major transactions. Discipline within the larger body is by the same two representative governing parties.

Money collected is budgeted and spent by the local ministries. They are not obligated to send these funds to the mother church. Expansion of facilities, however, is a matter beyond the authority of the ministries. Approval is needed before additions can be made.

The appointment of pastors to the satellite ministries is also a council decision made by the mother church's pastor and his own community of mission pastors. Pastor Macalao indicates that "some act like Baptists and act autonomously." When asked about fellowship among the ministries, he answers confidently, "We do not beat them, but they obey."

Among the 120 daughter churches of the Madureira Assembly, the largest participating ministry in Gurupi, Brazil, has approximately 3,000 members. The most distant ministry is 800 miles from the mother church. Often, members move to new communities and want the mother church to send them a pastor to begin a new ministry. At other times, relatives in distant cities ask the mother church to begin a chapel. Approximately three new "ministries" are begun each year.

Ecumenial attitudes of the church are inter-dependent: "We will cooperate with others as we did during the Billy Graham Crusade, but we do not cross denominational lines and do not choose to mix doctrine with practical Christian activities."

The mother church and her ministries teach both water and Holy Spirit baptisms. The Lord's Supper is closed except to certain trusted Christians outside this fellowship. Baptists, for example, are generally welcome to observe the ordinance at the church.

Many church officers make up the leadership of the Madureira Assembly. There are approximately 4,180 workers: 100 pastors, 180 evangelists, 300 *presbiteros* (elders), and 3,600 deacons.

Twenty-three gifts of the Spirit are recognized and exercised by the church.

Soul-Winning at Madureira

Paulo Macalao has estimated that approximately 60 percent of all adult members of the church participate in or support the church's visitation and evangelistic activities each week. He also estimates that the church has 2,000 soul-winners. More than 90 percent of all baptisms are for new believers. Baptisms at Madureira Assembly have continued to multiply annually. The church averaged 242 baptisms in 1966 and grew to almost 600 in 1980.

Conversion can be at any age past eight. A new member class is provided year-round by the church.

As soon as a person professes Jesus Christ as Lord and Savior, there is a four-month waiting period before baptism. During this period the new convert is assigned to a teacher in the local church for personal instruction and growth. Assembly members lead strict lives. Breaking rules of the church is grounds for exclusion from the body. This exclusion is exercised by the officers of the church.

The two main causes of growth at the church are prayer, and the church sanctifying itself for holiness. "When we quit these, we might as well shut our doors. Without prayer and holiness we are just a club," the pastor says.

The evangelistic strategy of the Madureira church and its 120 daughter ministries encourages open-air evangelism. Groups enthusiastically preach the gospel across the Rio area with loud-speakers. Each group uses musical instruments, songs, and testimonies on street corners and in city parks.

Concern for both members and non-members is demonstrated through active involvement in adult literacy classes, job training, tutoring services, preschool care, food and clothing distribution, medical clinics, legal assistance, aid to juvenile offenders, and aid for ex-prisoners and their families. A convalescent center operated by the church provides care for about sixty senior adults. Jail ministry and Bible study fellowships are also used to reach out in Jesus' name.

The church grew 46 percent from 1975 to 1980 and reaches more than six hundred new members each year.

The eight hundred active deacons of the church are appointed by the pastor of the mother church, with the advice of his pastors and the church. Their function is to missionize rather than to make management decisions.

Celebration and Instruction

The saints of Madureira hold very informal worship services. Regal treatment and respect are given to the pastor and pulpit guests.

In the tradition of other South American churches, services are held nightly at the church. Sunday services include an early morning prayer service attended by 300 to 400 intercessors. The morning worship service meets at 9:30 A.M. and will vary in attendance from 2,500 to 4,000. A Sunday evening service concludes the day.

The forty-member string and precussion instrument orchestra-band accompanies the one-hundred-voice choir in the cathedral sanctuary. The celebration service is punctuated throughout with both prayer requests and prayer from pew and pulpit. Everyone participates.

After the formal portion of the service is concluded, many attendants continue praying at their seats. When satisfied, members move up the aisle and back into the streets to another week of work. Members of the ministry staff linger to help.

The sermons are Bible-centered and usually follow the traditional Pentecostal pattern. Only Portuguese is spoken and the Almeida Version of the Bible published in Brazil is used. The version would be the equivalent of the King James Version in English.

Most Sunday school instruction is quite different at Madureira from most North American churches. Only fifty-five of the 455 teaching units meet at the main church campus. Classes meeting at the main church average nearly 1,000 in both enrollment and attendance.

Most of these classes meet in the homes of believers or supporters of the church. The home meetings are informal with much music, testimonies, and prayer requests. The lesson is usually determined in the monthly meeting when the pastors come together. At that time the pastors are taught the lessons for the upcoming month. These neighborhood home classes are usually not divided by age or sex. Everyone, from babies to grandparents, is present. Meetings usually last two or more hours.

The Sunday school is the least active organization of Assembly congregations in Brazil. Classes are held for children and young people. Some leaders have suggested that the low priority of Sunday school can be attributed to the Swedish Pentecostals who planted many of the first Assembly churches in Brazil. Sweden, like neighboring European countries, tended to be less Sunday school-oriented than North America.

Madureira and Church Planting

The church ministers in a commercial section of Rio with small factories along with professional people (doctors, lawyers, and dentists). The area developed along the central railroad serving greater Rio.

The inexpensive housing and cost of living attracted earlier settlers from the interior of Brazil. Today, the district has become a middle-class neighborhood mixed with poverty and wealth. Many schools and churches are located in this area and have contributed to community stability.

The influence of Madureira Assembly far exceeds the church's main campus and chapels. Churches have been planted throughout Brazil since 1926. See Table 43 for information on founding anniversaries as of 1980.

In a report issued in 1980 by the central church, a detailed summary of the church's larger ministry gave the following information:

Number of Churches. 850
Number of Missions 2,320
New Converts 28,645
Pastors. 344
Evangelists. 749
Elders (lay preachers) 3,861
Deacons (home visitors and Bible readers) 5,350
Workers (*Trabelhadores*). 7,800
Total Members. 458,792
Sunday School Classes 1,978
Sunday School Enrollment 185,000
Missionaries (Bolivia, Colombia, Venezuela). 10

A summary (Table 44) supplied by Pastor-President Paulo Macalao (1980) gives a capsule of the distribution of churches, missions, and preaching points.

These listings from the Madureira "convention" should silence critics who question earlier information given about daughter ministries. The

Table 43

Area	Anniversary	Pastors	Evangelists	Total
Guarabira	1926			
Goias	1936	78	160	238
Rio de Janeiro	1937	85	201	286
Sao Paulo	1938	125	230	355
Brasilia	1957	17	41	58
Parana		4	10	14

smaller cluster of 120 ministries does not constitute the North American equivalence of a denomination.

Table 44

Cities	Churches	Missions	Preaching Points
Sao Paulo	*526*	*829*	*930*
Minas Gerais	50	196	175
Goias	135	302	289
Parana	9	6	
Brasilia (DF)	6	42	
Espirito Santo	1	3	
Rio de Janeiro	85	542	1,635
Total	812	1,911	2,723

Brazil for Christ, Sao Paulo, Brazil

Terror mixed with rage must have rippled through the hearts of church members as they saw a wrecking crew destroy their new sanctuary. Within hours, a dream had been reduced to heaps of rubble.

Brasil para Christo (Portugese for Brazil for Christ) often has been recognized as the fastest growing religious group in Brazil. One key ingredient contributing to the church's growth has been the common man's identification with the political stance taken by Pastor Manoel de Melo.

Since the founding of Brazil for Christ in 1955, the pastor has led his people to support the election of city council members, the vice-mayor of Sao Paulo, federal senators, and even the vice-president of the republic. This involvement in political issues has, at times, penalized the congregation. The destruction of their sanctuary is one vivid example.

Out of the rubble of the demolished sanctuary, however, the congregation built a temple which seats 10,000 comfortably but can accommodate up to 25,000 for special events.

The new sanctuary, located in the western section of Sao Paulo, stands on a three-block area. The main auditorium occupies approximately 35,000 square feet. While designed to seat 15,000, church leaders estimated that 30,000 people crowded into the building on Good Friday in April, 1976.

William R. Read and Frank A. Ineson write:

> This church claims more than 300 satellite churches in Sao Paulo alone. The leaders of the satellite churches are under the training and constant surveillance of Manoel de Melo.[8]

Of all churches in South America, more ambiguity exists over the membership of the mother church of Brazil for Christ and its satellite chapels still awaiting autonomy than of any other large congregation. Repeated efforts have been made to gain accurate and current information about membership.

Two likely reasons seem to be a distrust of outside inquiry and a fear of government misuse of the information. A possible third reason could be hesitation to report information reflecting recent decline in membership.

A recent survey of attendance at various worship services (Table 46) reveals attendance trends.

Table 45   Profile of Brazil for Christ

	1955–6	57–8	59–60	61–2	63–4	65–6*	70–1†	1983‡
Membership								
Dec. 1st year	3118	4397	11,534	13,028	18,214	79,361	200,000	1,200,000
Dec. 2nd year	3381	4849	14,101	14,569	23,046	93,096		
Exclusions	592	210	777	724	968	2,405		
Growth Rate Percentage	8.4	10.6	22.5	12.0	26.1	14.3		
Central Churches in Denomination	31	35	51	58	92	108		6,000§
Satellite Churches Connected to Central Churches	0	75	120	152	251	359	300+	

* William R. Read and Frank A. Ineson, *Brazil 1980: The Protestant Handbook* (Monrovia, CA: Mission Advanced Research and Communications Center, 1973), p. 74.
† Read, *New Patterns of Church Growth in Brazil*, p. 33.
‡ Determined by personal survey in coordination with Dr. Larry Keys, director of Overseas Crusades of Santa Clara, California, March, 1983.
§

	Congregations	Membership	Pastors
In city of Sao Paulo	1,000	300,000	
Outside City of Sao Paulo	5,000	900,000	
Total	6,000	1,200,000	30,000

8. William R. Read and Frank A. Ineson, *Brazil 1980: The Protestant Handbook* (Monrovia, CA: MARC, 1973), p. 33.

Table 46

	Sunday	**Wednesday**	**Saturday**
Sunday School	250		
Evening Worship	5,000	4 services	10,000 to 15,000
First Sunday of Month (Lord's Supper)	15,000		

A Typical Celebration Service

The most popular weekly service at the central temple is on Saturday night at seven o'clock. The colossal concrete sanctuary of Brazil for Christ creates an awesome anticipation and quiet excitement. The building appears to cover at least one city block.

"*O Brasil para Cristo*" accents the outside arch of the fieldhouse-shaped national temple. Another bold sign above the main entrance informs the visitor that this building was built totally without government funds and is punctuated with the internationally recognized word of praise, "Alleluia!"

The church structure has fifty rooms but only two are visible to the visitor. The first room is a gift shop where posters, audio tapes and records, books, and other items are available. A small hallway leads to both the sanctuary on the left and an open courtyard on the right.

Both the courtyard and sanctuary are flooded with the sound of beautiful, majestic, and even militant, Christian singing and orchestration before the service begins. The dominant and surprising feature of the courtyard is the birdhouse, enclosing more than a hundred fluttering and singing birds. Across the music-filled courtyard is an office and reception building.

The sanctuary floor is paved with tinted blocks of concrete. The walls rise fifty-feet toward the ceiling in this assembly room. Approximately thirty arching ranks of pews fan across the front of the sanctuary facing the pulpit. Red concrete aisles flow toward the pulpit area which is suspended eight or ten feet above the floor.

There are two awesome features inside the temple. First, there is a wall-to-wall band of four-foot mirrors beneath the pulpit. Worshipers facing the pulpit all see themselves easily in this unusual wall mirror. Second, sunken into the floor immediately below the pulpit, are nine water fountains. They are not turned on until the end of the service when

Often recognized as the fastest growing religious group in Brazil, Sao Paulo's *Brasil para Christo* (Brazil for Christ) is also known for its involvement with political issues. Such involvement once led to the destruction by a wrecking crew of their new sanctuary. Manoel de Melo is pastor.

the building lights are turned off. The dancing waters light up like rainbows because of the colored floodlights built into the fountains.

The worship service begins at seven o'clock with the people singing hymns. All pastors are invited to occupy the front pew that circles the pulpit. Pastor Manoel de Melo speaks during this early segment of the service from a raised platform below the pulpit.

Members come forward to receive bank payment books with coupons in denominations of 250, 500, and 1,000 cruzeiros. Children's books are available in units of 50 cruzeiros. Ushers with green and white arm bands assist the hundred members who come to give their names and address. Music is provided by an eight-piece band of drums, electric guitars, organ, and trumpet directed by the pastor's son. The payment books are a special event rather than a regular event.

A precision adult choir of almost one hundred voices leads in special music. Congregational singing follows. One hour into the service a roll call of pastors and churches is given. Testimony is shared before the group by one of the pastors.

As the congregation sings, the offering is collected into red nets attached to the end of metal handles. Ushers walk down each aisle and receive the gifts in less than five minutes.

The pastor begins a captivating forty-minute sermon. Both pastor and congregation quote Psalm 23:1 spontaneously with concluding threefold "Amen!"

Two hours into the service, free expressions of praise are heard from the congregation. Again, with raised hands throughout the congregation, all join in a chorus as the sermon is completed.

Eight men join the pastor as he descends the steps to the left of the pulpit. Pastor de Melo extends a verbal invitation to give God first place in life by the visible expression of coming forward for surrender and prayer for the power of God. He specifies giving up cigarettes and drunkenness.

Almost immediately, multitudes of half-full cigarette packs are laid on the floor. Each person coming forward kisses the pastor's Bible. This is an intense time as a thunder of praise and the words, "Alleluiah, Jesus" are repeated.

As the pastor invites others to pray, one of the men following him holds a Bible over his head. During this time of prayer for healing, the pastor moves through the crowd.

A public call is given for those needing a miracle and for those needing surgery. Pastors are asked to come for the anointing oil for healing. A

AN EXPLANATION OF A TYPICAL SAT EVENING WORSHIP SERVICE ⟶

chant moves throughout the multitude, "For These Miracles, Glory to God." The pastor's son whispers into the microphone, "Holy Oil." Again recorded music begins to be heard over the public address speakers.

Pastor de Melo has olive oil poured over his hands as he rubs his palms gently across the face of those who have come forward. A tall elder is always at his side with the closed Bible lifted over the pastor's head as both move through the crowd.

Then asked to return to their seats, the pastor returns to the slightly elevated platform beneath the pulpit.

As a prayer of blessing is pronounced over the crowd, a mixed concert of praise, "Halleluiah, Jesus" and "Gloria Deus," spreads across the 15,000 worshipers.

The lights are then dimmed and the nine water fountains lighted like rainbows begin to spray water five feet into the air. As the pastors watch from the pulpit platform, worshipers gather in front of the mirrors below and allow their cupped hands and fingers to capture the water. When the lights are dimmed and the fountains are turned on, the music again is heard on the audio speakers in the sanctuary. Gradually, the people conclude their time of fellowship and return to their homes. The service is concluded and, after another thirty minutes, the sanctuary is empty.

The Brazil for Christ Story

Manoel de Melo was born August 20, 1929, in the city of Agua Preta, Pernambua, into a farming family. Before becoming a pastor, he worked as a farmer, bricklayer's assistant, bricklayer, carpenter, plumber, painter, and finally a builder.

During the late 1940s, with limited education but much experience, he began conducting evangelistic campaigns in Sao Paulo, Rio, and other Brazilian cities.

In 1955 he made a major decision to transfer his religious commitment from the Assembly of God to the Four Square Gospel Church. This was an era of widespread healing campaigns in Brazil. Often, several healing tents were set up in the same city simultaneously.

William R. Read records:

Special meetings were held each Sunday in large parks and squares; with great crowds gathering to hear the husky-throated preaching of Manoel de Melo and his pastor-friends who always accompanied him. Crowds up to one hundred thousand were not uncommon. In later days the crowds sometimes numbered more than two hundred thousand.[9]

March, 1955, marked the official organization and incorporation of his movement as *Brasil para Cristo*. By 1965, Pastor de Melo reported 1,100 organized churches throughout Brazil with 87 temples and 1,600 ordained pastors. Many organized Pentecostal groups joined ranks with him. As early as 1963, the movement was growing at a rate of 80,000 new members annually.[10]

Ministries of the church include a Bible Institute, several orphanages, a demonstration farm, a hospital, a home for expectant mothers, and several schools.

The church is governed by a board of directors composed of eight to thirteen pastors.

> From outward appearances, the movement "Brasil para Cristo" is a one-man organization. To be sure, a Board of directors . . . sets the policies and charts the course that the movement will follow, but it is commonly assumed that the guiding hand is that of Manoel de Melo. The movement would probably continue on in the event of his decease or if he for some reason relinquishes the leadership.[11]

Without question, the growth of the Brazil for Christ can be attributed to several factors: (1) God's leadership through Pastor Manoel de Melo, (2) the dynamic of the man Manoel de Melo, (3) the extensive saturation of Brazil through live daily radio broadcasts (seven hours daily) on 250 stations, (4) the weekly Saturday television broadcasts, (5) the controversy generated by the pastor as he attacks abuses of society and governmental policy.

Pastor de Melo is viewed by the masses as a defender of the faith and as a source of encouragement for the common man in the poverty of his daily life. He is well aware that many evangelical pastors do not share this sense of awe. He is a powerful and dynamic force for change that cannot be ignored in Brazil.

Other Superchurches of Brazil

A characteristic found among many Brazilian churches is their extension into other cities and states with daughter chapels. These "daughter"

9. Read, *New Patterns of Church Growth in Brazil*, p. 145.
10. Ibid., p. 154.
11. Ibid.

chapels or "ministries" can sometimes rival the size of the mother church (i.e., central church).

Gratitude is expressed to both Bernhard Johnson and Bruce Braithwaite of Bernhard Johnson Ministries of San Jose, California, for the information given in Table 47. They gathered the information from the Brazilian headquarters of the Assemblies of God. Appreciation is expressed to both organizations. Observers indicate that the reader should understand that these listings are very conservative and represent low tabulations. Special mention should be made about the Madureira Assemblies in Rio de Janeiro. After the death of this mother church's pastor, Paulo Leivas Macalao, the leadership of the congregation was transferred to Lupercio Verginano, pastor of the Bras Assemblies or "ministry" in Sao Paulo, Brazil. Both collective and separate figures for membership will be indicated since the transition occurred recently.

Table 47   Other Superchurches of Brazil

Congregation	Location	Total Members	Total Members in the State
Belenzinho Assembly	Sao Paulo	110,000	
Bras Assembly*	Sao Paulo	88,000	
Recife Assembly	Recife	48,000	120,000
Sao Luis Assembly	Sao Luis	47,000	104,000
Belo Horizonte Assembly	Belo Horizonte	45,000	
Salvador Assembly	Salvador	35,000	
Curitiba Assembly	Curitiba	20,000	100,000
Santos Assembly	Santos	20,000	
Porto Alegre	Porto Alegro	20,000	
Cidade Abreu a Lima	Permambuco	18,460	

*   Includes the 28,000 from Madureira Assembly in Rio.

The Future and Large Churches

Research among new churches planted by Southern Baptists in the Memphis, Tennessee, metropolitan area indicates that new churches tend to grow larger in less time than in past decades. This study of 118 congregations traces the growth pattern of churches from 1930–1980.[1] Rapid growth appears to be associated with new housing construction. Once a community becomes heavily saturated with single or multiple family housing units, the potential for quick growth rapidly decreases in most cases.

Several observable patterns surface as a result of the superchurches' survey.

The Principle of the Founding Pastor

Many of the pastors leading these superchurches are the same men who founded the congregations. Full Gospel Central Church, Brazil for Christ, Melodyland, Miracle Center, Thomas Road Baptist Church, and Calvary Chapel are blessed with their founding pastors. Pastors of the following

1. Research project conducted by the author for Southern Baptists in Shelby County (Memphis), Tennessee.

churches served under the ministry of their founding pastors or were immediate successors: Jotabeche Methodist Pentecostal Church, Young Nak Presbyterian Church, Akron Baptist Temple, and the Evangelistic Center of San Salvador.

Still others, following a series of pastors at the church, have been led by God to more than quadruple the size of the church. First Baptist Church of Hammond, Highland Park Baptist Church, First Baptist Church of Dallas, and others came alive under new leadership.

The founding or leading pastor is viewed as the key figure in the church's history. In most cases this image is created and reinforced by their tenure and effective leadership of the congregation.

The Principle of Pastoral Tenure

More than a decade ago, Dr. Elmer Towns wrote an interesting comment about the length of pastoral tenure:

> The average length of the pastor's tenure in the church is twenty-two years and one month among the ten largest Sunday Schools. . . . Perhaps the principle for building a large Sunday School is for a young minister to settle down in one church . . . rather than candidating at other churches, trying to climb the rungs on the ladder of success to the largest church possible.[2]

Today four of the churches listed by Towns also rank among the world's twenty largest churches in composite membership: First Baptist Church of Hammond, Highland Park Baptist Church, Thomas Road Baptist Church, and First Baptist Church of Dallas. Three other churches also appear in additional categories of the world's largest churches (see Appendices): Akron Baptist Temple, Landmark Baptist Temple, and Canton Baptist Temple.

Among these seven North American congregations, only two have changed pastors since 1970. At Akron Baptist Temple, Dr. Charles Billington followed his father as pastor. In Chattanooga, Dr. J. R. Faulkner became sole pastor of Highland Park Baptist Church in 1983. However, he had served as co-pastor with Dr. Lee Roberson since 1949.

Though the pastors of the world's twenty largest congregations come from many countries and cultures, their average length of service is twenty years.

2. Elmer Towns, *The Ten Largest Sunday Schools* (Grand Rapids: Baker, 1969), p. 115.

Dr. W. A. Criswell has the longest tenure: thirty-nine years at First Baptist Church in Dallas, Texas.

The Principle of Size: Bigness

Large churches are blessed with manpower, finances, high visibility, and community influence that often exceeds that of the small church.

The magnitude of these resources comes into focus when it is realized that the world's ten largest churches collectively have 649,286 members; 108,626 people attending Sunday school; and 269,545 worshipers each Sunday. These 649,286 members equal the population of a large metropolitan area such as Memphis, Tennessee.

Without exception, each of the ten largest churches functions like a large shopping center with varied attractions and resources. Some superchurches are more diverse than others. All of the churches place a high priority on the evangelistic penetration of their cities. Elmer Towns and Jerry Falwell give several reasons why the large church is important:

1. The large church is biblical (Acts 2:41, 4:4).
2. A church should be large because of the biblical mandate to evangelize (Matt. 28:19).
3. Large churches can reach large metropolitan areas (Acts 19:10).
4. The large church attracts the respect of the unsaved. Dr. Dallas Billington, former pastor of the world's largest Sunday school once remarked during an evangelistic invitation following his sermon, "Some of you folks don't want to join my church because it's big . . . then you won't like heaven. It's going to be big up there."
5. The large church can give a well-rounded ministry to the total needs of Christians. "The concept of multiple services is a practical application of spiritual gifts . . . (1 Cor. 7:7)."

Table 48

Pastoral Tenure Among World's 20 Largest Churches*

1– 9 Years	None
10–19 Years	Ten Men
20–29 Years	Six Men
30+ Years	Three Men

* Based on information received from nineteen churches.

6. A big church can be the conscience of the city.
7. The large church can operate functionally like a denomination. "The denominational church has historically provided many services to the small church such as financing, homes for orphans and senior citizens, literature, counsel, centralized programing and advertisement. However, the large church can provide all of these services for itself and does not run the risk of encouraging "institutionalization."
8. The large church is more efficient.

Falwell concludes, "We aren't going to argue with anyone about how big Sunday school should become. . . . We're just going to keep winning lost people to Jesus, keep teaching the Word of God to every convert, and when we have natural growth, we'll build another building for the new converts."[3]

The Principle of Size: Small Groups

Critics of the large church would benefit from an examination of how large churches have, in most cases, mastered the dynamics of smaller groups. The large churches that survive achieve and sustain their growth through effective subgroupings. A selection of the twenty largest churches is given in Table 49. Each church is analyzed by the number of attending pupils assigned to each teacher. This information is further classified by age groups.

Some of the twenty largest churches use auditorium or pastor's classes. Dr. Jack Hyles's class averages 2,500 each Sunday at First Baptist Church of Hammond, Indiana. Dr. J. R. Faulkner has taught the 800-member Tabernacle Sunday school class at Highland Park Baptist Church for years. Each of these classes, however, is divided into smaller groups. At Highland Park, for example, one teacher may teach fifty pupils while group leaders shepherd only ten or less within the classes.

Among the large, independent, charismatic churches, structure is less formal. Churches like Melodyland Christian Center in Anaheim, California, and Calvary Chapel in nearby Santa Ana, California, provide classes for children and young people, but adult groups tend to have a drop-in arrangement. The attitude appears to be that those who attend compose the body of the church. Staff members indicate that they do not practice

3. Elmer Towns and Jerry Falwell, *Church Aflame* (Nashville: Impact Books, 1971), pp. 34–42.

Table 49   Teacher/Pupil Ratio Among the World's Largest Churches

Church	Average Sunday School Attendance	Preschool	Children	Youth	Adult	Total (Average)
Central Church *Seoul, Korea*	12,100	1:15	1:30	1:35	Cells*	1:28
Jotabeche Church *Santiago, Chile*	11,100		1:18	1:22	1:17	1:19
Miracle Center *Benin City, Nigeria*	9,000	1:30	1:83	1:83	1:30	1:71
Young Nak Presbyterian *Seoul, Korea*	7,400	1:14	1:22	1:37	1:108	1:45
First Baptist Church *Dallas, Texas*	6,250	1:17	1:5	1:12	1:33	1:17
First Baptist Church *Houston, Texas*	3,750	1:5	1:4	1:6	1:12	1:7
Average	7,086	1:16	1:27†	1:32†	1:40	1:31

* Cell groups have a ceiling of fifteen or sixteen members each. Every cell has its own cell leader and assistant cell leader (a ratio of 8 pupils per teacher).

† Omits Miracle Center of Benin City, Nigeria.

sheep chasing. They provide a spiritual-based menu for healthy sheep and for those hunting for their menu. Dissatisfied sheep are free to feed in other pastures.

Whatever structure a church may decide to use, it is important to remember that large groups are in no way alien to scripture. For example, the Gospel of Mark records that Jesus spoke to 5,000 men (Mark 6:33–44) and again to 4,000 (Mark 8:1–9). Luke records that the church in Jerusalem was composed of at least 5,000 members (Acts 4:4). It is not until Acts 9:31 that a specific reference is made to the multiplication of churches by the Jerusalem church. It is understood that many churches were born from among the new converts gathered for Pentecost in Jerusalem. Chapters 3–9, however, focus on the growth of the Jerusalem church and this tends to be forgotten by many students of Acts and church growth.

The Principle of Multiple Models

A wide variety of models can be found among the world's largest congregations. Some churches are located in war zones, some are located only one hour from Communist borders, and another is located in a police state. Most are in the Free World.

Still other structural models have been adopted in the Communist countries of Asia and Europe. Because of the danger of high visibility in Communist-dominated countries, few churches become large churches. The house church is a common model under those socio-political conditions.

Several writers have attempted to classify various types of structural models. For example, Paul R. Orjala lists nine models or methods: parenting, satellite, multi-congregation, brothering, colonization, district team, catalytic, fusion, and task force.[4]

The churches considered in the previous chapters, and in the four statistical lists that follow this chapter, are classified as one or more of the following six types:

1. Mono-Congregational Model

This is the traditional model for the majority of churches in the United States. Most churches are single, corporate groups meeting under the same roof and location. Large churches of this type tend to create multiple services rather than multiple locations or satellite chapels.

This church-type may occasionally start a new mission church, but normally its evangelistic strategy focuses on reaching others through its own structure. External structures tend to be jail ministries, retirement centers, or other institutional ministries.

Most of the churches operating bus ministries are special adaptations of this model. The foremost example of a bus ministry church is First Baptist Church of Hammond, Indiana. In both fall and spring, 175 buses bring a weekly average of 6,000 riders to Sunday school at the main campus.

2. Multi-Congregational Model

Several congregations maintain separate services at different times in the same building. Some have several different cultural or language groups meeting simultaneously in the same building.

At least four churches in our listing have this structure. In addition many of the churches have services for the deaf, mentally retarded, and blind.

4. Paul R. Orjala, *Get Ready to Grow: Principles of Church Growth* (Kansas City: Beacon Hill Press, 1978), pp. 108–15.

First Baptist Church of Hammond, Indiana, conducts twelve Spanish services with more than one thousand attending each week.

First Baptist Church of Dallas, Texas, holds services for six language groups: Chinese, Spanish, Korean, Japanese, Portuguese, and Laotian.

Among the independent charismatic churches, Calvary Chapel of Santa Ana, California, has Spanish and Korean groups. They also have a Christian-Hebrew fellowship. Melodyland Christian Center of Anaheim, California, regularly has four hundred Romanians, more than one hundred Hispanics, and a small number of Koreans meeting.

3. Satellite Chapels, Branches, or Extension Classes

Traditionally, when a church in the United States decides to found a new congregation, only one new group is organized. This usually is due to the financial obligation involved in helping the new chapel or mission in the purchase of its own property and building.

However, there are exceptions to this model. As early as 1897, First Baptist Church of Dallas, Texas, operated three extension Sunday schools. That year 40 percent of the attendance was in extension Sunday schools. Even today, 25 percent of the total Sunday school attendance is in its chapels. These satellite chapels are the major channel for meeting benevolence needs throughout the Dallas area.

In 1956 the Dallas church began to target new areas of the city for chapels capable of becoming self-supporting, autonomous congregations. Several chapels have achieved this status. Others have not been as effective in their efforts and have requested continued support and membership as part of the mother church.

Around the world the names for satellite locations include chapels, missions, branches, temples, and extension classes. Most mother churches own, operate, and have final authority in the major decisions of these extension groups. As these groups grow larger they are usually encouraged to become independent congregations.

The Jotabeche Methodist Pentecostal Church of Santiago, Chile, is the second largest church in the world. The church begins an average of three new temples each year. A total of forty satellite units are operated by the church in addition to sixty locales or preaching points.

The foremost example of the satellite model is the Highland Park Baptist Church of Chattanooga, Tennessee. Highland Park began its first chapel in 1939 and now operates sixty within a seventy-mile radius of the mother church, in addition to its extensive bus evangelism ministry.

Because this model is used extensively by large churches of the world, Table 50 condenses information about satellite ministries.

4. Colonization Model

In this method an established congregation encourages a nucleus of its members to change residence in order to become part of a new congregation. A form of colonization was experienced by the emigration of Pentecostals from rural to urban areas in Brazil during the early years of the twentieth century.

The Miracle Center of Benin City, Nigeria, has experienced a unique form of colonization. The church's pastor, Benson Idahosa, began to see multitudes make public professions of faith in Jesus Christ in cities and villages where he led evangelistic crusades. Through his school he had a ready source of preachers who could gather the new converts and organize them into another branch of the mother church.

Table 50   Satellite Chapels Owned and Operated by Large Churches of the World, 1980–82

Church	Satellite Units	Comments
First Baptist Church Dallas, Texas	17	Begun prior to 1897.
Highland Park Baptist Church Chattanooga, Tennessee	60	Began first chapel in 1939.
First Assembly of God Phoenix, Arizona	10	Reports 700 attendance in the classes that meet Saturdays at the main facility (brought by bus).
Jotabeche Methodist Pentecostal Church Santiago, Chile	40	Begins 3 new units annually.
Congregacao Crista Sao Paulo, Brazil	157	157 in Sao Paulo and 203 outside the metro area. Had 18 under construction at the same time.
Bible Baptist Church Cebu City, Philippines	7	Also maintains 35 other preaching points.
Miracle Center Benin City, Nigeria	28	Also administers 572 other "branch" satellites outside the city.
Evangelistic Center San Salvador, El Salvador	12	Had 30 in 1961.
Madureira Assembly Rio de Janeiro	120	Largest has 3,000 members. Still under the authority and membership of the mother church.
Landmark Baptist Temple Cincinnati, Ohio	7	

Still another application, in reverse, is a common migration pattern of families interested in living near and benefiting from the superchurch. For example, families have actually moved to Lynchburg, Virginia, to be near the Liberty Baptist Academy, high school, college, and seminary owned and operated by Thomas Road Baptist Church.

5. Satellite Cell Groups

At least eight of the superchurches have networks of cell groups functioning outside the walls of their buildings. A cell is a unit of six to eighteen people, designed to meet in homes, factories, and other places.

Although Sunday school classes meet within the building, the cell group can meet anywhere. Usually, these groups meet on weekdays. Some have a prescribed curriculum; others do not.

Cell groups, because they are intended to ensure face-to-face fellowship, are the critical link for making initial contact with the unchurched in the neighborhood environment. This intimacy also assists in the conversion process.

In a rapidly growing church like Central Church in Seoul, cell groups can help to effectively assimilate new members and new converts into the larger congregation. Within the traditional Sunday school, this same cell concept is operative in regularly-graded, small Sunday school classes.

Cell groups are usually structured into men's, women's, young people's, and children's groups as a church grows larger. They tend to be mixed family groups in smaller churches. Activities in these groups include singing, praise, and personal testimony. Though designed for fellowship, their threefold purpose is nurture, evangelism, and assimilation.

6. Church-Planting Model

The superchurches, except for the denominationally-related large churches, tend to view themselves as a denomination in miniature.

Jerry Falwell and Elmer Towns express this view:

The large church replaces the need for denominations. The large church can have the enlarged ministry that is often delegated to denominations . . . the large church can provide all of these services for itself and does not run the risk of encouraging "institutionalization" or "centralization" of authority.[5]

5. Towns and Falwell, *Church Aflame,* pp. 41–42.

Table 51 Cell Groups in Operation
Among the World's Largest Churches,
January, 1984

Church	Cell Groups
Full Gospel Central Church *Seoul, Korea*	19,839
Young Nak Presbyterian Church *Seoul, Korea*	1,562
Soong-Eui Methodist Church *Inchon, Korea*	1,000
Sung Nak Baptist Church *Seoul, Korea*	767
Chung Hyeon Presbyterian Church *Seoul, Korea*	747
Quang Lim Methodist Church *Seoul, Korea*	750
Evangelistic Center *San Salvador, El Salvador*	280

However, if the small churches are to have adequate resources of their own adapted for the special needs of their congregations, cooperation among the small- and medium-sized churches is essential for survival in the shadow of the superchurches.

Since the resources of the superchurch are so awesome, they can function as a church-planting agency. This is why many smaller churches and some denominations accuse large churches, especially churches with satellites, of being denominations rather than congregations. Many denominations are many times smaller and less innovative than many of the churches surveyed in these pages. The superchurch, hopefully, will be aware of its role as part of the total community of churches, to be a biblical example and encouragement for smaller churches that desire to grow in kingdom skills and qualities. This does not suggest, however, that all churches can or want to grow.

Several large churches have excelled as church-planters. As they became larger, they reproduced themselves through the creation of numerous small congregations. Many of these new churches grew to reach thousands of members themselves.

An observation needs to be made about the churches planted by superchurches, especially those begun as satellite chapels or branches.

Unlike other small churches, these new churches often bear the marks of a predisposition to bigness.

Often, satellite churches are led by men nurtured within the structure of a larger church. This model molds their image of a church and tends to place fewer negative limits on size.

The expectations of the mother church reinforces the priorities and goals of the daughter church. Though a satellite begins small, it starts with an image quite different from the typical small congregation. Table 52 lists large churches with proven records as aggressive and consistent church planters:

Churches like *Congregacao Crista* in Sao Paulo and Madureira Assembly in Rio de Janeiro tend to be slower in releasing chapels. Madureira reports one daughter church with 3,000 members.

However, Brazil for Christ, also in Sao Paulo, rapidly led its satellite chapels to become autonomous in these last few years.

The Principle of Attendance

Perhaps no other area proved to be more of a challenge to interpret than attendance patterns among the twenty composite churches.

For some of the churches, total membership exceeds both worship attendance and Sunday school attendance.

Table 52 Record of Church Planters

Church	New Churches Planted
Miracle Center *Benin City, Nigeria*	1,000+
Thomas Road Baptist Church *Lynchburg, Virginia*	185
Young Nak Presbyterian Church *Seoul, Korea*	100
Full Gospel Central Church *Seoul, Korea*	120+
Calvary Chapel *Santa Ana, California*	27+
Highland Park Baptist Church *Chattanooga, Tennessee*	15+
Jotabeche Methodist Pentecostal *Santiago, Chile*	10

Other churches report worship services that numerically exceed membership or Sunday school attendance, or both. One church reports all three categories as being the same size. Another church has a Sunday school that far exceeds both total church membership and worship attendance.

One-half of the churches indicated that they are like many U.S. congregations with a ranking of the three indicators in descending order: total church membership, worship attendance, and Sunday school attendance. Another 30 percent of the churches ranked total membership as greatest, with attendance being equal in both their worship services and Sunday school. The remaining 20 percent of the churches indicated a variety of other combinations. Each category is shown below with all churches belonging to it.

Type: 1:

Large Total Church Membership
Medium Worship Attendance
Smaller Sunday School

These are churches where total membership exceeds worship attendance. Worship attendance exceeds Sunday school attendance. One-half of the churches are in this category.

Churches of this type are found distributed throughout the twenty largest composite churches, from largest to smallest. This is not true of the other five types of churches. Congregations among the twenty largest, by composite membership, include:

Full Gospel Central Church—Seoul, Korea

Jotabeche Methodist Pentecostal Church—Santiago, Chile

Young Nak Presbyterian Church—Seoul, Korea

First Baptist Church—Houston, Texas

First Baptist Church—Jacksonville, Florida

North Phoenix Baptist Church—Phoenix, Arizona

Bellevue Baptist Church—Memphis, Tennessee

Soong Eui Methodist Church—Inchon, Korea

Chung Hyeon Presbyterian Church—Seoul, Korea

Sung Nak Baptist Church—Seoul, Korea

Type 2:

Large Total Church Membership

Medium Worship Attendance

Medium Sunday School

Churches of this type have a large total membership. Both worship attendance and Sunday school attendance, of equal numerical size, are smaller than the total church membership. Examples include:

First Baptist Church—Hammond, Indiana

Highland Park Baptist Church—Chattanooga, Tennessee

Thomas Road Baptist Church—Lynchburg, Virginia

First Baptist Church—Dallas, Texas

First Southern Baptist Church—Del City (Oklahoma City), Oklahoma

Type 3:

Medium Total Church Membership

Large Worship Attendance

Medium Sunday School

None of the churches in the listing of the twenty largest churches, by composite membership, have this type of structure.

Type 4:

Large Total Church Membership

Large Worship Attendance

Large Sunday School

The Miracle Center of Benin City, Nigeria, is the only congregation reporting almost equal numerical information for all three areas.

Type 5:

Medium Total Church Membership

Medium Worship Attendance

Large Sunday School

This is the only category without a representative church model among the twenty largest (composite list) churches. Among the other lists, however, the Evangelistic Center of San Salvador, El Salvador, is representative of this type.

Type 6:

Small Total Church Membership
Medium Worship Attendance
Large Sunday School

A North American congregation, Grace Community Church of Panorama City, California, is the only church of this type among the twenty super-churches.

The Principle of Media

More than one-half of the twenty churches in the composite membership list are actively involved in either radio or television ministries. While the use of media does not guarantee growth, it appears to be a major contributor.

The potential for fulfilling the Great Commission in our lifetime already exists, with the use of broadcast satellites. Jim Bakker, President of the PTL Network, Charlotte, North Carolina, writes,

> The media of television and modern communication technology are quickly removing barriers so we will soon be speaking the Gospel message via satellite to all the world. . . . Ours is the first generation to be able to proclaim the Gospel to every nation.[6]

Among the world's largest churches, the ones known to have radio and/or television ministries are:

Full Gospel Central Church—Seoul, Korea

Thomas Road Baptist Church—Lynchburg, Virginia

First Baptist Church—Dallas, Texas

First Baptist Church—Houston, Texas

Brazil for Christ—Sao Paulo, Brazil

Miracle Center—Benin City, Nigeria

Melodyland Christian Center—Anaheim, California

Highland Park Baptist Church—Chattanooga, Tennessee

Bellevue Baptist Church—Memphis, Tennessee

6. Jan Struck, "Six Evangelists Share Their Final Word," *Christian Life* 11 (March 1978):39–53.

North Phoenix Baptist Church—Phoenix, Arizona

First Baptist Church—Jacksonville, Florida

Crystal Cathedral—Garden Grove, California

The Principle of People Movements

A "people movement" strategy of evangelism has a goal of reaching total social units and families rather than winning individuals in isolation. People movements have characteristics similar to those of mighty revival movements.

The distinguishing difference is that revival awakens the saints to service and holy living, whereas people movements are the mighty movements of God to awaken souls to salvation. A major aspect of this principle is its focus on those groups and individuals who indicate high receptivity to the gospel.

Several of the world's largest churches have been effective in identifying and reaching a receptive audience. Some of the churches use radio and television to accomplish both of these tasks. Others made their initial breakthroughs by door-to-door witnessing contacts. Others saw needs and met them during times of social and political upheaval.

Both Full Gospel Central Church and Young Nak Presbyterian Church of Seoul, Korea, began as tent churches and served as receiving centers for Korean refugees escaping the Communist invasion from North Korea. Santiago's Jotabeche Methodist Pentecostal Church experienced oppression during the reign of a Communist government in Chile. When the new government removed the Communist leaders and was rebuked by many national leaders, the Evangelicals and Pentecostals supported the new leaders. For the first time in modern history, a Catholic president of Chile participated in the public dedication of a major non-Catholic church sanctuary.

While some benefit from government favor, others, like Brazil for Christ, benefit at great expense and opposition from government disfavor. Their auditorium was once dismantled by bulldozers and demolition equipment. The powerful tool of radio has been used to identify their cause as one sympathetic to the hurts and hopes of the multitudes.

Also, migrations from Brazil's rural interior into the urban centers of Sao Paulo and Rio de Janeiro have greatly aided Pentecostal growth in South America. A major example of growth by population migration is the rapid growth of Sao Paulo's *Congregacao Crista* when Italians in that city identified with their evangelistic efforts.

In Nigeria, the evangelistic crusades of Bishop Benson Idahosa have provided ready-made groups of new converts who became the nucleus of many new churches.

A North American example of a people movement congregation is the explosive growth of Calvary Chapel in Santa Ana, California, during the latter half of the 1960s. The Jesus People Movement was the center of national focus as this church led in the baptism of thousands in the nearby Pacific Ocean. Also, its lead in the establishment of Christian communes invited curiosity and rage.

The Principle of Saturation Evangelism

As defined by Jerry Falwell, "saturation is preaching the gospel to every available person, at every available time by every available means. There must be a saturated population."[7]

Such evangelism is accomplished through door-to-door witness; street corner preaching; electronic media; printed books, articles, and tracts; and a myriad of other ways. The priority is to ensure the communication of the gospel every day in every place to all people.

Korean and North American churches have become specialists in employing almost every contemporary medium for extending their witness. Central Church in Seoul focuses on cell groups and broadcast media. Young Nak Presbyterian Church in Seoul stresses cell groups, Christian day-schools, and free medical clinics.

Thomas Road Baptist Church's thrust has moved from bus evangelism to secondary and graduate schools, Sunday school, and electronic media. First Baptist Church of Hammond, Indiana, is unmatched in its bus and confrontation evangelism throughout the metropolitan Chicago area. Jotabeche Methodist Pentecostal Church in Santiago provides many lessons and principles for saturation evangelism through street evangelism.

Even those critical of Crystal Cathedral often forget that the turning point of the church came when Dr. Robert Schuller began an intensive door-to-door search for the identifiable needs of the multitudes in southern Los Angeles. Armed with that information, he designed a strategy that gained an audience for the gospel. Today, the church has shifted its major method of saturation from door-to-door evangelism to electronic media.

Melodyland Christian Center discovered that the multitudes could best

7. Towns and Falwell, *Church Aflame*, p. 70.

be reached through a crisis telephone center. Churches across North America have used the center as their model.

While the methods differ, the principle of saturation is an essential key to multiplication growth in the Great Commission mode.

The Principle of Member Involvement

Without exception, every one of the world's largest churches have great pastors who built great congregations by the power of God's Holy Spirit. Holy Spirit-empowered pastors reproduce themselves among their people. In actuality, this principle is the Holy Spirit expanding His ministry among His leaders and people for the glory of God and conversion of the nations.

The people have a sense of both corporate and personal ministry. This awareness is the motivating source for explosive growth among these churches. They see themselves as a congregation of priests appointed by God with a divine mandate to glorify Him through evangelism and Bible teaching.

Education & Evangelism The heart beat of the Church.

Conclusion

Some pastors of large churches are almost apologetic about any mention of their congregation's size. Few dare to be brazen about size because they realize the truth of Psalm 75:5-7:

> Lift not up your horn on high: speak not with a stiff neck. For promotion cometh neither from the east, nor from the west, nor from the south. But God is the judge: he putteth down one, and setteth up another.

One of the reasons God chooses to "put down one and set up another" is that certain churches refuse to set limits on God. Another secret to growth is their willingness to have "eyes to see" what other churches do to cooperate with God as He provides almost unbelievable growth.

A crucial element in the stewardship of large churches is the responsibility to serve as willing teachers of what they understand to be biblical principles for building an effective servant church of Jesus Christ. Part of this teaching involves specific details of how the church has cooperated with God in the employment of the principles mentioned in this chapter. The temptation to hide the secrets of growth within the walls of the local membership equates to hiding one's candle under the proverbial basket.

A frequent reason for rationalization and hiding of the candle is rooted in the decline of a church's membership or attendance between statistical surveys. James 4:6 cautions us that "God resisteth the proud, but giveth grace to the humble." It would help others struggling with decline to know that the struggle against decline is a challenge for churches of all sizes.

Decline often cannot be avoided for valid reasons. Examples include the decline of churches in Detroit where sizeable out-migration has resulted from massive unemployment among automotive workers. Church members experience unemployment alongside the unchurched. Both must often relocate to find employment.

In districts of New York City, the rising cost of living and simultaneous high unemployment among both white and black churches does affect church growth and decline.

On occasion, relocation of entire populations of people by government direction can cause loss of members and can alter the growth strategy of a congregation. One example is the decline of Rev. N. Bhengu's congregation in southern Africa. The congregation met in a 10,000-seat auditorium before the membership was repopulated to another district. The large congregation divided into several smaller churches.

Another example in Durban, South Africa, is the Bethesda Temple (Church of God) that declined after the death of its founding pastor. When Dr. John Rowlands died in 1981, Bethesda Temple owned and operated 90 temples throughout the territory with approximately 40,000 members. All were members of the mother temple and usually were baptized by Dr. Rowlands and the assistants he designated.

Today Dr. Alex Thompson, the present pastor of the congregation, indicates that two factors led to the division of the mother church into the present twelve large churches with their chapels. First, the rapid growth rate soon led the church to outgrow its mother worship center. Second, the exodus of many Indian residents exclusively reached by the church. New Indian cities created by the South African Government provided more suitable housing for these former residents.

Dr. Douglas W. Slocumb of Church of God Missions in Cleveland, Tennessee, writes about another large congregation that has experienced recent decline:

In Port-au-Prince, Haiti, we have a church which currently averages 3,000-3,500 in attendance per Sunday. Until recently, this church had several daughter churches throughout Port-au-Prince. The mother church and

The Bethesda Temple (Church of God) in Durban, South Africa, provides an example of church growth and decline. A rapid growth rate eventually led the church to outgrow its mother worship center, leading to the development of 12 large churches with their chapels.

daughter churches together comprise a membership of 14,000. However, in the past few years, these daughter churches have been organized into independent churches.[8]

No church can continue growing indefinitely without experiencing eventual decline. Decline is as real as the coming of illness and death among men. Often, demographic transitions within communities surrounding a church lead to major identity and membership loss by the congregation.

Several prospects appear certain for the future of large congregations.

1. The number of large churches will continue to increase. Recent reports state that a church in Sao Paulo, *Deus e Amor*, fills a renovated warehouse with a crowd of 12,000 people weekly.
2. These churches will continue to be conservative congregations rather than theologically liberal churches.
3. The large churches will, in many instances, continue to grow even larger.
4. Continued research will explore the role of small group substructures in the growth mechanisms of the large church.
5. Future church growth researchers will focus on rate of growth, rather than size, among large churches and smaller ones.
6. Intense efforts are being made today to develop research tools to measure Christian maturity and its role in church growth.
7. Large churches are able to encourage other large churches to plant new daughter churches. Smaller churches are less likely to follow the example or the encouragement of the large church, since the large church is perceived as able to contribute members and other resources to begin new congregations.
8. Increasingly, there will be intense interest, recognition, and encouragement of extension growth through church planting. While all large churches (and smaller churches for that matter) do not see a responsibility to multiply themselves in this manner, many churches have proven their willingness to contribute members, staff, finances, experience, and influence as resources to ensure strong beginnings of daughter churches. Southern Baptists reported the commitment to plant 2,000 new churches on one day (Pentecost, 1983). Their goal is to increase their present 36,000

8. Personal correspondence from Dr. Douglas W. Slocumb, February 5, 1982.

congregations to 50,000 by the year A.D. 2000. Among Independent Baptists, Dr. Jerry Falwell's goal is to begin 5,000 new churches in North America through his own congregation.

9. The issue of chapels constituting membership in a mother church, and the ownership of these chapels and their members, will continue to stir theological debate on the definition of church.

10. While Baptists presently constitute the largest congregations in the U.S., a larger number of major Pentecostal and Independent congregations will appear in both the U.S. and the world. Today, auditoriums seating 10,000 people either exist or are being built by First Assembly of God in Lakeland, Florida; Huffman Assembly of God in Birmingham, Alabama; and Bellevue Baptist Church of Memphis.

11. Large churches throughout the 1980s will be adult churches, rather than for children alone, as families are reached and demographic shifts continue to occur.

12. Researchers will continue to substantiate the key role of membership involvement among large growing congregations.

13. Previous efforts by researchers of North American church growth tended to omit ethnic congregations in the listings of large churches. This will change in the future. Success in this area, however, will only be effective in proportion to the willingness of these churches to provide information.

The future belongs to the church that is alert and open to change, that honors God's Word and that is concerned for souls and organizes for their assimilation and growth.

Composite Membership of the World's Largest Churches, 1981-82

1.	*Full Gospel Central Church* Seoul, Korea	130,000
2.	*Jotabeche Methodist Pentecostal Church* Santiago, Chile	50,336
3.	*First Baptist Church* Hammond, Indiana	37,133
4.	*Young Nak Presbyterian Church* Seoul, Korea	29,600
5.	*Highland Park Baptist Church* Chattanooga, Tennessee	25,646
6.	*Miracle Center* Benin City, Nigeria	14,433
7.	*Soong-Eui Methodist Church* Inchon, Korea	12,167
8.	*Thomas Road Baptist Church* Lynchburg, Virginia	11,666
9.	*First Baptist Church* Dallas, Texas	11,650

10.	*Melodyland Christian Center*	11,000
	Anaheim, California	
11.	*Calvary Chapel*	10,175
	Santa Ana, California	
12.	*First Baptist Church*	8,216
	Houston, Texas	
13.	*Sung Nak Baptist Church*	8,079
	Seoul, Korea	
14.	*Chung-Hyeon Presbyterian Church*	8,066
	Seoul, Korea	
15.	*First Baptist Church*	7,999
	Jacksonville, Florida	
16.	*North Phoenix Baptist Church*	7,902
	Phoenix, Arizona	
17.	*First Southern Baptist Church*	7,900
	Del City, Oklahoma	
18.	*Bellevue Baptist Church*	7,878
	Memphis, Tennessee	
19.	*Grace Community Church*	7,333
	Panorama City, California	
20.	*Kwang Lim Methodist Church*	7,076
	Seoul, Korea	

A list of Brazilian churches are listed separately in the chapter on "Brazilian Superchurches."

Total Membership of the World's 20 Largest Churches, 1981-82

1. *Full Gospel Central Church* Seoul, Korea	275,000
2. *Jotabeche Methodist Pentecostal Church* Santiago, Chile	80,000
3. *First Baptist Church* Hammond, Indiana	74,400
4. *Highland Park Baptist Church* Chattanooga, Tennessee	57,322
5. *Young Nak Presbyterian Church* Seoul, Korea	55,614
6. *Soong-Eui Methodist Church* Inchon, Korea	28,000
7. *First Baptist Church* Dallas, Texas	22,700
8. *Melodyland Christian Center* Anaheim, California	20,000
9. *Thomas Road Baptist Church* Lynchburg, Virginia	19,000

10.	*First Southern Baptist Church* Del City, Oklahoma	17,250
11.	*Calvary Chapel* Santa Ana, California	15,625
12.	*First Baptist Church* Houston, Texas	14,900
13.	*Akron Baptist Temple* Akron, Ohio	14,000
14.	*Brazil For Christ* Sao Paulo, Brazil	14,000
15.	*Chung Hyeon Presbyterian Church* Seoul, Korea	14,000
16.	*Bellevue Baptist Church* Memphis, Tennessee	13,249
17.	*First Baptist Church* Jacksonville, Florida	13,249
18.	*North Phoenix Baptist Church* Phoenix, Arizona	12,845
19.	*First Methodist Church* Houston, Texas	12,330
20.	*Sung Nak Baptist Church* Seoul, Korea	12,320

A list of Brazilian churches appears separately in the chapter "Brazilian Superchurches."

Average Worship Attendance, 1981-82

1.	*Full Gospel Central Church* Seoul, Korea	105,000
2.	*Jotabeche Methodist Pentecostal Church* Santiago, Chile	60,000
3.	*Young Nak Presbyterian Church* Seoul, Korea	20,000
4.	*First Baptist Church* Hammond, Indiana	18,500
5.	*Calvary Chapel* Santa Ana, California	12,500
6.	*Deus e Amor* Sao Paulo, Brazil	12,000
7.	*Miracle Center* Benin City, Nigeria	10,000
8.	*Melodyland Christian Center* Anaheim, California	10,000
9.	*Brazil for Christ* Sao Paulo, Brazil	10,000
10.	*Sung Nak Baptist Church* Seoul, Korea	9,960

11.	*Highland Park Baptist Church* Chattanooga, Tennessee	9,800
12.	*Thomas Road Baptist Church* Lynchburg, Virginia	8,000
13.	*Crystal Cathedral* Garden Grove, California	7,027
14.	*First Baptist Church* Dallas, Texas	7,000
15.	*Bellevue Baptist Church* Memphis, Tennessee	7,000
16.	*North Phoenix Baptist Church* Phoenix, Arizona	7,000
17.	*Soong-Eui Methodist Church* Seoul, Korea	7,000
18.	*Grace Community Church* Panorama City, California	7,000
19.	*Mt. Olivet Lutheran Church* Minneapolis, Minnesota	6,125
20.	*First Baptist Church* Jacksonville, Florida	6,000
21.	*Chung Hyeon Presbyterian Church* Seoul, Korea	6,000
22.	*First Baptist Church* Houston, Texas	6,000
23.	*Akron Baptist Temple* Akron, Ohio	6,000
24.	*Mo'en Church* Shanghai, Peoples Republic of China	6,000

A list of Brazilian churches appears separately in the chapter on "Brazilian Superchurches."

Average Weekly Sunday School Attendance, 1981-82

1.	*First Baptist Church* Hammond, Indiana	18,500
2.	*Full Gospel Central Church* Seoul, Korea	12,100
3.	*Young Nak Presbyterian Church* Seoul, Korea	11,500
4.	*Jotabeche Methodist Pentecostal Church* Santiago, Chile	11,100
5.	*Grace Community Church* Panorama City, California	10,000
6.	*Bible Baptist Church* Cebu City, Philippines	9,200
7.	*Miracle Center* Benin City, Nigeria	9,200
8.	*Highland Park Baptist Church* Chattanooga, Tennessee	9,026
9.	*Thomas Road Baptist Church* Lynchburg, Virginia	8,000
10.	*Evangelistic Center* San Salvador, El Salvador	7,700

11. *First Baptist Church*   6,250
    Dallas, Texas
12. *Calvary Temple* (Assembly of God)   5,429
    Springfield, Illinois
13. *First Baptist Church*   4,747
    Jacksonville, Florida
14. *First Assembly of God*   4,339
    Phoenix, Arizona
15. *Landmark Baptist Temple*   4,200
    Cincinnati, Ohio
16. *Chung Hyeon Presbyterian Church*   4,200
    Seoul, Korea
17. *Canton Baptist Temple*   4,200
    Canton, Ohio
18. *Kwang Lim Methodist Church*   4,095
    Seoul, Korea
19. *Bellevue Baptist Church*   3,921
    Memphis, Tennessee
20. *North Phoenix Baptist Church*   3,863
    Phoenix, Arizona

A list of Brazilian churches appears separately in the chapter "Brazilian Superchurches."

Bibliography

Books

Cho, Paul Yonggi. *Successful Home Cell Groups*. Plainfield, NJ: Logos International, 1981.

Cho, Paul Yonggi. *The Fourth Dimension*. Plainfield, NJ: Logos International, 1979.

Collins, J. B. *Get A Glimpse of the World's Largest Church*. Chattanooga: Private Publication, 1973.

Criswell, W. A. *Criswell's Guidebook for Pastors*. Nashville: Broadman Press, 1980.

Dudley, Carl S. *Making the Small Church Effective*. Nashville: Abingdon Press, 1978.

Entzminger, Louis. *How to Organize and Administer a Great Sunday School*. Ft. Worth: Manning, 1949.

Falwell, Jerry and Elmer Towns. *Capturing a Town for Christ*. Old Tappan, NJ: Revell, 1973.

Garlock, Ruthanne. *Fire In His Bones*. Plainfield, NJ: Logos International, 1981.

Hyles, Jack. *Let's Baptize More Converts*. Murfreesboro, TN: Sword of the Lord, 1967.

Hyles, Jack. *Let's Build an Evangelistic Church*. Murfreesboro, TN: Sword of the Lord, 1962.

Hyles, Jack. *The Hyles Sunday School Manual*. Murfreesboro, TN: Sword of the Lord, 1969.

Johnston, P. J. *Operation World*. Bramley, Kent, England: STL Publications, 1978.

Kennedy, Nell L. *Dream Your Way to Success*. Plainfield, NJ: Logos International, 1980.

Kessler, J. B. A. *A Study of the Older Protestant Missions and Churches in Peru and Chile*. Oosterbaan and le Cointre N.V., 1967.

Lepp, Ralph E. *The Logarithmic Century.* Englewood Cliffs, NJ: Prentice-Hall, 1973.

Lindsay, Homer G. *How We're Building a New Testament Church.* Decatur, GA: The Southern Baptist Journal, 1975.

McBeth, Leon. *The First Baptist Church of Dallas.* Grand Rapids: Zondervan, 1968.

Peters, George W. *A Theology of Church Growth.* Grand Rapids: Zondervan, 1981.

Read, William R. *New Patterns of Church Growth in Brazil.* Grand Rapids: Eerdmans, 1965.

Read, William R. and Frank A. Ineson. *Brazil 1980: The Protestant Handbook.* Monrovia, CA: MARC, 1973.

Schaller, Lyle E. *The Small Church Is Different!* Nashville: Abingdon Press, 1978.

Skelton, Eugene. *Ten Fastest Growing Southern Baptist Sunday Schools.* Nashville: Broadman Press, 1974.

Smith, Chuck and Hugh Steven. *The Reproducers.* Glendale, CA: Regal Books, 1972.

Towns, Elmer and Jerry Falwell. *Church Aflame.* Nashville: Impact Books, 1971.

Towns, Elmer L.; John N. Vaughan; and David J. Seifert. *The Complete Book of Church Growth.* Wheaton, IL: Tyndale, 1981.

Towns, Elmer. *The Ten Largest Sunday Schools.* Grand Rapids: Baker, 1969.

Towns, Elmer L. *World's Largest Sunday School.* Nashville: Thomas Nelson, 1974.

Wagner, C. Peter. *Look Out! The Pentecostals Are Coming.* Carol Stream, IL. Creation House, 1973.

Articles

Bell, L. Nelson. "Korean Missions: Triumph and Shadow." *Christianity Today* 10 (February 18, 1957): 1–16.

Cho, Paul Yonggi. "Outreach: Life of the Church." *World of Faith* 1 (Winter 1981): 3–4.

Clark, Michael. "Bellevue Baptist Unveils Huge Project." *Commercial Appeal,* September 14, 1982, pp. A-1, 12.

Corvin, R. O. "*Gloria a Dios:* World's Largest Pentecostal Sanctuary Dedicated." *The Pentecostal Holiness Advocate,* February 9, 1975, pp. 4–5.

Hitt, Russell T., "California God Rush." *Eternity,* March 1978, pp. 21–32.

"How Did Calvary Chapel Do It?" *Eternity,* March 1978, p. 32.

Hurston, Karen. "Freedom to Mature: Home Cell Units in Central Church." *World of Faith* 3 (Summer Fall 1980): 2–11.

Kennedy, Nell L. "Troubled South Korea Manages a Very Big Bash for Missions." *Christianity Today* 16 (September 19, 1980): 24–44.

Moffett, Samuel. "The Church in Asia: Getting on the Charts." *Christianity Today* 17 (October 2, 1981): 25–39.

Moffett, Samuel H. "The Gospel in Korea: Struggle and Triumph." *World Vision* 8 (September 1973): 17–9.

Schaller, Lyle E. "Twenty Questions for Self-Evaluation in the Small and Middle Sized Church." *Church Management,* April 1977, p. 18.

Struck, Jan. "Six Evangelists Share Their Final Word." *Christian Life* 11 (March 1978): 39–53.

Swanson, Allen. "Not in Vain." *World of Faith* 1 (Winter 1980): 2–17.

Synan, Vinson. "Mission to Chile." *International Pentecostal Holiness Advocate* 6 (July 13, 1980): 64–4–5.

Towns, Elmer. "50 Largest Sunday Schools in the U.S. Today." *Christian Life* 6 (October 1969): 31–46.

Towns, Elmer L. "Trends in Sunday School Growth." *Christian Life* 6 (October 1976): 38–101.

Ward, Larry. "Dr. Han Kyung Chik, Korea's Quiet Dynamo." *World Vision* 3 (March 1968): 12–18.

Correspondence

Slocumb, Dr. Douglas W. Correspondence dated February 5, 1982.

Notebooks

First Baptist Church of Del City, Oklahoma. "Education, Church Administration," *School of Ministry Notebook.*

Research Papers

Towns, Elmer L. *An Accurate Picture of the Thomas Road Baptist Church.* An unpublished research study for Fuller Theological Seminary, Pasadena, California, 1982.

Willard, F. Burleigh. *An Accurate Picture of Calvary Chapel.* An unpublished research study for Fuller Theological Seminary, Pasadena, California, 1982.

Sermon

Roberson, Lee. "The Day Before." A sermon based on Joshua 3:5. From the *Evangelist,* a publication of Highland Park Baptist Church, Chattanooga, Tennessee. December 29, 1982, p. 1.

Church Publications

Bellevue Messenger. A publication of Bellevue Baptist Church, Memphis, Tennessee. September 2, 1977; March 17, 1983.

Evangel. A publication of First Baptist Church of Jacksonville, Florida.

Evangelist. A publication of Highland Park Baptist Church of Chattanooga, Tennessee. October 13, 1976; September 7, 1977; September 6, 1978; February 10, 1982; December 1, 1982; January 26, 1983.

Orbit. A publication of First Baptist Church of Houston, Texas. October 3, 1980; November 21, 1980; February 20, 1981; July 16, 1982; May 13, 1983.

Word. A publication of North Phoenix Baptist Church of Phoenix, Arizona.

First Baptist Church. *The By-Laws of First Baptist Church,* Dallas, Texas. 1979 ed.